Life after Stress

Martin Shaffer, Ph.D.

Contemporary Books, Inc.
Chicago

Library of Congress Cataloging in Publication Data

Shaffer, Martin.
　Life after stress.

　Originally published: New York : Plenum Press, c1982.
　Bibliography: p.
　Includes index.
　1. Stress (Psychology)　　2. Stress (Psychology)—
Prevention.　　I. Title.
[BF575.S75S48　　1982]　　　158′.1　　　82-22096
ISBN 0-8092-5622-3 (pbk.)

This edition published by arrangement with Plenum Press.

Published by Contemporary Books, Inc.
180 North Michigan Avenue, Chicago, Illinois 60601
Manufactured in the United States of America
Library of Congress Catalog Card Number: 82-22096
International Standard Book Number: 0-8092-5622-3

Published simultaneously in Canada by
Beaverbooks, Ltd.
150 Lesmill Road
Don Mills, Ontario M3B 2T5
Canada

To Judy,

my loving wife and partner,
for her support in completing this challenge.

To Rachel and Jay,

my children who teach me to play.

And to Ean Dennis Roby,

for his enthusiasm and skill in
reshaping the manuscript.

CONTENTS

INTRODUCTION

STRESS STYLES

It is late afternoon on the last Friday of the month. At the bank, the lines of customers waiting to deposit their paychecks or to withdraw money for the weekend have stretched practically to the front doors. At one window, a customer finishes and the next person, a merchant, steps up. He opens a cloth bag and produces a stack of checks, cash, and deposit slips almost two inches thick. The teller's eyes widen. This will be at least ten minutes' work, maybe fifteen. What about those other customers waiting in line? How will they react?

Interestingly enough, the reactions of the customers waiting in line behind the merchant vary considerably. Gary Johnson, for instance, is furious. He grinds his cigarette under his heel and mutters about inconsiderate jerks who wait until the last minute to deposit their week's receipts. Gary shifts back and forth from foot to foot, the swaying of his body telegraphing his frustration. He probes his pockets to see whether any of his antacid mints are left. Finding none, he curses under his breath and lights another cigarette.

Several places behind Gary, Mike Harlow is waiting in a different way. Mike has a dinner date at six, and he felt his anger rise when the merchant at the head of the line began his lengthy transaction. Unlike Gary, however, Mike is working hard to cope with his irritation. He takes several deep breaths, reminds himself that there is nothing he can do to speed up the line, and then gazes out the windows—focusing his attention upon the beautiful trees that line the street.

Directly behind Mike, Ginny Caldwell is dealing with the situation in yet another way. Before she came into the bank, Ginny knew that she might be in for a long and frustrating wait, what with it being Friday afternoon and payday as well. So she made sure she had plenty of time to spend, and she brought along an Agatha Christie novel to occupy her time. Ginny vaguely noticed when the merchant stepped up to the window to deposit his time-consuming pile of work, but she thought little or nothing about it. She simply adjusted her stance to feel more comfortable and continued reading Chapter Six. Would Miss Marple, she wondered, really be able to figure out who had murdered the Duchess?

Gary, Mike, and Ginny have all been subjected to a typically stressful situation, not unlike the stresses each of us is subjected to every day. What is significant, however, is that each of them has reacted to that stress in a dramatically *different* way. But how is this possible? Why do their reactions differ so much? The answer lies in the nature of stress and in our reaction to it.

People who know little about stress often assume that it is some kind of powerful external force, over which they have little control. They seem to feel that stress is to be avoided if possible, but endured if one cannot escape. Gary is a good example of this attitude in action. He fumes and blames the merchant at the head of the line for the delay. Gary sees the problem as outside himself. He has no control over it. It's all that other guy's fault!

Nothing could be further from the truth. There is nothing automatic or inescapable about stress. Each of us has the choice of how we will respond when we are confronted with a potentially stressful situation. We may choose to make ourselves miserable, as Gary did, or we may elect to react differently—coping calmly as Mike did, or actually enjoying the experience as Ginny was able to do. Each person's reaction to stress is unique and highly personal, and grows out of a complex pattern of thoughts and behavior. We respond to stress, for instance, on the basis of what we believe about ourselves and the world, and of what we say to ourselves (remember Gary muttering in line?). Our stress response also depends upon how much we feel in control of our lives, upon the nature of our personal interactions, and upon our physical condition. These factors and many more combine to create a distinctive stress style for each of us.

Gary, for instance, did not just happen to feel stressed at the bank. His response was actually the end result of a complex interaction among different aspects of his thought and behavior. He had planned poorly (or not at all), to start with, arriving at the bank with only a few moments to spare before he needed to be off on his way to an important meeting. And what about his naive assumption that his banking wouldn't take very long—late on Friday afternoon? Add his fatigue at the end of a long week, his incessant smoking, and far too many cups of coffee earlier in the afternoon—and you have a problem waiting to happen. Add Gary's tendency to blame others (instead of taking responsibility for the consequences of his own actions), and his repeated agitation of himself by muttering insults, and you have a full-blown stress reaction. The reaction, however, is the direct result of Gary's personal style.

Given his ineffective stress style, is Gary doomed? That is, will he continue to repeat this destructive behavior over and over whenever a stressful situation presents itself? The answer is that it depends on what Gary wants. If he desires, there is nothing to prevent him from continuing to act much as he has in the past, an angry victim trapped by stress. But there is also another possibility. Gary may decide that he has suffered enough and that he deserves a better and happier life. Gary may, in short, decide that he would like to change. This personal decision is crucial, for if Gary wants to change, there are ways that he can learn to change. If he wants to, Gary can learn to cope better with stress, or he may even learn to overcome stress and turn it to his own advantage.

Assuming that Gary decides he wants to change, how does he go about doing it? There might be many approaches, but this book offers a comprehensive and highly personalized method for gaining control over stress. By reading this book and performing the tasks that it presents, Gary could develop a better understanding of stress itself and his own stress style. He could, in turn, learn about the particular features of his own style that predispose him to stress, and he could learn and master a variety of new, stress-reducing behaviors. With time and practice of the skills set forth here, Gary could learn to cope more effectively and, if he wished, could even learn tactics for overcoming stress and turning it to his own advantage.

The same opportunity is available to you as you read this book. Chapter 1 explains the stress reaction in detail, showing how physiological responses occur in response to psychological judgments. Stress is largely a matter of how we look at things! Chapter 2 continues on to describe the most common signs or symptoms of stress—physical, psychological, and behavioral. If you are not sure whether you are under stress or not, this is the place to check.

Chapter 3 offers the first real step toward meaningful personal control over stress. Here, you will undertake a personal stress analysis, examining your own life to determine those aspects that are stress-producing. Various techniques are described to help you interpret your stress behavior in useful and revealing ways. Chapter 4 offers practical suggestions to help you alleviate some of the obvious bodily signs of stress by providing proven relaxation exercises that reduce tension.

Chapter 5 turns to the question of resistance. Stress cannot predominate when the body is ready and able to resist its advances. In this chapter, you will learn how to bolster your personal resistance to stress and stress-induced illness by proper sleep, adequate exercise, and correct nutrition. Such increased resistance will then provide the foundation for further efforts to control, or even overcome, stress.

Chapters 6 and 7 both deal with the world of work—a common and powerful source of stress. Chapter 6 focuses on environmental causes of stress, aspects of your work environment that may actually be stress-producing. Chapter 7, in turn, emphasizes the role that personal relationships can play in creating stress on the job. By following the instructions given in these chapters, you should learn methods that will contribute to more healthy and productive interactions at work.

Chapter 8 addresses another common source of stress: the family itself. Here too, as with the preceding chapters that dealt with work, the emphasis is on practical techniques that can reduce, or even eliminate, sources of stress in the home environment.

The last two chapters deal with the role of personality in the stress reaction. Chapter 9 focuses upon the stress-prone person and upon those behaviors that generate stressful reactions. Here, the focus is upon people who react sharply to stressful situations in their lives. The final chapter, Chapter 10, examines the opposite case. This chapter looks at those who have learned to go beyond stress, and beyond everyday coping with stress. Here, the emphasis is upon those who have learned to challenge the stress reaction and to turn it to their own advantage. Unlike those who fall victim to stress, or those who struggle to survive its influence, these stress masters have learned to thrive on stress—and to use it as a stimulus to effective action, rather than see it as a problem. Finally, for those who might wish to continue learning about stress and stress styles, the book ends with a bibliography of recommended readings.

These chapters have been laid out in such an order as to guide you, the reader, to a better understanding of stress and to offer you the chance to increase your own mastery over stressful situations. The exercises and explanations offered in this book will take time; they will be of little value if you attempt to rush through them. A careful and thorough examination, however, should yield more satisfactory results. So read thoughtfully, and experience the opportunity to gain more meaningful personal control over stress in your life!

CHAPTER 1

ON THE NATURE OF STRESS

Until the year 1936, the meanings of the term *stress* were clear enough. The basic sense of the word traced back to at least the 15th century, when, according to the *Oxford English Dictionary*, it was used in the sense of "physical strain or pressure." Subsequent usage retained this specific meaning (particularly in fields such as engineering or architecture, where one might speak of the "stress" on a wall or against the piling of a bridge), but also generalized it. By the year 1704, for instance, "stress" was used to describe "hardship, straits, or adversity"—pressure upon a person instead of a thing. By the mid-19th century, the notion of stress was broadened even more to include "strain upon a bodily organ or mental power." Still other, related meanings continued to appear, but they too seemed to cluster around the basic notion of "stress" as some sort of force. At least that was the case until 1936.

In that year, a young researcher at Canada's McGill University published a paper that was destined to revolutionize our concepts of illness and to create a new and radically different definition of stress. Although that researcher, Dr. Hans Selye, at first consciously avoided the term *stress* in describing the state that his research had discovered, he subsequently changed his mind. By the mid-1940s, he began to speak of his findings in terms of "stress." His use of the term was novel in several respects, but the brilliance of his research, coupled with his vast number of publications, helped to establish this new usage in the scientific community.

The most significant aspect of Selye's definition of "stress" was that he reversed the traditional usage. Instead of viewing stress as an agent or force, he instead regarded stress as the *result* produced within an organism by the presence of some other agent or force. It is also important to note that Selye's conception of stress is physiological, rooted in the biological processes of the organism. This is not surprising given Selye's training as a physician and endocrinologist—a specialist in the study of hormones secreted by the various glands of the body. Selye's biological model serves as a foundation for other approaches to stress that were to follow.

THE PHYSIOLOGY OF STRESS

Selye describes stress as "a state manifested by a syndrome." That is, physiological stress is revealed by a specific sequence of events. Selye terms this sequence the general adaptation syndrome (GAS) and distinguishes three stages therein. The first stage is an "alarm reaction," the second a "stage of resistance," and the third a "stage of exhaustion." Let us examine each of these stages in turn.

The alarm reaction is a physiologically complex response, triggered by what Selye terms a *stressor*. We will investigate the concept of the stressor in more detail shortly. For now, let us simply accept Selye's definition that a stressor is "that which produces stress." If a stressor is present, the alarm reaction will follow.

Probably the most familiar element of the alarm reaction is release of adrenaline into the bloodstream. All of us have felt, at one time or another, the racing of the heart that comes when we are excited or frightened. This sudden increase in heartbeat is triggered by the secretion of adrenaline by the adrenal gland, which rests atop the kidneys. At the same time, a number of other bodily changes take place. Breathing becomes shallower, and blood flows from the skin and viscera to the muscles and the brain. As a result, the hands and feet become cooler. (This is why cold hands normally indicate nervousness.) Finally, nourishment is redistributed to those parts of the body that would be needed to respond during this emergency, particularly the musculature.

Underlying these familiar sensations are many more that we cannot perceive. The hypothalamus, a part of the midbrain that controls such feelings as fear, anger, joy, sadness, and disappointment, is a key component of the hormonal-alarm system. When our brain registers a "danger" response, the hypothalamus sends electrochemical signals to the pituitary gland, which is located at the base of the skull. The pituitary secretes a hormone called ACTH (adrenocorticotrophic hormone) to activate the adrenal glands. These glands in turn release into the bloodstream substances called corticoids, which carry messages to other glands and organs.

The spleen, for example, is mobilized for action and releases red blood cells into the bloodstream. These additional red blood cells, which carry oxygen and nourishment to other cells throughout the body, are needed to handle the increased demands of the body during the alarm stage of the stress reaction. Similarly, the ability of the blood to clot is increased, and the liver releases stored vitamins and nutrients in the form of sucrose, which will then be converted into nourishment for the body's cells. In addition, the body uses large amounts of B vitamins, vitamin C, pantothenic acid (one of the B vitamins), and other nutrients during the alarm stage.

But the hormonal system is not the only network activated when a stressor is identified and the alarm stage is triggered. Walter B. Cannon, an eminent physiologist who performed pioneering studies of the stress reaction, explored the involvement of the autonomic nervous system (ANS), a series of nerve pathways that connect many of our internal organs. (The ANS is the route by which messages are sent to the adrenals in order to release adrenaline and speed up our heartbeat and respiration.)

Cannon also described what he termed the *emergency reaction*, a response that we might best describe as an acute case of Selye's alarm reaction. This extreme reaction, Cannon showed, sought to guarantee the survival of the organism by the principle of "fight or flight." That is, in the face of extreme danger, the organism would either confront the danger or flee from it. In animals, as well as in man, this reaction involves an interplay between genetic endowment and actual circumstances. Thus, when confronted with danger, most animals—even a bear or a lion—will flee. On the other hand, even a normally docile creature such as a household pet may fight ferociously if cornered. It is important to realize, however, that Cannon's "emergency reaction" is a much more specific and extreme case than Selye's "alarm reaction." In most situations, human experience with stress requires far less strenuous measures than those Cannon describes!

Several other concomitants of the alarm reaction need to be mentioned. One is muscular tension. Whenever the body enters into the alarm reaction, one of the consequences is tension in the musculature. Such tension often occurs particularly in the lower back, in the neck and shoulders, and in the form of tension headaches. Unfortunately, the tension often persists even after the alarm reaction that initiated it has ceased. We will see in subsequent chapters that this tension is a principal indicator of stress and, as such, can be of great value both as a measure of how stressed we are and as a tool for helping us to gain control over stress. It is also worth mentioning that Chapter 4 will present a variety of relaxation techniques that might be of particular value in counteracting the effects of such muscular tension.

Another consequence of the alarm reaction is that it causes the stomach to release hydrochloric acid, which normally is utilized in the digestion of food. If acid is released when the stomach is empty, however, it can burn the linings of the stomach, the esophagus, and the upper intestines. Such burning of tissue, if repeated over a period of time, could lead to the development of ulcers. Obviously, a prolonged series of alarm reactions, each of which triggered such secretions of hydrochloric acid, could be extremely harmful. A similar situation occurs with the cardiovascular system, where continued mobilization in response to repeated alarm reactions could eventually lead to cardiovascular disease or even heart attacks. It is no wonder that continuous stress reactions among executives and professionals frequently lead to ulcers or heart disease!

This, then, is the alarm reaction, a complex physiological response involving a number of interacting bodily systems. Assuming that the stressor that initiated the alarm response is still present, that response will then be followed by a stage of resistance. During this second phase of the GAS, the body will mobilize to actively combat the stressor. The distinctive indicators of the alarm reaction will disappear during this period of resistance, and the body will seem to have "returned to normal" as it vigorously fights the stressor. There is a danger, however, that this stage of resistance will last too long. If the body remains mobilized for too long a time, its resources will begin to become depleted. When this happens, the stage is set for the final stage of the GAS: exhaustion. When the stage of resistance has been completed and exhaustion sets in, the body once again exhibits symptoms similar to those of the alarm reaction itself. Even more important, however, this third phase of the GAS also means that the body is increasingly vulnerable to disease and organic dysfunction. Indeed, this is the point at which stress-related diseases begin to be most evident.

It is worth noting at this point, as Selye himself stresses, that there is no way to avoid the GAS entirely. The stress reaction will be initiated again and again—as we shall shortly see—by any of a wide range of stressors, both positive and negative. Excitement, joy, and unexpected happiness can evoke the alarm response as effectively as grief and sudden tragedy. It is possible to reduce the frequency and intensity of the alarm response, but not to eliminate it. The initial reaction to a stressor is as natural as eating or breathing. The same might be said of the stage of resistance. Just as with the alarm reaction, the body is programmed to resist disease and stress over a period of time. The final stage of the GAS, however, is to be avoided if at all possible. Repeated evocations of the alarm reaction are tolerable, even repeated forays into the realm of resistance. But journeys into the land of exhaustion are dangerous—far too dangerous to tolerate if they can be avoided. But how can this final slippage into exhaustion be avoided? Is it possible to slow down—or even stop—the progress of the GAS? Interestingly enough, to answer these questions, we need to consider the role that human psychology plays in the stress reaction.

PSYCHOLOGICAL FACTORS IN THE STRESS REACTION

Body and mind together form an integrated whole, although it is often convenient to treat them as separate for purposes of scientific study. This interaction between the mental and the physical is particularly evident in two aspects of the GAS: first in the concept of the stressor itself, and second in the duration of the GAS reaction. Let us begin by looking at the stressor.

Selye, you will recall, defined the stressor very briefly as "that which produces stress." But exactly what kind of thing can be a stressor? And exactly how does it trigger the alarm reaction of the GAS?

The answer to the first question is surprising, because we are used to thinking of things that happen to our bodies as having specific causes. If we get the mumps, for instance, we regard that as the consequence of being infected by a particular organism. If someone else were to be infected by the same organism, we would expect him to get the mumps—not the measles or influenza. Each of those other diseases would be caused in turn by still another organism, and so on. But this kind of orderly relationship between cause and effect does not hold in the case of stress. In fact, almost the opposite is true, because many different events, potentially a great many, can all serve as stressors that trigger the alarm reaction. This is in part the reason that Selye himself refers to stress as a "nonspecific" response, by which he means that there is no one, specific cause that acts to produce stress and its accompanying GAS. Rather, the stress reaction, which is a nonspecific mobilization of the body, can be set in motion by any number of causes.

As was mentioned earlier, stressors can be either positive or negative. A wedding can evoke just as strong an alarm response as a funeral, and winning the state lottery can be just as stressful as losing your shirt in Las Vegas. But stressors can vary in a number of other respects as well. The alarm reaction can be set off by external events, or by internal thoughts and memories, or by a blend of both.

Stressors may include, for example, environmental conditions such as noise or air pollution—or social ones such as overcrowding or unpleasant, dangerous surroundings. They may appear in interpersonal relationships at home or at work, or they may directly involve the body itself, as with illness or injury. Or stressors may be private and internal—ranging from bad memories to unrealistic expectations or unresolved conflicts. The only element that these and other potential stressors share in common is their capacity to initiate the stress reaction.

This leads to the second question posed above: Just how does a stressor trigger the GAS? The answer is more complicated than we might suspect at first, because something becomes a stressor only when the mind identifies it as one. This means that the triggering of the stress reaction depends on cognition, the process by which our mind comes to have knowledge of both the external world and our internal experience of thoughts and feelings. The mind, in short, signals the body that a stressor is present—and the alarm reaction follows.

Exactly how the mind identifies a stimulus as a "stressor" is a complex and controversial issue that ranges far beyond the scope of a practical book on stress control. For our purposes, however, it is important to emphasize that this "identification" can take place at different levels of awareness. Some stressors, for example, are recognized by the mind more or less automatically. In such cases, the alarm reaction is triggered almost immediately, though we often remain totally unaware of the reaction or of the stressor that evoked it. Air pollution may trigger a stress response even though we take the smog for granted; high-decibel noise from jets may do the same for those who live in the flight path near an airport, whether they pay attention to the jets any more or not. Even commuting in heavy traffic can set off such a "silent" stress response! The difficulty in such cases is that the connection between mind and body is so direct that it eludes attempts at conscious control. Knowing that pollution, or noise, or driving in heavy traffic evokes the stress response cannot prevent that reaction; the GAS proceeds in spite of our insight. From the point of view of stress control, the immutability of such reactions suggests a significant point: These stressors (primarily chemical or environmental ones) must be dealt with actively. One can avoid them, modify them, or use other methods—such as the relaxation techniques in Chapter 4—to reduce their effects.

Other stressors are somewhat more accessible to our control. For the sake of our discussion, these can be conveniently divided into three groups. Let us call them "hidden" stressors, "unnoticed" stressors, and "obvious" stressors. Each type exhibits a somewhat different relationship between the cognitive processes of the mind and the stress reaction that follows—and each one can be dealt with in a somewhat different way. Let us begin by looking at the "hidden" variety of stressor.

THE HIDDEN STRESSOR

Amelia Brown is a heavyset woman in her mid-40s, recently promoted to office supervisor in a small corporation. Amelia was widowed over 4 years ago when her husband Frank died suddenly from a heart attack. About 6 months after his death, she began suffering a variety of symptoms for which her doctor can find no organic cause. The symptoms have persisted ever since. She suffers from nervousness and does not sleep well. Her energy is constantly low, and she sometimes finds it hard to concentrate. During the past few years, she has also had a weight problem due to constant overeating. Amelia recently began psychotherapy in an attempt to solve her problems. One of the results of her therapy is that she has begun to discover some very unexpected feelings within herself, particularly feelings of anger toward her husband's withdrawn coldness during their marriage and feelings of rage at his unexpected death, which left her with little money and few job skills. During therapy sessions, Amelia has found herself screaming, crying, even shaking with rage. Somehow it seems as though she's only scratched the surface, but she already has noticed that she is sleeping better, has more energy, and has stayed on her diet for more than 2 weeks!

Amelia's experience illustrates a common form of "hidden" stress. She has been caught in an unconscious conflict between negative feelings that she felt toward her late husband and her own judgment that such thoughts were unacceptable. As a result, she remained unaware of her negativity, but she also paid the price of an almost constant stress reaction during most of the time since her husband's death. In Amelia's case, the conflict is so deep-seated that it has taken some professional help to lead her to discovering it. This is not always the case. Often, thoughtful self-examination of the type recommended in Chapter 3 will provide the opportunity to bring such hidden conflicts to the surface.

THE UNNOTICED STRESSOR

Such "hidden" sources of stress as discussed above often arise from interpersonal or even intrapersonal difficulties. These are also likely sources for "unnoticed" stressors, although this second form of stressor usually does not produce such profound conflicts and is consequently easier to manage.

Consider the case of Max Brammer: Every year, as winter turns into spring, Max begins to feel a vague discomfort. When his tax man calls to arrange his yearly appointment, Max chooses the latest possible date and then finds his discomfort noticeably worse. He begins to feel vaguely irritable and notices that his digestion is behaving strangely, bubbling and gurgling. Sometimes his abdomen is inexplicably distended with gas. When the day of the appointment finally arrives, Max is suddenly compulsive, scurrying around in search of the necessary records scattered throughout the house. He even experiences a half hour of pure horror when he realizes that he has misplaced last year's tax return. (He finally locates it underneath a stack of old magazines!) When the tax man arrives, the session seems to drag on forever, punctuated by Max's burping and fidgeting. Finally, when it is over, Max begins to feel a whole lot better—and not just because he is to receive a refund of $275. Within a week, Max suddenly realizes that his "stomach problem" has cleared up.

Unlike Amelia, whose stress-producing conflict was locked

deep within her psyche, Max is confronted with a much more obvious problem. Tax time is, for whatever reason, a source of particular stress for Max, and his body responds appropriately to his perception of the stress-producing event of having to prepare his return. Max, however, actually has a great deal of control over this stress reaction, control that he has largely failed to exercise. He has intentionally chosen to wait until the last moment to prepare his return, thereby prolonging his stress. Furthermore, he has failed to keep his records in a convenient, central location. In fact, he has done so little that he has to spend the morning of his tax day tracking down his records—hardly a soothing or relaxing activity. He has even gone so far as to misplace his last year's return! Clearly, Max is making trouble for himself, creating a situation in which he will feel stressed and uncomfortable—just as his stomach repeatedly reminds him. While Max might profit from introspection or possibly even professional help, most of the stressful nature of tax time could be alleviated by a few simple actions on his part. He could, for instance, schedule his appointment earlier and avoid subjecting himself to such prolonged stress. Furthermore, he could keep his records more carefully and in one, convenient location—along with his previous tax returns. These few simple changes might not eliminate his negative, stressful response to taxpaying, but they might very well reduce the level of stress and shorten the length of time for the entire stress reaction.

Max's case illustrates several features of stress reactions that involve "unnoticed" stressors. First, these situations are far more subject to conscious intention and change than the more unconscious or "hidden" kind. The sort of stress that Max experiences may respond nicely to practical alterations in behavior—such as rescheduling appointments or paying more careful attention to record-keeping. Second, cases such as Max's illustrate a property of the stress reaction demonstrated by Selye: that the intensity of the stress response is in proportion to the perceived intensity of the stressor itself. To put this in terms of Max's problem, the less control Max believes himself to have over the taxpaying process, the more stress he experiences. The more he regards taxpaying as something dreadful that he has to put off to the last moment, something that he is forced to gather records for only under compulsion at the last minute, the more Max will feel stressed and powerless. This observation leads to a third point: Max himself is responsible for the stress reaction he is suffering. He has chosen a course of action (last-minute appointment, scattered records, lost return) that conforms to his own perception of a stressor. He has guaranteed that tax time will be a stressful and unpleasant event. Simply becoming aware of how he has set himself up to be stressed may help Max to choose other, more productive ways of dealing with the problem of his taxes.

THE OBVIOUS STRESSOR

Amelia was genuinely ignorant of the conflicts that had produced the stress reaction in her life; Max has simply avoided paying attention to how he has created his own stress. There is still another possibility, however: the "obvious" stressor. Here, the relationship between stressor and alarm reaction is far more conscious and evident, but even its obviousness doesn't guarantee that the stress reaction will be discontinued. Take, for example, the case of Jack, an assistant professor with a heavy teaching load. Over the past few years, Jack has noticed that sometimes he experiences a curious collection of symptoms: His muscles become tight and painful, particularly in his shoulders and in the small of his back; he begins to eat and drink too much, particularly late in the evening; he feels disorganized and overwhelmed by responsibilities; and he finds himself jogging less, sleeping less, and wanting to lock himself up away from everyone. Jack has also noticed that this odd cluster arises near the end of each semester—when students' exams and term papers suddenly appear in large numbers and troubled students fill the hall outside his office. "It's all because of my damn job," he tells his wife. Yet Jack keeps working as he has worked for years, and every semester brings the same curious collection of symptoms.

Jack's situation illustrates that merely being aware of the source of our stress does not necessarily lead to stress relief. Sudden and dramatic insight, such as into unconscious conflicts, may produce gratifying results, but even in such cases, insight is not enough. Effective stress control usually demands changes in one's behavior. In this sense, Jack's problem is like Max's difficulty with taxes—the only difference is that Jack's is even more basically rooted in his life-style. Jack seems to regard his problem as necessary—that is, the way he teaches seems to require the bizarre collection of symptoms he experiences at the end of each term. This seems obvious to him, so obvious that it masks his own contribution to the problem. Jack suffers because he has chosen to structure his job in terms of a last-minute sprint. Even more, he has failed to prepare himself for that onslaught of work at the end and, as a result, is repeatedly overwhelmed by it. Like Max, Jack could also learn to reorganize his life to better meet his needs, restructuring his workload and his responsibilities so that they are more evenly distributed and not all bunched up at the end. But Jack seems unwilling to do this, and part of the reason is that Jack is quite confident that he knows what his problem is: It is his job. He has no control, no responsibility; he is an innocent victim. This is the attraction of the "obvious" stressor: It is a convenient source of blame—and a handy way to avoid dealing with the real issue.

Taken together, these three descriptions of stressors that we can more or less control tell a similar tale. It is our minds—our expectations, our fears, our mistaken certainties—that lead us into unproductive, stressful situations. By becoming aware of what these stressors are, and of the ways we create environments in which these stressors thrive, we can take significant steps toward achieving stress control.

COGNITION AND THE STRESS REACTION

The stressor is not the only point where the mind influences the stress reaction, however. Cognition plays a similar role in the GAS reaction itself. This occurs because the stress reaction not only needs a stressor to trigger it, but also requires the continued presence of that stressor to maintain the reaction. Without the mind's continuing awareness of the presence of the stressor, the alarm reaction (or the stage of resistance if the GAS had progressed that far) would simply stop, and the organism would return to a normal, unstressed state. This need for continuing identification of the stressor throughout the life of the stress reaction suggests several options for stress control.

A stimulus originally regarded as dangerous and identified as a stressor, for example, might be reevaluated later and judged to be safe. In such a case, the alarm reaction originally triggered by the mind's labeling of the stressor would be shut down as soon as the mental reevaluation had occurred. Such stoppage of the GAS might occur if, say, a young lady was going skiing for the first time and was fearful about injuring herself. She might regard going skiing as fun, but her mind would also view it as potentially dangerous and initiate a stress reaction as the time for the trip approached. Once the novice skier is on the slopes, however, and has gained confidence in her ability to control speed and direction, she may relax and no longer be fearful. The act of skiing, initially regarded as a source of stress, has been reevaluated by the mind and relabeled as a source of pleasure.

Alternatively, what was originally regarded as a stressor may simply be forgotten. A child who is fearful of swimming might experience the alarm reaction if he were forced to go into the pool. After a while, however, he might discover that frolicking in the shallow end is very pleasurable—and simply forget to attend any further to his original feeling of fear. Once he ceases to label his experience in the pool as dangerous, the GAS will cease as well. This may seem obvious, but it is a significant point as far as stress control is concerned. Many events remain stressors for us only because we continually remind ourselves about them. Normally, this reminding is done in the form of internal dialogues—"talking to ourselves." If our beginning skier had continually reminded herself of how dangerous skiing can be, telling herself to "watch out" and "be careful," she would have remained stressed and fearful for a longer time. Thus, each negative statement functions as a specific stressor.

Such negative internal dialogue might also have inhibited her learning of skiing skills and prevented the development of her self-confidence as a skier. On the other hand, if we stop reminding ourselves about the threat posed by a particular event, we may discover that our stress has vanished. A similar result may occur if we alter what we are saying to ourselves. By using more positive language in our internal dialogues, we may discover that what our mind had originally labeled as a stressor is, in fact, far less dangerous. Like the child in the swimming pool, we can use such mental reappraisal to help us let go of fear and the stress that follows from it.

The mind, then, plays an active role both in triggering the stress response and in maintaining it. The physiological response of the GAS starts and stops in accordance with our mental evaluation of both external and internal events. Understanding this interaction between the cognitive activity of the mind and the physical response of the GAS is fundamental if we are to learn how to control the cycle of stress.

STRESS COPING—AND BEYOND

Both body and mind are involved in the stress reaction in another way as well. Whenever a stress reaction occurs, both body and mind seek to adapt to the stressful alarm reaction, seeking to reduce or even stop the reaction. The behaviors that the organism exhibits in this adaptation response are referred to as forms of *coping*. As was the case with stressors, these coping behaviors form a broad spectrum, ranging from automatic physical responses, such as jumping out of the path of a speeding car, to cognitively determined strategies, such as responding assertively to a badgering salesperson.

Coping behavior is either effective or ineffective, depending on whether it is able to reduce or even remove a stressor, or to diminish or even short-circuit a full-blown GAS reaction before serious damage has been done to the organism. The role of coping in the stress cycle is illustrated in Fig. 1.

An external or internal event triggers the alarm response. If the event is evaluated as dangerous by the mind, the response continues, and coping behaviors are called into play. Effective coping is able to reduce significantly the intensity of the GAS, or

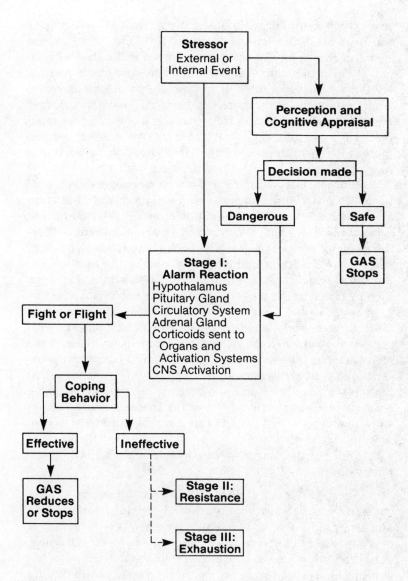

FIGURE 1. Sequence of events in the general adaptation syndrome (GAS). CNS, Central nervous system.

may even stop the stress response entirely. Ineffective coping, on the other hand, fails to slow down the GAS, and the alarm reaction continues and may eventually proceed to the stage of resistance or even exhaustion, depending on the strength of the stressor that initiated the reaction and the length of time the mind continues to label it as dangerous. From the viewpoint of stress management and control, effective coping is obviously desirable. Ineffective coping simply does not work well enough; furthermore, ineffective efforts to cope often prove to be additional sources of stress.

Consider Mary's coping behavior: Whenever Mary finds herself in a stressful situation, she feels jumpy and uncomfortable. She has learned that she can temporarily alleviate at least some of that feeling of discomfort by smoking cigarettes. Smoking does not remove the stress, however, and it actually sets off its own stress reaction in the body by introducing nicotine into the bloodstream and carrying tars and resins into the lungs, thereby lowering the lungs' efficiency. Like most smokers, Mary is unaware of her body's almost automatic alarm response to tobacco smoke, and she notices only the superficial sense of relief she experiences when she smokes. So, she smokes whenever she feels "nervous" and wonders why her cigarette consumption has slowly risen to over a pack and a half a day. The answer is that Mary relies heavily on an ineffective coping strategy. Smoking produces temporary effects, but leaves the real sources of her stress untouched—and triggers a small stress response of its own as well!

Other popular but counterproductive strategies include the following:

Alcohol. This is one of the most common ways of coping with stress in our society. Alcohol is a central nervous system depressant that produces a sense of euphoria when used in sufficient quantity. Alcohol often creates a temporary sense of well-being, but at the same time it creates a physiological alarm response within the organism and encourages the user to avoid dealing with the problems—often interpersonal or intrapersonal—that led to the use of alcohol as a coping behavior in the first place.

Drugs. As with alcohol, the main effect of drugs is to distract the user from the reality of his or her own situation. Although the effects of specific drugs vary enormously, their use as a coping behavior normally indicates a desire to avoid dealing with the real sources of stress.

Overwork or Hyperactivity. The key element here is activity for its own sake. The husband who works late every night to avoid having to interact with his family is avoiding stressful conflict just as surely as the homemaker who fills every moment with activity for fear that silence and rest will bring uncomfortable and confusing feelings to the surface. The same use of activity as a coping device can be seen in the person who devotes enormous amounts of time to a hobby or sport—the perpetual gardener, for instance, or the compulsive jogger. It should be stressed that none of these time-consuming activities is, by itself, an ineffective coping mechanism. Productive work or pleasurable recreation can be a healthy and wholesome way of dealing with stress. These methods become ineffective when they are overdone, when "keeping busy" becomes an attempt to avoid problems and run from stress.

Overeating. Another common but ineffective coping behavior is overeating. Those who turn to food when under stress have learned to associate the various acts associated with eating—smelling, tasting, chewing, swallowing, or the feeling of a full stomach—with a sense of relief or relaxation. But here, as with other ineffective strategies, this temporary pleasantness is offset by several more long-lasting and unpleasant effects. The primary difficulty is that overeating is simply a palliative; it offers a temporary sense of well-being, but avoids the real stressors. Another drawback of overeating is that it produces its own physiological and psychological side effects. Excessive weight, gained through overeating, can itself create stress in the organism and may contribute to disease or the dysfunction of bodily organs. Overweight may also affect a person's self-esteem and produce feelings of guilt or powerlessness. Clearly, overeating is not a productive form of coping behavior.

Ineffective coping can take many other forms besides the

few discussed here, but all forms of such behavior have the same consequences. Stress that has not been coped with effectively continues to affect the organism unabated. If such uncontrolled stress persists, the GAS will eventually take its toll as the organism slowly slips from alarm, to resistance, and finally to exhaustion. As the GAS continues through its cycle, the chance of stress-related disease increases as well. This increased chance of illness reveals another consequence of ineffective coping: Superficial, temporary, or palliative measures not only fail to affect the source of the stress reaction, but also tend to distract our attention from that source. Ineffective coping often does little more than make us believe that problems are minor and that they will "go away."

Imagine, for example, the case of Raphael, the owner of a small chain of restaurants. The last 2 years have been difficult ones for Raphael and his business. Managerial and financial problems, coupled with labor strife, have made Raphael anxious and fatigued. With each new crisis, he becomes more upset. His body signals his distress with a series of headaches and chronic gastritis, or "upset stomach." Raphael ignores these warning signals that his body is under serious stress and continues to cope as he has in the past: smoking heavily, working long hours, and eating and drinking far too much. After some months, his resistance begins to fail, and his body slowly slips into the exhaustion stage of the GAS. Raphael now begins to get infections, an even stronger signal that his body is suffering under the stressful burden that his life-style (not to mention his way of coping) has imposed on it.

But Raphael is not listening to his body. His coping behaviors, though ultimately of little use, do manage to keep him busy and distracted. So Raphael goes to his physician and receives antibiotics for the infection. This initiates a new stage in Raphael's attempts to cope with stress. Since his body is now in the exhaustion stage, Raphael will have little resistance and will become increasingly susceptible to infection or other illness. Instead of noticing his failing health, however, Raphael will use his physician as he has used other means of coping. Whenever he falls ill, Raphael will go to his doctor and demand medication.

While such medication may help Raphael's body fight off infection, it can also cause problems of its own. Antibiotics, for example, can disrupt the intestinal flora, the beneficial bacteria that inhabit the intestine and contribute to the proper absorption of nutrients by the body. Such disruption can produce diarrhea and result in decreased absorption of vitamins, minerals, and essential amino acids from the intestinal tract. The medication designed to cure Raphael's infection may actually lay the foundation for other, even more serious disorders.

Raphael, however, still does not pay attention to what his body is telling him. He continues to live in the same style, subjecting himself to even more pressure at work and continuing to depend upon ineffective coping strategies. After another year or so, his symptoms become more severe. He develops hypertension, and his heart begins to malfunction under the strain. One morning, Raphael collapses at his desk, the victim of a heart attack. Had he listened to his body's repeated warnings that it was suffering under stress, he might have prevented this debilitating and potentially lethal sequence. Raphael might have been in a far better position to attend to his body and what it was telling him if he had not put so much time and energy into inefficient—and useless—coping behavior.

The case of Raphael illustrates a point that is crucial for stress management and control. To cope effectively, it is first necessary to understand the stress reaction and how it works. Then we must become aware of the ways in which stress presents itself in our own lives. It is only when we recognize that we are under stress that we can begin to search out the stressors and develop effective coping behaviors. The next chapter will discuss some of the common manifestations of stress, so you can gain a better understanding of how stressed you are. In Chapter 3 you will find a program of stress self-analysis, designed to identify stressors in your life and to lead you to imaginative and effective coping.

CHAPTER 2

THE SIGNS OF STRESS

TENSION AND PHYSICAL ILLNESS

The signs of stress are many, and they can vary greatly in different persons. Some manifestations of stress, however, are more usual than others. By examining some of these more common ways in which stress shows its presence, we can better gauge the degree to which stress is present in our lives. As an example, consider the following situation: You are driving along the expressway when another car, without warning, cuts in front of you and then brakes suddenly. You react immediately as the threat of danger triggers an intense alarm reaction of the general adaptation syndrome (GAS): Your heart races, respiration quickens, and the pupils of your eyes dilate. You also cope automatically, swerving into an empty lane or slamming on your brakes. By now, you are also beginning to react emotionally as well, perhaps even to the extent of shouting or cursing at the offending driver. As the immediate danger passes, you begin to notice other things as well. Your muscles may be very tense, so tense that you experience a headache or backache. You might even feel sick to your stomach.

After a few minutes, most of the acute signs of the alarm reaction will have passed. Your heartbeat and respiration will have returned to normal, as will the pupils of your eyes. Your emotions will probably have moderated as well (unless you choose to keep the stress reaction going by continually reminding yourself in internal dialogue about "how irresponsible that other driver was" and so on). Some things will not have changed, however. The muscular tension triggered by the alarm reaction does not just vanish; it persists as a residual effect of your having been in a state of stress. Depending on the severity of your reaction to that near-accident, your stomach might remain upset for a time, too. These consequences of the alarm reaction provide a valuable clue to determining your own level of stress, for if muscular tension is a residual effect of stress, then determining how tense you are ought to provide some indication of your present level of stress.

In addition to tension in our muscles, there are a number of other physical effects that often appear as a consequence of stress reactions. Here is a series of questions that deals with the most common of these effects. Read through the questions carefully and keep track of how many you answer "Yes." The larger the number of positive answers, the greater the chance that your body is actively manifesting the signs of stress. Here are the questions:

Do you experience nervous tics or muscle spasms frequently? Do you find your eyelids twitching, your fingers picking at one another, or your hands rubbing parts of your body in repetitive ways?

Do you find yourself often clearing your throat? Do you sneeze a lot, or get sniffles and runny noses frequently? Do you find yourself short of breath or breathing shallowly? Does your mouth go dry in anticipation of events? Do you get colds often?

Do you experience pain in your lower back, chest, shoulder, or in the joints or other parts of your body? How about abdominal pains? Do you frequently get indigestion or "upset stomach"? Do you frequently feel bloated or pass gas? Does your skin itch for no reason, or do you find yourself scratching a lot?

When you sit, is your posture slumped? Do you sit with your arms crossed tightly as you talk to people? Do you drag your feet when you walk? In traffic, do you find yourself clutching the steering wheel? Does standing in line put you on edge? Do you startle easily in response to noises or sudden motion? Do you find that you get tension headaches?

The more of these questions you answered "Yes," the better the chance that you may be experiencing the effects from a stress reaction. If that reaction is strong and has been operating for some time, you may be at or near the stage of exhaustion. At that point in the GAS, bodily resistance is dramatically weakened, and the organism becomes subject to more serious disease and organic dysfunction. If you answered "Yes" to many of the previous set of questions, try the following questions as well. The more "Yes" answers you give to this second group, the greater the likelihood that your stress has progressed perilously close to, or actually moved on to, the exhaustion stage. Here are the questions:

Do you have hypertension, ulcers, heart disease, or emphysema? (At least 20 million Americans suffer from these stress-related diseases!) Or do you suffer from ulcerative colitis, spastic colon, or hemorrhoids? Do you get recurrent infections of the genitourinary tract? How about acne as an adult—or dermatitis, eczema, or some other recurrent, unexplained rashes? Finally, do you have debilitating lower back pain? Or migraine headaches?

These conditions, like the somewhat less severe ones described in the first group of questions, are physical indicators of stress. Through such symptoms and illnesses, your body is sending a powerful message to you. Your body acts like a mirror, reflecting the stresses to which it is subjected. One of the first steps toward real stress control is to learn how to pay attention to this powerful communication.

PSYCHOLOGICAL SIGNS OF STRESS

The body, however, is not the only vehicle by which information about stress is communicated. Behavior and feelings are also potent indicators of whether you are suffering from stress or not. During the alarm reaction and on into the stage of resistance, a variety of behavioral indicators can reveal the presence of the GAS taking place in your body. Some of the most obvious are those common but ineffective coping patterns that people so often turn to when under stress—smoking, drinking, and overeating. Other common indicators are agitation and increased activity. People under stress tend to walk faster, talk faster, even breathe faster. A good sign of this is the urge to rush or hurry wherever one is going; people under stress normally find it frustrating to get caught in traffic or have to wait for an elevator.

Besides such behavioral indications, there are other psychological signs that a person is under stress. Cognitive processing is disrupted, for example. As a result, normal patterns of organization can be changed by stress. A usually neat and well-organized person might become disorganized and untidy under stress conditions. The reverse might happen with a person who is normally a careless housekeeper; in the midst of the stress reaction, such a person might become compulsively neat and orderly. Cognitive responses to stress can also be more subtle. Stress can cause memory problems, for instance. When stressed, a person may have trouble keeping things straight or become confused about details. Another sign is repetitive thinking. A person under stress tends to narrow his range of interests and to think repeatedly about certain ideas. Often, this takes the form of what is popularly called "worrying."

Stress can also affect the emotions. One example common under stress is "fixated affect" (*affect* being a term used by psychologists to denote a person's subjective response to his environment); this occurs when a person clings to a feeling, much as someone might worry endlessly over a single disturbing thought. An illustration might be a person who, when subjected to stress, holds a grudge. Other examples of how stress can affect emotion are sudden outbursts of anger or joy, or sharp changes in mood toward either depression or hyperactivity. In the first two stages of the GAS, a person might exhibit either depression or a hyperactive, "up" mood. The depression involves such symptoms as lack of energy, loss of sense of humor, lack of smiling, and apathy that may last for days. The hyperactive state is much the opposite; the person is euphoric, frenetic, and probably boisterous, and often behaves irrelevantly. Obviously, to be considered depressive or hyperactive, the mood must represent a sharp departure from the person's normal emotional behavior.

Taken together, these various behavioral, cognitive, and emotional signs all point toward the experience of stress. As with physical symptoms in the body, the number of these psychological signals—and their intensity—will give a clue as to how stressed one is. If you find yourself manifesting a number of these psychological indicators of stress, then the chances are good that you are suffering from the ravages of stress. This possibility becomes even stronger if you earlier found a number of physical symptoms in yourself that are stress-related.

The psychological signs of stress are like the physical in another respect as well. Here, too, the signals become more dramatic and forceful as the person nears the stages of exhaustion. Physically, this approaching of the exhaustion threshold is signaled by the onset of serious disease. Psychologically, the clue to the approach toward exhaustion is low energy and its associated fatigue. To understand how and why this takes place, it is first necessary to examine energy and the role it plays in the body and mind.

LOW ENERGY AND FATIGUE

Both life itself and efficient functioning depend upon a continuous flow of energy. Energy is the force that moves us through life and that ebbs and flows in response to how we live. When there are strong demands on us externally—when we are under stress, for example—there are simultaneous demands on our internal resources, both physical and psychological. The greater the pressures of life, the more energy we need for survival.

Biologically, our survival depends in part on our nutrition. The foods we eat are digested, and the absorbed nutrients are transformed into energy—chemical, electrical, or psychological. These energies provide the forces that drive our thinking, feeling, physical movement, and all other biological functioning. Here, the primary process involves the conversion of matter into energy. Additionally, however, psychological energy can transform matter. When a person rests, relaxes, or sleeps, there is a reorganization of psychological energy that stimulates a reorganization of the body's biochemistry. Research has demonstrated that relaxation facilitates healing and prevents biological breakdown. In this way, psychological energy can affect the body

Energy is of crucial importance in our understanding of

stress because the body and mind draw upon energy reserves to provide the high level of energy output needed to meet conditions of stress. This reserve of energy is held in the form of vitamins, minerals, and energy-producing materials stored in the form of fats and carbohydrates. The liver serves as the major storage depot. In times of stress, when more energy is needed, the liver is signaled to release sucrose and other nutrients into the bloodstream. Because the body is able to store such energy in the form of nutrients, it is able to meet the demands of stress even if its present nutritional intake cannot keep pace with the demand for energy.

Continued mobilization of the body to deal with stressors, however, increases the demand for energy. As our adrenal, thymus, and pituitary glands work hard to mobilize our bodies in response to the alarm reaction of the GAS, we require more vitamin C, B vitamins, and pantothenic acid to maintain our energy levels. If our nutritional reserves are already drained from chronic exposure to stressful life events, then we will be less able to produce the needed levels of energy, and biological breakdown will be more likely. This is exactly what happens as the exhaustion stage of the GAS approaches. Bodily energy reserves have been depleted during the long stage of resistance, and as a result, the body's ability to provide necessary extra energy—chemical, electrical, or psychological—is seriously impaired. Without such energy, the ability of the body and mind to cope and resist the ravages of stress is considerably reduced, hence the increased incidence of serious disease during the exhaustion stage.

Psychologically, this gradual depletion of the body's energy reserves manifests itself in a cycle of low energy and fatigue that seems to feed upon itself, slowly winding down to total mental and physical exhaustion. The elements of this cycle can be seen in homes across the nation where people drag themselves home from work, only to flop down on the sofa wondering whether they will have the energy to make it through the evening. They may manage to get themselves to the dinner table to eat with barely an awareness of what is set before them, but they soon return to the sofa to watch television—a ready opiate for a fatigued and overworked population.

After they have watched television for a while, their eyes begin to sag and close, and many fall asleep right there. Those who do not will muddle lifelessly through the evening until bedtime, only to find that their sleep is often fitful and that they awaken with barely enough energy to get out of bed and go to work.

These, then, are people living on the edge, slowly slipping into the exhaustion stage of the GAS. Unfortunately, unless they get some relief from stressors, this downward-spiraling cycle will continue. Its victims will feel increasingly lifeless, listless, and numb. Their work will seem duller and more boring, and even minor additional stresses will be difficult to cope with. These people will also lose their perspective; molehills will really become mountains as their range of interest continues to narrow and intensify.

As people sink deeper into the stage of exhaustion, their behavior appears more and more like depression: They experience fatigue that, typically, is not alleviated by sleep, and feel a vague sense of anxiety. They become apathetic and humorless— and withdraw even further into sleep, television, or fantasy. These people continue to use ineffective coping behaviors, particularly smoking or abuse of alcohol or drugs, and generally feel helpless and unable to deal with their problems. They begin to doubt that they can ever overcome their difficulties and feel better.

Although these symptoms seem to match those of a clinical depression, there is usually one important difference between these victims of the fatigue–low energy cycle at the end of a sustained stress reaction and the clinically depressed patient: Clinically, depression is a response to loss, or perhaps to internal conflict or the suppression of anger. In such cases, the depression is tinged with sadness or a sense of loss. In cases of physical and mental fatigue arising from stress, however, there is no such sense of loss or conflict. The victim is simply exhausted— drained of energy and unable to cope either physically or mentally. The energy needed to perform normally is no longer there, and the person hovers at the brink of total collapse. The fatigue–low energy cycle is, in a sense, an attempt to cope with such vanishing energy reserves.

Both body and mind, then, respond to the challenges of the stress reaction. Their responses cover a broad range, but the symptoms of both bodily and mental reactions to stress are distinctive enough that they can serve as valuable indicators that a stress reaction is under way—and of how intense and persistent it is. By studying the bodily symptoms of stress and comparing them with the psychological ones of behavior, thought, and emotion, you should begin to have an accurate impression of the role that stress is currently playing in your life. There is, however, still a third way to measure this—a way that focuses upon the relationship between stress and change.

CHANGE AS A SIGN OF STRESS

Everyday life is filled with events that themselves evoke the stress response. A myriad of activities—ranging from loud noises, air pollution, or physical dangers to job demands, arguments at home, or overeating—can trigger a state of physical and mental mobilization. It was noted in Chapter 1 and should be repeated here that there is no way to avoid all these potential stressors. Indeed, Dr. Hans Selye, the father of modern stress research, has emphasized that some amount of stress is necessary and healthful. Stress, he feels, can provide the "spice of life." Total avoidance of stressors would be not only impractical, but also monotonous!

Selye's point is well-taken. Stress is a necessary element in all our lives, and there is no way to avoid it. In fact, although our discussion has tended to focus upon negative examples of stress, it is true that positive, exciting events can trigger the alarm response of the GAS just as well as negative, frightening ones. Stress is simply a given in our lives. What counts from the perspective of stress control is that we understand what stress is and how it affects us. Such knowledge gives us the foundation needed for effective stress control. One of the factors that is of great importance in such control is the understanding—and management—of change.

Human beings generally feel calm when their worlds are

ordered, predictable, and stable. When changes occur (and these changes can be either positive or negative), attitudes and expectations must be altered and new choices must often be made. This re-ordering or rearrangement of one's priorities is stressful and stimulates a state of vigilance. Intense feelings are often evoked as changes alter previous rules or understandings, change family configurations, or create new and unexpected situations. Change, in short, evokes a stress response from the organism, a response that is often intense and energy-demanding.

As a result, when people experience many changes over a short period of time, they become vulnerable to exhaustion and disease. Research has demonstrated, for instance, that within 2 weeks after experiencing some interpersonal crisis, a person is four times more likely to contract a streptococcal infection than to contract other types of infections. Similarly, college football players who have experienced many life changes during a one-year period prior to playing football are twice as likely to have injuries during the season as those who did not experience so many changes. Patients hospitalized with a heart attack are more likely to have experienced some interpersonal crisis just prior to the attack. There are also a number of reports that indicate that up to 75% of persons who contract cancer have suffered the loss of a relative or close friend in the 2-year period prior to the onset of the carcinoma.

Clearly, changes in people's lives—particularly changes in interpersonal relationships—seem to correlate with loss of resistance and energy and with the onset of disease. Two researchers, Dr. Thomas Holmes and Dr. Richard Rahe, have devised a rating scale designed to take this consequence of change into account. Their scale, which they called a "Life Events Survey," lists 43 events that involve some life change (see Fig. 2). A score (termed the "mean value" in Fig. 2) has been assigned to each event. This score was determined according to the rankings and ratings assigned to these events by a large sample of persons.

Since change is such an important element in creating stress, it will be very valuable for you to fill out the Life Events Survey form before you continue reading. Follow the directions carefully. Drs. Holmes and Rahe termed the numbers in the right-

Instructions: Please check the life events that occurred during the previous 2 years. Circle the "mean value" for each item checked, and add all mean values for a total LCU score. If an event occurred more than once, then multiply the number of occurrences by its mean value. Thus, if you were divorced twice during the 2-year period, then the score for "Divorce" is $2 \times 73 = 146$.

Rank	Check if occurred	Life event	Number of occurrences	Mean value
1	☐	Death of a spouse	___	100
2	☐	Divorce	___	73
3	☐	Marital separation	___	65
4	☐	Jail term	___	63
5	☐	Death of a close family member	___	63
6	☐	Personal injury or illness	___	53
7	☐	Marriage	___	50
8	☐	Fired at work	___	47
9	☐	Marital reconciliation	___	45
10	☐	Retirement	___	45
11	☐	Change in health of a family member	___	44
12	☐	Pregnancy (score applies for both spouses)	___	40
13	☐	Sexual difficulties	___	39
14	☐	Gain of a new family member	___	39
15	☐	Business readjustment	___	39
16	☐	Change in financial state	___	38
17	☐	Death of a close friend	___	37
18	☐	Change to different line of work	___	36
19	☐	Change in number of arguments with spouse	___	35
20	☐	Mortgage over $10,000	___	31
21	☐	Foreclosure of mortgage or loan	___	30
22	☐	Change in responsibilities at work	___	29
23	☐	Son or daughter leaving home	___	29
24	☐	Trouble with in-laws	___	29
25	☐	Outstanding personal achievement	___	28
26	☐	Spouse began or stopped work	___	26
27	☐	Began or ended schooling	___	26
28	☐	Change in living conditions	___	25
29	☐	Revision of personal habits	___	24
30	☐	Trouble with boss	___	23
31	☐	Change in work hours or conditions	___	20
32	☐	Change in residence	___	20
33	☐	Change in schools	___	20
34	☐	Change in recreation	___	19
35	☐	Change in church activities	___	19
36	☐	Change in social activities	___	18
37	☐	Mortgage or loan less than $10,000	___	17
38	☐	Change in sleeping habits	___	16

Rank	Check if occurred	Life event	Number of occurrences	Mean value
39	☐	Change in number of family get-togethers	____	15
40	☐	Change in eating habits	____	15
41	☐	Vacation	____	13
42	☐	Christmas	____	12
43	☐	Minor violations of the law	____	11
			Total LCU score:	____

FIGURE 2. Life Events Survey.

hand column (the numbers given for the "life events") *LCUs,* which stands for "Life Change Units." Multiply each LCU by the number of times that event has occurred in the past 2 years; then add these products to get your final LCU score. Go ahead and mark the chart. When you have finished scoring it, you will want to read on.

Basically, your score on the Life Events Survey indicates your probable level of resistance and how likely you are to become ill from the changes you have been through during the past 2 years. It should be emphasized before we go into this further that these are probabilities. Given a group of people who have filled out the Life Events Survey and received the same score, all of them will have the same probability (or odds) of becoming ill as a result of the changes they have experienced. But interestingly enough, only some of those people will actually become ill. Part of the reason that only some fall ill is that those who cope successfully are more likely to be healthy, regardless of how much change they have been through. We will talk later about how to maximize such effective coping—and even how to live so as to anticipate stress and thrive upon it. For now, it is important to remember that your score is just that, a score. Whether you remain well or eventually become sick will depend more upon how you live and cope from here on than upon what score you got. A high score, however, should serve as a warning that you may need to attend to stress in your life and devote yourself to the more effective ways of coping—many of which are discussed later in this book.

With this caveat in mind, you can interpret your score on the Life Events Survey as follows:

Your total LCU score	Your chance of illness or injury*	Your level of resistance
150–199	Low (9–33%)	High resistance
200–299	Moderate (30–52%)	Borderline resistance
300 or more	High (50–86%)	Low resistance—high vulnerability

If your total LCU score falls between 150 and 199, your resistance is high and you have a small chance of contracting illness because of the stress induced by changes in your life over the past 2 years. If your score is within the range from 200 to 299, however, your resistance is likely to be less and your chance of illness has increased to moderate. Finally, if your LCU exceeds 300, the odds are that your resistance is low, perhaps even dangerously so, and you are at a relatively high risk for illness. The reason for this high likelihood of illness is that an LCU of over 300 probably indicates that you have entered the exhaustion stage of the GAS.

An example might clarify why this is the case. Consider Mike, a 28-year-old man who comes to his family physician at midweek complaining of chest pain, headaches, and a general sense of irritability. His doctor cannot find anything organically wrong with this young, athletic, and otherwise apparently healthy person. The only obvious stressor in Mike's life seems to be some tension at work, so the physician tells him that he is anxious and must relax more, perhaps even take a vacation. Mike takes his doctor's advice and, together with his wife and newborn child, goes on a short vacation. After he gets back, though, he contracts a cold that lingers for weeks. Mike is perplexed. He cannot understand why a person so obviously healthy as he is should not be able to get rid of something as minor as a cold—especially right after a relaxing vacation!

A review of Mike's recent life reveals, however, that he is

*The range of percentages (e.g., 9–33%) indicates the range of findings drawn from a variety of research studies.

actually under a considerable amount of stress due to a series of significant life changes. During the previous 2-year period, he married (LCU of 50), his wife became pregnant (LCU of 40), and they subsequently gained a new family member (LCU of 39) and bought a house (LCU of 31). His wife stopped working (LCU of 26), they changed living conditions by moving from an apartment into their new house (LCU of 25), and Mike himself revised his personal habits and routines (LCU of 24). Mike also had problems with his boss (LCU of 23) and changed his social activities because of his single primary relationship with his wife (LCU of 18), and the family celebrated Christmas (LCU of 12). His total LCU score was 288!

Mike appears both normal and healthy, but his score on the Life Events Survey indicates that his body is paying the price for all the changes he has experienced over the past 2 years. His resistance has been lowered by these stressful changes, and although he has not yet reached the stage of exhaustion, his body is sufficiently depleted that it is unable to cast off his cold. Instead, the body fights a rear-guard action, and the cold lingers on for weeks. This physical symptom of persistent illness, coupled with Mike's high score on the Life Events Survey, indicates that he needs to cope more effectively with the stresses of his life.

Your score on the Life Events Survey may communicate a similar message. Like the physical and psychological signs of stress discussed earlier, your total LCU score is an indicator of your personal level of stress—and the level of your body's resistance. A high LCU score, together with evident physical or psychological indications of stress, signals a need to slow down, seek stability, and begin a careful personal investigation of the role that stress plays in your life. A lower LCU score, along with fewer psychological or physical signs of stress, indicates a less urgent situation. However, you may find that you will also profit from an examination of how stress affects your life.

The signs of stress discussed in this chapter—physical and psychological symptoms, together with their extent—form the foundation upon which any personal stress analysis can be built. By familiarizing yourself with these various signs, you will be ready to undertake the next step: observing your own daily behavior to see whether, when, and under what conditions these signs of stress emerge. Such observation is the first step in undertaking a *stress self-analysis*. The next chapter will describe in detail how you can use such an analysis to increase your own awareness of stress and enhance your ability to gain control over it.

CHAPTER 3

YOUR STRESS SELF-ANALYSIS

There is an old joke about a man who went to a psychiatrist because of a problem with thumb-sucking. After several months of therapy, the patient was delighted with the results and was describing them to a friend. "So," the friend said, "you don't suck your thumb any more?" "Oh, no," replied the patient, "I still suck it as much as ever. But now I know why!"

Learning about stress can produce similar problems. You can understand the stress reaction, and even note the signs of stress in your everyday life, yet still have little idea of what to do about it. Simply knowing about stress is not enough. Achieving real control over stress requires something more: an understanding of the unique patterns that stress takes in your life. This personal understanding is necessary because the actual patterns that trigger stress reactions vary enormously from one person to the next.

Jack, for instance, has recently discovered the game of soccer. Although he never played the game when he was younger, he learned about it several years ago when his son began playing soccer at school. Practicing with his boy sparked Jack's interest, and he soon found the game a pleasurable way to exercise. After some months, Jack heard about a league for older players and eventually joined a team as a substitute. Now, having improved his skills somewhat, he plays every weekend. Jack really looks forward to the games. They are both fun and a great workout. He even enjoys the friendly competition and the occasional body contact. It reminds him of how much he enjoyed athletics when he was younger. Playing soccer, for Jack, is relaxing and pleasurable.

Another person, however, might experience the same situation in a very different way. Consider Luigi. Raised in Italy, Luigi had athletic ability that was noticed at an early age and praised by his father, a skilled soccer player. During childhood, Luigi was encouraged to play soccer and to develop his skill. His father spent many evenings drilling Luigi on the fundamentals of the game, often criticizing the boy harshly for errors. As his considerable ability developed, Luigi found himself selected by better and better local and school teams. Here, too, the emphasis was on excellent performance: Either he could do the job or the team would find someone else who could. Luigi drove himself to excel and, by his early 20s, was an excellent player on a respected semiprofessional team. There was even the prospect of a professional career. Soon thereafter, Luigi's family moved to the United States, and he worked in the family's grocery store. After a time, Luigi found a local soccer team, made up largely of immigrants, and he began to play once again. The level of competition was far lower than what he was used to, and many of the players really didn't seem to try too hard. Luigi, however, gave his all in every game, playing as hard as he could. As each game approached, he would become nervous and agitated. Sometimes he would even vomit before the game began.

Jack and Luigi illustrate that the same situation can be stressful for one person and harmless, or actually self-enhancing, for another. What makes the difference, of course, is the way each person interprets the situation. For Jack, the prospect of playing soccer is pleasant exercise, tinged with positive memories of earlier athletic competition. Luigi, on the other hand, sees each game as a mortal contest, yet another test of his personal worth. He cannot separate playing soccer from his personal expectation of excellence and success, and as a result, he becomes acutely stressed as each game approaches. It might be argued that the stress drives him to excellent levels of performance, but it is far more certain that the repeated stress will take its toll on Luigi, both physically and mentally. Soccer will be a source of distress and fatigue, instead of an opportunity for relaxation and enjoyment.

Clearly, Jack has no stress problem as far as his soccer playing is concerned, but Luigi does. Yet Luigi's problem would not go away if Luigi were to read a book or article that described the stress reaction—not even if Luigi himself were to check over his signs of stress and discover that he is far more stressed than he had imagined. Such knowledge, like the insight of the thumb-sucking patient in the joke, is not enough. Before Luigi could really begin to cope effectively with the stress he feels whenever he plays soccer, he would need to understand the entire *stress pattern* that he is involved in. He would need to comprehend the overall sequence of events that lead up to, and trigger, his stress response. Without this personal insight into his own, unique stress-producing process, Luigi will probably be doomed to repeat his stressful behavior before every game.

Like Luigi, each of us experiences uniquely stressful situations—events in our lives that we customarily react to with alarm, resistance, and—if the reaction continues long enough—exhaustion. Since these stress-inducing situations are personally determined, however, the only way to detect them—and thereby begin to gain some sense of control over them—is by mapping out the role they play in our lives. This can be done in several steps. First, we can sensitize ourselves to potential stressors in our environment. (Luigi might ask himself, for instance, when it is that he feels stressed and discover--surprise!—that it is usually before a soccer game.) The next step is to build upon that initial awareness of possible sources of stress, and one excellent way of doing this is to keep a *stress journal* or notebook, a day-by-day account of when and where the signs of stress appear in our lives. Such a journal is really the key to developing your own stress control because it, above all else, will reveal the patterns of stress, those unique configurations of stressor and response that operate in your life. Finally, the stress journal provides the raw material for a personal *stress analysis,* a method by which you systematically evaluate and interpret the information in the journal. This analysis, when well grounded in your examination of potential stressors and in your careful observation of your own behavior, can then serve as the basis for the subsequent development of a comprehensive program of stress management. Knowing your personal stressors and how you react to them provides a tremendous opportunity for you to alter your behavior, coping more efficiently or perhaps avoiding stressful situations altogether.

EXTERNAL AND INTERNAL DIMENSIONS OF STRESS

Almost anything is potentially a stressor. All that is needed is that the cognitive processes of the mind identify something as dangerous, and the alarm reaction of the general adaptation syndrome (GAS) springs into operation. Because the potential range of stressors is so great, it is useful to divide possible sources of stress into two groups, depending on whether they are located in the external environment or whether they are experienced internally. Both these dimensions of stress, external and internal, will be examined below by means of a series of questions designed to reveal which aspects of the internal or external environments might be stressful for you. For each set of questions, there is a comprehensive chart that will help you summarize and interpret your responses.

External Dimensions

Beginning with the external environment, there are nine major sources, or dimensions, that can induce a stress reaction. These dimensions are listed below. Each is followed by several questions for you to answer. Positive responses to any of the questions suggest that the dimension in question may be a potential source of stress for you; several positive answers to questions for that same dimension increase the likelihood that this particular dimension should be examined more carefully later to determine its exact role in your pattern of stress.

1. *Noise*. Do you work in a noisy environment? Are you especially sensitive to noise? Do you startle easily in response to noises? Are you more relaxed when you are quiet, rather than when you are in an active or noisy environment?

2. *Air Pollution.* Do you live or work in a major urban environment? On the job, do you work in a setting where many people smoke? Do you smoke yourself, or do you find cigarette smoke unpleasant or irritating? Is there adequate ventilation at home and work? Are there any unpleasant or irritating odors that constantly permeate the air at home or work?

3. *Adverse Lighting.* Do your eyes feel strained during the day at work? Do you rub your eyes often? When you have to perform tasks that are visually demanding, do you get headaches? Does working indoors under artificial light make you feel less energetic or depressed? (Lack of exposure to ultraviolet light, an invisible but biologically essential component of sunlight, can contribute to energy loss and depression.)

4. *Overcrowding.* Do you work or live in a setting in which there are many people in a small area? Do you find yourself being interrupted by the movement of others into your work or living space? Do you find yourself wanting to escape from that environment so that you can be alone?

5. *Negative Personal Interactions.* Do you have many negative interactions with people at work? Are you in conflict with your boss or co-workers? At home, do you argue or fight frequently? Do you spend much of your time thinking about conflicts or difficulties you have had with others? Overall, do you feel negative about your relationships with your spouse, children, friends, or relatives?

6. *Adverse Work Conditions.* Is your work setting too hot, too cold, or otherwise physically uncomfortable? Do you find your work monotonous or uninteresting? Are you usually under pressures to perform? Do the conditions at work lead you to feel exhausted by the end of the day? Does the nature of your work—or the physical layout of your work space—make you feel tense or inefficient?

7. *Major Life Changes.* Have you experienced many major life changes over the past 2 years? (These might include such things as a new job, new geographic location, career change, loss of a loved one, marriage or divorce, or economic changes.) Do you feel that you have not coped adequately with these changes? Do you feel that these changes raised issues that are still unresolved?

Have you been seriously or chronically ill during the past 2 years?

8. *Availability of Choices.* Are you required to make too many decisions at work? Or does your work make you feel bored or powerless? Do you feel you have too many responsibilities to cope with, either on the job or at home? Do you feel that you are not permitted to think or act for yourself?

9. *Rules of Living.* Do the rules you live by at home or work restrict your life too much? Do you regard those rules as too inflexible or feel trapped by them? Is your expression of your feelings or creativity restricted or stifled by those rules? Are you dissatisfied with the lack of change, either at work or in your home life?

As you can see, there are many potential sources for stress in your external environment. Using Fig. 3, review your responses to the questions about each of the nine external dimensions. Note the number of questions you answered "Yes" for each dimension and use the space for comments to make any additional observations that may come to mind as you reflect upon how each of these external dimensions affects your life.

Internal Dimensions

As far as internal dimensions of stress are concerned, there are ten different areas that should be examined. Answer the questions following each dimension.

1. *Nutritional Adequacy.* Do you eat irregularly or have an unbalanced diet? Do you find that your energy level fluctuates throughout the day? Do you eat too much? Or do you eat too much of one kind of food? Do you crave sweets when you feel tired?

2. *Junk Foods and Nonfoods.* Do you use alcohol or drugs frequently? Do you often eat junk foods? (Junk foods are highly refined or processed foods, often high in sugars, fats, and food additives. Examples are presweetened cereals, soft drinks, and potato chips and other snack foods.) Do you feel flushed or anx-

Dimensions	Number of "Yes" responses	Additional comments or observations
1. Noise		
2. Air pollution		
3. Adverse lighting		
4. Overcrowding		
5. Negative personal interactions		
6. Adverse work conditions		
7. Major life changes		
8. Availability of choices		
9. Rules of living		

FIGURE 3. External dimensions of stress.

ious after eating or drinking? Do you experience unexplained feelings of anxiety or rushes of energy? Do you notice mood swings after eating or drinking?

3. *Exercise.* Do you get enough exercise to keep your heart and lungs in peak physical condition? Do you get winded after climbing a flight of stairs? If you exercise infrequently, do you still try to "go all out" and try for maximum performance? (Such sudden outbursts of energy can be dangerous; it is possible to precipitate a coronary this way!) At the end of the day, do you feel enervated or lackadaisical?

4. *Posture.* Do you stand or sit for long hours? Does your work require that you remain in one position for long periods of time? Do you get backaches, headaches, neckaches, or leg cramps during the day or after work? When you go to sleep, does your body ache or feel tense?

5. *Rhythm and Pacing.* Do you push yourself at work? Is your working pace rushed or abrupt? When you work, do you set your own comfortable pace, or do you tend to match the work rhythms of those around you? When caught in a traffic jam, do you often get angry or frustrated? Do you become irritable if you have to wait in a line?

6. *Personal Psychology.* Are you in conflict about your work or some other aspect of your life? Do you feel as though you need to hurry and that you must be doing something at all times? Do you dislike or not respect yourself? Do you take yourself, your work, or your life too seriously and avoid relaxing or "goofing off"? Are you unrealistically ambitious? Are you depressed about work or your family or personal life?

7. *Sexual Fulfillment.* Do you feel comfortable about sex? Are your sexual needs adequately met? Can you "let yourself go" sexually, or do you limit your sexual expression? After having sex, do you feel good? Are you satisfied with your partner and yourself sexually?

8. *Spiritual and Creative Fulfillment.* Do you feel a lack of meaning in your work or life? Do your activities seem empty or purposeless? Do you have areas of interest or self-expression that you feel are blocked or unfulfilled? Do you avoid being creative or imaginative?

Dimensions	Number of "Yes" responses	Additional comments or observations
1. Nutritional adequacy	___	_____
2. Junk foods and nonfoods	___	_____
3. Exercise	___	_____
4. Posture	___	_____
5. Rhythm and pacing	___	_____
6. Personal psychology	___	_____
7. Sexual fulfillment	___	_____
8. Spiritual and creative fulfillment	___	_____
9. Sensory and neurological behavior	___	_____
10. Personal interests	___	_____

FIGURE 4. Internal dimensions of stress.

9. *Sensory and Neurological Behavior.* Are you the type of person who startles at noises or visual stimulation? Do you get uncomfortable or "motion sick" in moving vehicles? Does walking up or down stairs make you feel dizzy or off-balance? Do you take a long time to recover from stressful events?

10. *Personal Interests.* Do you fail to take time to do things for yourself? Would you feel guilty if you did something just to satisfy yourself—not for anyone or anything else? Do you make excuses to avoid doing things that you would really like to do by yourself?

These, then, are the dimensions of the internal environment that can serve as sources of stress. Review your responses to the questions for each dimension and record the number of "Yes" responses in Fig. 4. Then reflect upon your answers and make any additional comments or observations you wish in the spaces provided on the chart.

BEGINNING YOUR STRESS SELF-ANALYSIS

By this point in the book, you will have learned several important things. First, you have been introduced to the concepts of the "stressor" and physiological "stress reaction" of the GAS. Furthermore, you have been shown the active role that the cognitive processes of the mind play in triggering the stress reaction and in determining both the intensity and duration of that reaction. You have also had a chance to assess the degree of stress in your life by examining how tense or ill you are and what behavioral signs of stress appear in your life and by determining how much change you have recently experienced. Finally, you have investigated both external and internal dimensions of stress, potential sources of stressors in your own life. Now comes the opportunity to put all this learning to work on your own behalf by starting your stress self-analysis. This analysis will help you to discover the unique *patterns* of stress that operate in your life. Knowledge of these patterns—and how they work to create stress for you—is the first step toward overcoming the destructive effects of stress and living a more productive and satisfying life.

This stress self-analysis is grounded upon several principles that have already been discussed. The most important is that both our bodies and our minds respond to stress in various ways. If we are aware of these signs of physical and mental response to stress, we can begin to notice when we become stressed. Noticing that we are under stress then provides the foundation for the next step: observing the events that preceded the stress reaction. By working backward from the point at which we first noticed that we were experiencing stress, it is usually possible to detect the events that triggered the alarm reaction in the first place. This detection introduces us to the specific stressors at work in the situation. Knowing what these stressors are, and the situation or situations in which they customarily appear, prepares us for the final step—actually analyzing the relationship between the stress reaction and the stressful situation that evoked it. Such analysis, as will be shown in a subsequent section, often provides the insight necessary to devise new, more efficient ways of coping with the stress in question. Sometimes, because of such understanding, it is even possible to reduce or even eliminate the stress reaction entirely. Thus, stress self-analysis is a powerful step toward realistic and effective stress control

You can begin your stress self-analysis in either of two ways: by "stress brainstorming" or by keeping a "stress journal." Both methods accomplish the same purpose, but the brainstorming method is more loosely organized and spontaneous, while the journal tends to be a more carefully structured and methodical approach. Choose whichever method you prefer. You may find that you will want to switch at a later time, or you may discover that a combination of both methods works best for you. Whatever method or combination you use, the important thing is that the stress self-analysis puts you in touch with stressors and stress-producing situations in your life.

Both stress brainstorming and the stress journal start in the same way, by asking you to review a list of the most common physical and mental signs of stress. This list summarizes much of the material discussed in Chapter 2, so you might wish to review that chapter before beginning your own analysis. You might also want to review your responses to the external and internal dimensions of stress discussed earlier in this chapter. Your answers to those questions about stress dimensions may have alerted you to signs of stress in your own life that you might want to add to the list of common stress signals given below. When you have completed any reviewing you might want to do of Chapter 2 and the earlier part of this chapter, study the following list of frequent indicators of stress:

Body Symptoms

Flushing	Constipation
Sweating	Fatigue
Dry mouth	Loss of appetite
Shallow breathing	Nervous chill
Chest oppression and pain	Insomnia
Heart palpitation	Breathlessness
Pounding pulse	Flatus (passing gas)
Increased blood pressure	Belching
Headache	Abdominal cramping
Backache	"Irritable colon"
Feeling of weakness	Dizziness or faintness
Intestinal distress	Paresthesias (illusory prickly-
Vomiting	skin sensations)
Diarrhea	

Feeling States

Agitation	Panicky feeling
Shakiness	Depression (feeling blue)
Easy tiring	Irritability

Cognitive States

Worry	Forgetfulness
Dread	Nightmares
Inattention	Fear of death
Distractibility	

Motor Symptoms (muscles involved)

Muscular tightness	Incoordination
Tremors	Sighing
Tics (spasms)	Freezing, feeling immobilized
Increased startle reaction	

With this list in mind (together with any additional signs of stress you have noticed while reading earlier in the book), here is how to start stress brainstorming: First, make a list of all the signs of stress that you remember experiencing during the past week. After you have made the list, remember and describe the situation surrounding each experience of stress. Your recall does not have to be perfect. Just write down whatever you can remember about what happened before and after the stressful event. (Incidentally, if you don't enjoy writing, it is also possible to do brainstorming with a tape recorder. Talk into the tape recorder as you review various symptoms of stress, and when you discover a symptom you have experienced during the past week, simply talk about that experience, when and where it happened, what preceded it, what came after, and so on. Then go on to the next symptom of stress you experienced and do the same.) You can also do brainstorming on a daily basis, sitting down at the end of the day and reviewing your activities to see whether there were any stressful situations. Describe the circumstances surrounding each such situation.

The next step is to look for *patterns* of stress. You may discover such a pattern if it is obvious or particularly strong. In more subtle cases of stress, it may take repeated observation of your life and behavior before a pattern will emerge. The important thing to remember is that these patterns *are* there; your mind is identifying stressors and triggering the GAS response. Careful observation of the events of your life will lead you to a better understanding of what the stressors are and what sets of circumstances lead the mind to identify them as stressors.

As an example of this pattern-identification process, consider the case of Fern, a housewife and working mother in her late 20s. When Fern began stress brainstorming, she soon noticed that a number of indicators of stress tended to appear together early in the evening, and particularly on weekdays when she worked. She began to observe herself more carefully during those periods and then brainstormed about what she had noticed. She soon realized that there was a more or less regular pattern. Every evening after she had come home from work, picked up her daughter at the baby sitter, and fixed dinner, Fern began to feel listless and depressed. Frequently, her back began to ache, and sometimes she developed a headache as well. As she continued to observe her own behavior, Fern noticed that these feelings usually began as she cleaned up after dinner, doing the dishes and straightening the kitchen, while her husband relaxed in the family room and watched the news. She also observed that the symptoms were worse on evenings when her daughter was demanding or cranky, constantly interrupting Fern as she tried to finish her work. Once the details of this stressful pattern became clear, Fern used some additional techniques (to be described shortly) to help herself determine more accurately just what it was about this situation that made it so stressful. She soon discovered her resentment over her husband's lack of support and his failure to help with either the dinner, the dishes, or their daughter. Using self-assertiveness (also discussed later in the book), Fern was able to confront her husband about her needs for support and assistance. Eventually, they were able to work out a compromise that alleviated much of Fern's stress and made the dinner hour a relaxing and rejuvenating part of her day.

Fern was able to learn about the causes of her stress because she paid attention to her own behavior. She observed the pain of backaches and headaches in her body, and she noticed the sense of depression and fatigue she experienced at the same time. These were physical and psychological messages that Fern was constantly sending to herself, and by paying careful attention to them, she was able to arrive at a realistic understanding of what was causing her distress. She was then able to take steps that enabled her to cope more effectively and, eventually, to completely eliminate the problem.

The stress journal offers a similar opportunity for you to explore the sources of your own stress. Like stress brainstorming, the journal gives you the opportunity to pay attention to your own life, noticing when stressful events occur and attending to the circumstances that trigger them or that cause them to stop. Unlike brainstorming, however, the stress journal is a somewhat more methodical and carefully structured exercise. You may find this more systematic approach to stress observation more to your liking than the more spontaneous style of brainstorming. If so, give the journal a try. You may also discover that some combination of the two methods works best for you.

To keep a stress journal, you will need some sort of notebook in which you can write your daily observations. Select any size or shape you like, as long as there is adequate room to write down the necessary information. The format in Fig. 5 is recommended.

To illustrate how the journal works, consider the case of Jeff, a junior executive in an insurance firm. By use of the brainstorming method, Jeff became aware that his greatest difficulty with stress involved his work. He decided to keep a stress journal to see whether he could discover specifically what was troubling him. The next morning, Jeff began work and felt no strong indications that he was under stress. About half-past-nine, however, he suddenly became aware that his stomach felt as though it had been tied in a knot. Jeff immediately made an entry in his journal. As he wrote, Jeff became aware that he had been feeling great until his boss came into his office and said a few words to him. He also noticed that the upset feeling in his stomach persisted until the boss left the office to attend a meeting. Jeff's journal entry appears in Fig. 6.

Jeff's entry is an excellent example of the way the journal works because it helps him to associate his symptom (the message that his body sent him that it was under stress) with the event that triggered off the alarm reaction of the GAS. In Jeff's case, the event had something to do with his boss's visit. Note that Jeff is still far from understanding exactly what it was that triggered his distress, but making the journal entry has alerted him to a possible pattern behind his experience of stress at work. By continuing to observe himself, Jeff will be able to get a more accurate impression of precisely what it is the boss does that

Date and time:

Signal(s) of stress:

Duration of symptom:

Event(s) prior to symptom:

Event when symptom stopped:

Comments:

FIGURE 5. Recommended format for a stress journal.

Date and time: Thursday, 9:30 A.M.

Signal(s) of stress: Knot in my stomach

Duration of symptom: I felt it strongly for about 10 or 15 minutes, but the feeling kept on for about an hour more.

Event(s) prior to symptom: The boss came into my office and spoke to me. I can't remember what he said.

Event when symptom stopped: The feeling finally went away when the boss left the office.

Comments: I'm not sure what it was about the boss coming to my office and talking to me. But something he said or did drive set off my stress reaction?

FIGURE 6. Sample entry in Jeff's stress journal.

causes Jeff to react with an upset stomach. Once he has a clearer idea of the cause of his stress, Jeff will be in a much better position to take action to alleviate, or even eliminate, his stress reaction.

As with brainstorming, the stress journal will work best for you if you keep it regularly over a period of at least several weeks. Some insights may come more quickly, of course, but ingrained patterns of stress-producing behavior often take repeated observation and thoughtful reflection before they become comprehensible. In stress self-analysis, the degree of success is often directly related to the amount of time given to brainstorming or the keeping of the journal.

TECHNIQUES FOR INTERPRETATION

As you become aware of a pattern between a particular stress signal that you experience and a sequence of events that seems to trigger that stress, the next step is to *interpret* the meaning of that pattern. Sometimes the interpretation will occur spontaneously. A man might notice, for instance, that he is always tense and tired after he arrives home from work. Yet as he checks over his journal, he sees that he seldom if ever feels those signs of stress before he leaves for home. Suddenly he realizes the stressful toll taken by his daily commute in heavy traffic. "That's it," he thinks, "that damn drive is killing me!" With this insight, the meaning of his stress pattern becomes clear, and the man is ready to consider what he might do to reduce the stress of driving— take the bus or train, for example, or join a car pool.

Not all interpretation is so spontaneous, however. In many cases, it requires more effort to discover the meaning of a particular stress pattern. Two techniques that are often helpful in doing this are: (1) language association and (2) self-questioning. The first of these methods, language association, depends upon commonly used phrases or expressions that mention either a part of the body or some other sensation that indicates tension or stress. Examples might include expressions such as "He's a pain in the neck," "Her heart ached," or "I can't stomach that."

It is no accident that expressions such as these occur in our language, for these expressions communicate feelings—and feelings are often connected metaphorically with the body. Our postures, facial expression, tone of voice, gait, gestures—or all of these—are bodily ways of reflecting feelings. Our language merely takes the process one step further, using words for various body parts or sensations to describe feelings. If we are angry, for example, we may communicate that feeling simultaneously on a variety of channels: through posture (sharp, angular movements), facial expression (narrowed eyes, flared nostrils), tone of voice (harsh), gait (aggressive), gestures (forceful, threatening), and language ("You burn me up").

This regular use of words that describe body or sensations as a way of expressing feeling provides us with a powerful tool for interpreting patterns of stress. If you discover in your stress self-analysis that you are experiencing a pattern of stress response that involves a part of your body, allow yourself to free-associate to the name of that body part. That is, make yourself comfortable and relaxed, and then begin to think about the body part that is involved in your stress pattern. Try to think of some common expression that refers to that part of the body, and then see whether that expression applies in any way to the stress pattern you are trying to learn about.

For example, suppose you have discovered a pattern that results in your experiencing gastritis (a burning sensation in the esophagus caused by excess stomach acid) or stomach pains. Using language association, you might think about your stomach and any common phrases that might refer to it. You might think of an expression such as "I can't stomach that." Then try to apply that phrase to your own situation. Usually, this is best done in the form of a question: "Whom or what can't I stomach?" By such free association, simply playing with the word "stomach" and seeing what sort of fanciful connections you can make, you may discover connections between the way we talk about "stomachs" and the gastric distress you have been experiencing.

A useful variation of this technique is to use writing, instead of just thinking, as the means of free association. You can simply write down the name of the body parts or sensations involved in your stress pattern, and then just write about them, jotting down whatever comes into your mind. If you choose this method, it is important to realize that this is an exercise in self-discovery— not in fancy or formal writing. If you free-associate in writing, it is important to write quickly and without reflection. Write rapidly and spontaneously, concentrating only on getting words onto the paper. Later, you can be critical and reflective; the free-association method of writing simply provides you with raw material that you can then investigate more carefully to see what relation it bears to your stress pattern. If you have trouble writing freely and spontaneously, you might want to make a contract with yourself that you will write *without stopping* for a set period of time, usually 5 or 10 minutes. Don't remove your pencil or pen from the paper (or your fingers from the typewriter), and make no corrections. Just write whatever comes into your mind about the body part that is involved in your stress pattern. Like the brainstorming process discussed earlier, free association— whether in the mind or on paper—will often lead spontaneously to insight into the nature of the stressful patterns that affect your life. Also, like brainstorming or the journal, this free-association technique usually works best if it is practiced regularly.

This technique is exemplified by the case of Cindy, a nurse who had been referred for psychological examination by her physician. Cindy's problem was chronic neck pain, for which no organic cause could be found. As part of her treatment, Cindy began to keep a stress journal. After a few weeks, she became aware that the pain tended to peak at certain times and diminish at others. Further observation revealed that such increases normally occurred at home. Cindy continued her journal until she had a clear conception of her stress pattern. Then she began to use language association. Because the journal had worked so well, Cindy decided to try writing as her vehicle for free association, and she soon discovered that she had written the following entry:

> My neck has been hurting so bad. Why does it hurt? Who is giving me this bad pain in the neck? When does it hurt? My mother! My mother! It's her. She is a real pain in the neck. I mean in *my* neck!

Cindy went on to discover that she deeply resented her mother's intrusion into Cindy's recent marriage. The pain correlated, she discovered, with her mother's numerous phone calls and unannounced visits. Once Cindy became aware of the source of her pain, she was able to learn to express her anger toward her mother and to demand appropriate restrictions on her mother's visits and calls. After this was resolved, Cindy's mysterious neck pains gradually disappeared.

In addition to language association, there is also a second technique for interpreting the meaning of your stress patterns. Self-questioning is a more direct, straightforward technique. You may find that you can use it more easily, or you may try it if the free-association technique is not productive. Before beginning the self-questioning procedure, use brainstorming or the stress journal to reveal your stress pattern to you. Once you have a clear picture of that pattern in mind, ask yourself the following sequence of questions:

1. What am I doing when I get the distress signal? Whom am I with?
2. Is it always the same person? Or the same activity?
3. If different situations are involved, do they have common characteristics?
4. To which common characteristics do I react?
5. Does this person or situation remind me of someone or something that I have felt negative about in the past?
6. What is it about the context of the stress pattern that sets off my stress reaction?
7. When the stress reaction occurs, what are my primary feelings?
8. What do I tell myself that keeps me from expressing those feelings? (Or: What personal rules keep me from expressing those feelings?)
9. If I could express those feelings at the time I felt them, what would I feel like?
10. I am binding myself by not expressing the feelings the situation arouses. In what alternative ways could I release the tension generated by those bound feelings?

The systematic use of this series of questions can often help to extricate us from the stress pattern in which we have been caught. Let us look at an example of the use of the self-questioning technique: Jim is an upper-level manager who finds that he experiences a stress pattern when he interacts with his boss in certain ways. More specifically, whenever he and the boss disagree about company policy, Jim finds his heart beating irregularly and he feels chest pains. Jim is frightened about these symptoms, and he uses both brainstorming and the stress journal to clarify some of the details of these interactions between his boss and himself. Then he asks the ten-question series. Both the questions and Jim's answers are given below.

1.	Whom am I with when I get the chest pain and heart-beat problems?	My boss, Mr. Bradley.
2.	Is it always him?	Yes, it is.
3.	Are there common characteristics in these situations?	Yes, he is always so arrogant!
4.	What do I react to?	He's such a know-it-all. He won't give me credit for anything.
5.	Does this remind me of anyone from my past?	Yes. . . . He's just as pigheaded as my father was. Couldn't tell him anything either.
6.	What about the context?	He usually pulls his routine in front of other employees, and I feel I shouldn't confront him in public.
7.	What are my primary feelings?	Frustration and sometimes rage.
8.	How do I keep myself from expressing those feelings?	I say, "Control yourself. He's the boss. Don't embarrass him in front of the others. The bastard might fire me if I did."

9. If I could express those feelings, how would I feel?	Really relieved.
10. What alternatives do I have?	Talk with him in private. Or tell him off and quit. Play racquet ball to relax. Don't take him so seriously. Talk to a friend to vent my feelings.

As you can see, self-questioning not only clarifies the nature and meaning of the stress pattern itself but also helps you to generate new ideas about other, more effective ways to cope with the situation. Here, too, as with the language-association technique, practice often leads to better results. Many of us are not used to examining our behavior carefully, and it can take time to become comfortable and confident about our ability to learn from the messages that our body and mind send us about stress. Careful, repeated observation forms the foundation for our self-analysis. Brainstorming and the stress journal are both valuable tools with which to conduct such observation. Once stress patterns begin to emerge as a result of such careful attention, then is the time to apply various techniques of interpretation to help provide understanding of why the stress pattern operates as it does. Sometimes such understanding is nearly spontaneous, but other situations require the use of techniques such as language association or self-questioning. Taken together, these various methods of observation and interpretation offer a unique opportunity for you to practice your own stress self-analysis. While many of the topics that will be discussed subsequently will be of value, none of them can substitute for an effective, personal stress self-analysis!

CHAPTER 4

RELAXATION

YOUR FIRST LINE OF DEFENSE

Learning about stress and how to cope with its effects takes time. We need time to learn, time to observe, time to analyze, and time to change and grow. Yet while all this learning, insight, and growth take place, stress continues to affect us. Stressors continue to be identified by the mind, and alarm reactions are triggered, persisting perhaps to the stage of resistance or even exhaustion. Clearly, there is a need for stress-reduction strategies that are effective and easy to use, strategies that we can use at any time, even before we have learned other, more sophisticated methods for controlling or even eliminating stress. Fortunately, such a simple and effective stress-reduction strategy is readily available: It is called *relaxation*.

Recent research has demonstrated the preventative power of relaxation. In one study, it was found that college students who napped or relaxed daily for up to 20 minutes during the daytime had significantly fewer illnesses than those who did not rest. Other research has demonstrated that people who regularly meditate—a powerful form of relaxation—report that they sleep better, feel more prepared to cope with stressful life events, and perceive themselves as being more integrated than before meditating. And no research is needed to explain those moments in each of our lives when we have felt truly relaxed: calm, centered, yet full of energy and zest for life. Truly, relaxation is a potent antidote to the ravages of stress.

In a sense, all of us are aware of this already, and each of us has found some ways to "relax." The only problem is that many of the activities that people consider to be relaxing are, in fact, not relaxing at all. Some "relaxation" is just pausing, a temporary escape from stress that leaves us no more able to cope with stress than when we began. Other forms of "relaxing" can actually be counterproductive, producing additional stress instead of reducing the original stress problem. A good example of these very unrelaxing strategies would be this: Imagine a group of people taking a short break from a stressful meeting. As they walk outside the conference room, many go immediately to a nearby table where coffee and tea are being served. While these people might well describe what they were doing as "having a cup of coffee or tea to relax," what they are doing will actually produce the opposite effect. Coffee and tea are stimulants and act upon our bodies to arouse the central nervous system (CNS), not to quiet it. Granted, the stimulant effect may produce a temporary energy boost and a sense of well-being, but drinking coffee or tea actually drains our energy reserves in the long run—using up reserves of B vitamins, minerals, and other nutriments that the body needs to cope with stress.

The same can be said for the doughnuts and sweet rolls being served with the tea and coffee. Such foods, which are high in sugar content and usually made with white flour and other highly processed ingredients, often provide a temporary "lift" as their refined sugars pass quickly into the bloodstream. This sudden increase in sugar is tempered, however, by a massive secretion of insulin from the pancreas, and the level of blood sugar soon drops precipitously. This sudden lowering of blood sugar level triggers the urge for more sugary foods, capable of pouring energy quickly into the bloodstream. When this is done, the cycle repeats itself. Should the person fail to ingest additional sugar to compensate for the drop in blood sugar, he or she may experience nervousness and trembling and perspire heavily. These unpleasant side effects help to explain why people who eat candy bars, pastries, or other sweet treats during the morning often have to snack throughout the day. They are attempting to raise their plummeting blood sugar, but by turning to sugary, refined foods, they are actually restarting the very cycle they seek to end. Clearly, such activity is far from "relaxing."

The same can be said for another popular way that our friends on their break from the meeting choose to relax: smoking. With smoking, too, as with sugary foods or coffee, there is an initial sense of relaxation or pleasure, followed by a longer and more persistent series of side effects. In this case, the source of relaxation is itself stress-inducing. As was discussed in Chapter 1, smoking actually triggers a stress response on its own because of its introduction of nicotine into the bloodstream and tars and resins into the lungs. And as with coffee or tea, smoking also has a stimulant effect, increasing stress rather than reducing it.

None of these supposedly "relaxing" activities is, in fact, very relaxing. They are truly "pausing" activities, socially approved ways of temporarily alleviating stress. Unfortunately, such methods do not really get to the sources of stress, nor do they provide authentic, rejuvenating relaxation. Before moving on, let us review some of the more common examples of this kind of "unrelaxing" method of coping with stress:

Pausing activities	Purposes	Effects
Smoking cigarettes, tobaccos	Pick-me-up Pausing, arousal Social activity	Increased energy, nutrient drain, poor sleep, indigestion
Drinking coffee or tea (nonherbal)	Pausing, arousal Social activity	Energy boost, nutrient drain, poor sleep, indigestion
Drugs: cocaine, methadrine ("uppers")	Pick-me-up Arousal	Energy boost, nutrient drain, poor sleep, incoordination, hyperactivity
Drinking hard alcoholic beverages	Pausing, social acts CNS depressant	Energy drain, digestive imbalance, potential brain impairment

Pausing activities	Purposes	Effects
Drinking wines	Pausing, social acts CNS depressant Muscle relaxant	Energy drain

Drugs: marijuana and others	Pausing, social acts
	Muscle relaxant
	Vascular
	  expansion
		Energy drain,
		  feeling "wasted"

Eating sugary or
  highly refined foods
	Pausing, arousal
	Pick-me-up
	Social activity
		Poor nutrition,
		  possible low
		  blood sugar,
		  possible
		  indigestion

These kinds of activities—drinking coffee or alcohol, smoking, and the like—may have their uses. They have become incorporated into our social structure and are frequently indulged in by many of us. But it must be stressed that whatever short-term effects these methods may have, they are *not* effective ways to relax. Anyone seeking true relaxation as a means of coping with stress must look elsewhere. One way to begin the search for authentic relaxation is to become aware of the elements that characterize a true state of relaxation. These elements would include the following:

1. The heart rate slows and becomes even.
2. Breathing becomes deeper and more even.
3. Muscles loosen and relax.
4. Hands and feet feel warm, or heavy, or both.
5. The mind feels at peace.
6. The body has energy for at least several hours of work.
7. The entire body feels refreshed.

These sensations and experiences within our bodies signal a state of true relaxation. When we achieve such successful relaxation, we will feel refreshed and recharged, more prepared to work and to continue with our other interests.

But what sort of activity creates such authentic, refreshing relaxation? There are a variety of them:

Relaxation methods	Purposes	Effects
Deep muscle relaxation	Relax muscles and internal organs	Better sleep Energy recharge Normalization of functioning of internal organs Less tension
Deep-breathing exercises	Relax muscles Vasodilation	Energy recharge Deeper breathing Less tension
Meditation	Relax muscles Feel calm and in control	Energy recharge Improved health Less tension Less irritability Better sleep
Stretching exercises (including yoga)	Release tension Increase flexibility	Muscles more flexible
Biofeedback	General relaxation Relax specific muscles and organ systems	Biological self-regulation Less tension Improved healing
Autogenic training	General relaxation Lower blood pressure Increase warmth of limbs Improve circulation	Increase blood circulation Less muscular tension Lowered blood pressure Better sleep

As can be seen from this list, effective relaxation methods have both long- and short-term positive benefits. These coping strategies can be used to relax, to pause, to improve blood flow, to increase body temperature, and to increase our energy level. The long-term effects include creating a general state of calm and relaxation in the musculature, creating a state of biological self-regulation (body heals itself), increasing blood flow to extremities, improving the depth and evenness of breathing (better oxygenation of blood), increasing availability of energy for work and action, creating a positive state of well-being, and improving our ability to cope.

Relaxation strategies can be used for different purposes. We can relax to pause as well as to release tensions. We can increase our energy level, dissipate a negative feeling, and even create a positive mood. We can also use some methods to rest briefly in order to give us temporary energy when we have not had enough sleep. Finally, we can use these methods to maintain a feeling of equanimity throughout our work day. This will allow us to go calmly from task to task and to cope effectively with stressors. In such a positive state of mind, we can go beyond coping to come through crises in a viable way.

The following sections provide detailed instructions for relaxing. Several different relaxation methods are outlined. They are presented in such a way that a friend can read them to you, or, if you have a tape recorder available, you can read the instructions and record them on tape. You can then play the tape back so that you can concentrate on the exercise. With each exercise, there are examples of where and how to make best use of that technique.

GENERAL RULES FOR RELAXATION EXERCISES

Preparation for relaxation is vital to the full effectiveness of any relaxation technique. Failure to prepare amply and to adhere to some general principles that aid in relaxation will interfere with the effects of an exercise. For example, if you do an exercise for deep muscle relaxation while wearing tight clothes (e.g., girdle, ties, watches, belts), then you will find that certain areas of your body will not relax. You will become aware of tensions at the surface of your body. These tensions are simply the result of the pressure created by the outer garment. Some people are so annoyed by these tensions that they become more tense rather than relaxed. The following are general rules that prepare you for relaxation exercises:

1. *Assume a comfortable position.* If you are trying to relax, the position of your body can significantly influence the effective-

ness of relaxing. This first rule is based upon the fact that when your muscles work, they are in a state of tension; thus, if you assume a position that uses your muscles, you create a state of tension. More specifically, you should assume a comfortable position in which your muscles are supported by some structure and do not have to work to support your body. Lying down on a sofa or bed or sitting in a reclining chair are the two ways of supporting the body most completely. When lying down, place a pillow beneath the knees. If no chair that supports the head is available, then at least use one with arms so that the arms are supported.

2. *Loosen constricting garments and remove jewelry.* Muscle tension can be triggered by afferent stimulation—information that comes from our sense receptors for touch and passes through nerve pathways to the brain. To facilitate relaxation, therefore, it is best to minimize such tactile input and the tension it can produce. One way to do this is by loosening your garments and taking off any jewelry.

3. *Relax in a quiet, peaceful environment.* In line with the previous principle, you will want to minimize all forms of stimulation. These include noise, light, odor, and movement. Ideally, you should practice your relaxation exercises in an environment that is quiet and removed from noisy distractions and intrusions (take the phone off the hook or don't permit incoming calls), that is dark or at least dim, and that is free from distracting odors. Finally, you will want to minimize or avoid being in motion. Movement stimulates the middle ear and triggers arousal of your balance system.

4. *Assume an observing attitude.* In performing any of the relaxation exercises described below, the objective is not to make some feeling or sensation happen. Take a passive, *observing* attitude. Simply notice what you experience. Make no attempt to control your body. To assume such an attitude requires that you appreciate this paradoxical situation: You control or regulate your body by not controlling it. You can become relaxed by observing what you experience when you take specific actions. You cannot force your body to relax! You can breathe and move and observe—relaxation will follow. Some people may find that taking a passive, observing attitude is frustrating, and they may

become impatient. These people need to relax even more. It is a fact of life that we cannot directly control everything. But we can control or influence many events indirectly—that is, control by observing and *not* controlling.

5. *Allow enough time.* Initially, you will want to allow longer periods in which to practice the relaxation exercises. Some exercises will require up to 30 minutes to complete, while others can be done in as little as 5 or 10 minutes. To avoid being frustrated from the outset, it is important to be prepared to spend up to 30 minutes initially in your practice sessions. Each technique has some time recommendations along with the instructions. For a matter of perspective, you will find that as you practice regularly, the amount of time that you need to experience a relaxation response will decrease. Through practice, you become more skilled and more efficient. You are acquiring the skill of learning to relax. Very skillful relaxers can achieve a beneficial response in a few minutes.

6. *Schedule a relaxation period regularly.* It is preferable to practice relaxing daily. Two times a day is a good start. If you don't want to make quite so strong a commitment, then practice at least once a day. Most people find it easier to learn to relax when they treat this like any other skill they learn. To learn to play a musical instrument, you have to practice regularly. This holds true for relaxing, the instrument in this case being your body. It is helpful to set up a routine in which you practice at the same time each day. A consistent daily routine increases your likelihood of success. Some people prefer bedtime, or the time just after a day's work, while other people prefer the early morning. Relaxation prior to sleeping will improve the quality of your sleep. I usually recommend bedtime as the ideal time to begin learning a relaxation process, for the reason that bedtime capitalizes on the fact that you are already expecting to unwind, and adding a period of relaxation practice time seems most fitting.

7. *Practice, practice, practice.* Although it may seem contradictory that anyone should need to work at relaxing, relaxing is a skill. We all learned to walk and to talk, but few of us have yet learned to relax. Instead, most of us have learned how to become tense. The more we practice relaxing, however, the more effective and efficient we will become. And if we lead high-pressure,

fast-paced work lives, then it is imperative to be efficient. So remember the wise old saying, "Practice makes you ... perfectly relaxed."

RELAXATION EXERCISE INSTRUCTIONS

Deep Diaphragmatic Breathing

You will begin with a relatively brief relaxation exercise. Initially, you want to spend about 10 minutes practicing this exercise with the eventual goal of being effective in only 2 to 3 minutes. Deep diaphragmatic breathing is just that—breathing deeply with the diaphragm.

The diaphragm is a large sheet of muscle that extends across the lower edge of the rib cage under the lungs and attaches to the back. When we are using our diaphragms correctly, our abdomens move *out* as we *inhale* and pull *in* as we *exhale*. Animals breathe correctly: Observe a dog or cow and notice how its abdomen goes in and out as it breathes. Most people breathe with their chests and not with their diaphragms. Chest breathing is shallow, whereas diaphragmatic breathing is deep. Deep breathing means that the lungs fill more fully and the body gets more oxygen.

Most people are not aware of this, but deep diaphragmatic breathing makes use of a built-in, natural relaxation response. We were all biologically and genetically programmed to relax, but over the course of the ages, we have unlearned this process. The relaxation response occurs when we exhale. When we exhale, our muscles tend to let go, and when muscles release, they relax.

Try the exercise and discover this natural relaxation response. You can have someone read the following instructions to you:

Assume a comfortable position. It is easiest to do this sitting in a chair.

Close your eyes.

Let yourself be aware of your breathing. Notice whether you are breathing through your mouth or your nose. Notice the pace of your breathing.

Now observe your body. In your mind, inspect all the muscle groups of your body and notice where you feel tension. Do this for a minute.

Return to your breathing. Begin breathing in deeply through your nose. Then exhale through your mouth. Continue breathing in deeply through your nose and exhaling through your mouth. Breathe deeply and evenly. As you exhale, notice what your muscles do. Notice how they begin to let go. Go on breathing deeply and evenly for a minute and notice what you feel throughout your body.

Each time you inhale, your diaphragm expands and your abdomen pushes out. Each time you exhale, your abdomen pulls inward. (If you are having difficulty, then it may help to place one hand on your abdomen so that you can monitor the movements of the diaphragm. Your hand should move out as you inhale. Your hand should move in as you exhale. You may have to force yourself to use your diaphragm at first.)

Continue breathing in and out: slowly . . . deeply . . . evenly.

Now let's inhale to a count of four. Inhale . . . one, two, three, four . . . and HOLD IT. Hold your breath to a count of four: one, two, three four. And, exhale. Slowly to a count of eight: one, two, three, four, five, six, seven, eight.

And, repeat. Inhale to a count of four. Hold your breath to a count of four. And exhale to a count of eight. Breathe slowly and evenly.

As you exhale slowly, notice what you feel throughout your body. Each time you exhale, your muscles feel warm. They may begin to feel heavy or light. You may begin to feel tingly all over. Breathe deeply and evenly. Just let yourself enjoy whatever sensations you experience. Breathe deeply and evenly.

Continue to breathe deeply and evenly, and notice how energy begins to flow throughout your body. Breathe in to a count of four. Hold to a count of four. And exhale to a count of eight. Go on breathing and observing what you experience. Just let whatever happens, happen. Observe and enjoy. Continue to breathe in this way for several minutes.

After 3 minutes, continue with these directions:

Before opening your eyes, it is helpful to return to the awakened state by doing several movements. First, move your hands and arms about. Second, move your feet and legs about. Third, rotate your head. Fourth, open your eyes and sit up. Notice how you feel.

For some people, diaphragmatic breathing is very difficult at first. The usual reason is that these people have learned incorrectly to do chest breathing. In deep diaphragmatic breathing, the chest and shoulders remain motionless at first. The abdomen moves out as the bottoms of the lungs expand. Once the bottoms of the lungs are filled with air, then the chest can expand and the tops of the lungs fill with air. On exhalation, the diaphragm pulls in and forces the air out, and then the chest collapses to force the last air out.

If you initially have difficulty with your abdomen moving in and out, it is often helpful to first practice a pant breath. A pant breath is a form of throat breathing. Start by forming an "O" with your lips, and breathe quickly in and out through your mouth. Pant in short, quick breaths. Each time you inhale, push your abdomen out. Practice panting and synchronize the panting with your abdominal movements. Breathe in and out . . . one, two . . . one, two . . . one, two. In on "one," out on "two." Place your hand on your abdomen so that you can feel the movement of your abdomen.

As soon as you have mastered this quick, panting technique, shift to breathing more deeply and evenly as outlined above. Keep your hand on your abdomen for feedback as to how you are doing with your diaphragm.

Once you have learned to correctly synchronize your diaphragm movement with your inhalation and exhalation, then mastering deep diaphragmatic breathing can be done quickly. Breathing is a natural relaxation response. It can be done in most of the more stressful situations. You can do this breathing unobtrusively, at work, at home, or at play. The benefits will surprise you.

Deep Muscle Relaxation

In 1938, Dr. E. Jacobson published a book, *Progressive Relaxation*, wherein he described his use of deep muscle relaxation. Dr. Jacobson applied a simple biological principle to create a systematic method to relax the muscles of the body. When a muscle group releases and smooths out, the muscle relaxes. To get a muscle to relax, we can first tense it, then release it. Dr. Jacobson developed a systematic series of tension–release cycles to achieve a relaxation response. His research demonstrated that the long-term effect of progressive relaxation was the normalization of the dysfunctioning body organs. He found, for example, that when the colon was constricted and ulcerated, daily practicing of the relaxation response led to the recovery of the large intestine. Ulcerative colitis would heal. The colon would expand to its normal size and shape, and the ulcers would heal completely.

Since the first research project, Dr. Jacobson and others have refined the technique. In recent applications, Dr. Jacobson was able to demonstrate that a person can learn progressive relaxation to such a high degree that he or she can learn to use one part of the body and maintain a complete state of relaxation in the remainder of the body. It is possible, for instance, to learn to differentiate the body to such a degree that one can type (and hence tense fingers, hands, and arms) and yet keep the remainder of the body perfectly relaxed.

Progressive relaxation is an ideal relaxation method for people who experience tensions in specific muscles. When people work, the nature of their jobs often places them in certain postures (e.g., sitting, standing, walking, lifting) that can generate tensions. For example, sitting cuts down blood flow to the legs and can cause cramping and stiffness. Sitting can also create back pains. Common muscle-tension complaints include eyestrain, low or middle back pain, stiff legs, neck stiffness, hoarse voice, gas pains, and chest pains. All of these can be relieved with regular use of progressive deep muscle relaxation. Few of us are likely to become as adept at isolating muscle groups as Harry Houdini, but the effort will do us good.

There is a list of general instructions that should be understood before this technique. First, you should practice at least once per day for at least 20 to 30 minutes. As you become more skilled, you will need less time. Next, follow a general order of the muscle groups to be relaxed. Begin with the hands and arms, then go to the head region, then down the body to the trunk, and then to the lower limbs and feet. The progressive nature of the process will create a feeling that a wave of relaxation is flowing from muscle group to muscle group. Then, do each muscle tension–release cycle twice. As you tense and then release a muscle group, focus your attention on the difference between a state of tension and a state of relaxation. In your mind, compare the sensations and allow yourself to remember the feelings. Each tension–release cycle consists of first tensing a specific muscle group, holding the muscles in a tensed state for 8 to 10 seconds, and then abruptly releasing them. The best position is either lying down or reclining in a full chair to keep the body fully supported.

You will find it helpful, before continuing with a step-by-step set of instructions, to practice a sequence of exercises for relaxing the muscle groups in their progressive order. The exercises are listed below and most are illustrated in the series of photographs following page 72. You can practice these exercises in front of a mirror to familiarize yourself with them.

1. Relaxation of arms:
   a. Clench right hand (make a fist) and tense forearm.
   b. Clench left hand and tense left forearm.
   c. Tense both right and left hands and forearms.
   d. Tense right biceps (front of upper arm) by bending right arm at elbow.
   e. Tense left biceps by bending left arm at elbow.
   f. Tense right triceps (back muscle, upper arm) by stiffening right arm.
   g. Tense left triceps by stiffening left arm.

2. Relaxation of head area:
   a. Wrinkle forehead.
   b. Frown and crease brows.
   c. Close eyelids tightly and keep them closed throughout the remaining exercises.
   d. Rotate eyes in clockwise circles. Return to center.
   e. Rotate eyes in counterclockwise circles. Return to center.

    f. Rotate eyes to far right.

    g. Rotate eyes to far left.

    h. Rotate eyes to top of sockets.

    i. Rotate eyes to bottom of sockets.

    j. Wrinkle nose and cheeks.

    k. Press lips together tightly (or purse them).

    l. Clench jaws.

    m. Press chin against chest.

    n. Press tongue against roof of mouth.

    o. Begin to swallow, and hold. Tense throat.

    p. Tense throat and larynx muscles by humming a high note without making any sounds. Then hum down the scale to a low note.

3. Relaxation of trunk:

    a. Tense shoulder muscles by raising shoulders as though touching ears.

    b. Pull shoulders back and tighten upper back muscles.

    c. Arch lower back and tighten lower back muscles.

    d. Pull shoulders inward to the front and tighten chest muscles.

    e. Tighten stomach muscles by pulling inward and downward.

    f. Tighten pelvic muscles in groin area. (Same as stopping urination in the middle of urinating. Known as the Kegal exercise.)

    g. Tighten buttocks. Pull them together.

4. Relaxation of legs:

    a. Tighten right upper leg.

    b. Tighten left upper leg.

    c. Tense both upper legs. Pull legs together at knees and straighten legs.

    d. Tense right calf and shin (raise foot as though to touch leg).

    e. Tense left calf and shin.

    f. Tense right foot and toes.

    g. Tense left foot and toes.

5. Intensification of relaxation throughout body:
   a. Inhale to a count of four. Hold breath to count of four and focus on tension. Exhale slowly.
   b. Breathe deeply and evenly while inspecting all muscle groups.

6. Return to aroused state through movements:
   a. Move hands and arms.
   b. Move feet and legs.
   c. Rotate head.
   d. Open eyes and sit up.

Now that you are familiar with the nature of the entire sequence, the following is a detailed narrative to induce a state of deep muscle relaxation through tension–release cycles.

First, assume a comfortable position. Either lie down or sit in a supportive chair. Be sure your arms and head are supported. You will proceed by tensing different muscle groups throughout your body. The idea of progressive relaxation is to tense a muscle group, hold the state of tension, abruptly release the muscle group, and relax. As you release the muscles, notice the sensations of muscles relaxing. You can read the following instructions into a tape recorder:

Begin with the right hand and forearm. Make a fist with the right hand and bend it at the wrist. Feel the tension there. Hold it for 10 seconds. Release! Notice the change and the sensations in your right hand and forearm. Pay attention to these sensations and compare them to what you felt when you tensed the right hand and forearm. Keeping the rest of your body still, tense the right hand and forearm again. Make a really tight fist and hold it for 10 seconds. Notice the feelings of tension. Release! And now focus on the sensations that occur after you released. Go on appreciating these sensations. You may begin to feel sensations of heaviness, lightness, or tingling. These are all sensations of relaxation.

After 20 seconds of focusing on sensations of relaxation, continue:

Now, keeping your right hand and arm still, tense the left hand and forearm. Tense that left hand and forearm. Notice the sensations of tension. Hold it for 10 seconds, and release. And notice the sensations that happen when you let go of the left hand. Compare these to what you are experiencing in your right hand and forearm. Appreciate these feelings in your left lower arm. Again, tense the left hand and forearm. Hold it *(10 seconds)*, then release. Notice what you feel in your left hand and forearm. Continue to let go and flow with the sensations. Compare your left lower arm to your right. Observe what you experience in both.

After 20 seconds of focusing on sensations of relaxation, continue:

Keeping your right lower arm as loose as possible, tense the right upper arm. Tense the right biceps. Hold it *(10 seconds)*, and release. Notice the sensations after you let go. Remember them. They are sensations of relaxation. Compare what you feel in your right biceps with what you feel in your right forearm and hand.

After 20 seconds:

Again, tense the right biceps muscle. Hold it *(10 seconds)*. Notice the sensations of tension. Now, release. Appreciate the sensations in your right biceps when you let go. You may notice feelings of warmth or heaviness. These are signs of relaxation. Go on appreciating what you feel.

After 20 seconds, continue:

Now tense the left upper arm, while keeping the right arm still. Tense the left biceps. Notice the feelings of tension there. Remember the feeling of tension. Compare this to what you now feel in your right biceps. Notice the differences between tension and relaxation. Appreciate the differences. Again, tense the left biceps while keeping the left lower arm as still as possible. Hold it *(10 seconds)*, then release. Just let go of the left biceps muscle. Compare what you feel there to what you feel in the left lower arm. Compare it to what you experience in the right arm. Continue appreciating the feelings in both arms.

After about 20 seconds, continue:

Now go to the back of the upper right arm. Tense the right triceps muscle. You can do this by straightening the right arm. But keep your hand loose. That's it, tense that right triceps. Hold it *(10 seconds)*, and release. Just let it go and notice how the sensations of relaxation go from your right hand to the right forearm, across the elbow, up the right biceps, and around to the triceps. Again, tense the right triceps. Keep the remainder of your body relaxed. Hold it *(10 seconds)*, and release.

Again, notice how the right triceps feels when you let go. Just observe what happens there. Let your entire right arm continue to relax. Appreciate what you feel there.

After 20 seconds, continue:

Keeping your right arm relaxed, tense the left triceps muscle. Straighten the left arm, while keeping the left hand loose. Notice the tension in back of the left upper arm. Hold it *(10 seconds)*, then release. Notice the feelings of relaxation that flow into the back of your left upper arm. The sensations flow into the triceps, and a flow of energy happens all up and down your left arm. Observe these feelings. Again, tense the left triceps. Hold it *(10 seconds)*. Release! And notice the full flow of relaxation up and down your left arm. Compare the left upper arm to the left lower arm. Compare what you feel in your left arm to what you feel in your right arm. Just let the sensation flow.

After 20 seconds, continue:

Now, keeping your arms quiet and relaxed, proceed to the muscles in your head. Beginning from the top downward, tense the muscles in your forehead. Wrinkle your forehead, as you would do when you are either worried or angry. Hold the tension *(10 seconds)*. Release! Notice what you feel in your forehead as you release these muscles. Pay attention to the difference from when you tensed these muscles. Let these muscles smooth out and let go. Again, tense the muscles in your forehead. Wrinkle your forehead as tightly as you can. Hold it *(10 seconds)*. Release! Just smooth out your forehead and relax. Notice the sensations that happen there. Compare the sensations in your forehead with the sensations in your arms. Let them all go.

After 30 seconds, continue:

Now tighten the muscles around your eyebrows. Frown and crease the eyebrows. Hold it *(10 seconds)*. Notice the feelings of tension. Remember these tense feelings in your eyebrows. Then release. And notice what you feel when you let go. Notice that the eyebrows smooth out and there is a flow from your scalp to your eyebrows. Continue to appreciate the sensations there.

After 30 seconds, continue:

Now, tense the muscles of the eyelids. Squeeze the eyelids tightly together. The eyes are constantly in use, and most of us keep a lot of tension there. Hold it *(10 seconds)*. Notice the tension there. Now, release. Let the eyelids go and relax. Let your eyelids smooth out. Appreciate the sensations there. If they twitch, this just signals that you have a lot of tension there. Again, tense the eyelids. Squeeze them tightly together. Hold them *(10 seconds)*, and release! Let your eyelids go and smooth out. Notice the sensations that travel from your hairline down your forehead across the eyebrows and down into your eyelids. Appreciate the feelings of relaxation that begin to flow down your face.

After 30 seconds, continue:

Now that the eyelids are released, go inside to the extraocular muscles that control the movements of the eyeballs. The extraocular muscles move the eyeballs in six ways, and you will do six tension–release cycles to relax all these muscles. First, rotate your eyeballs upward as high as you can roll them. Hold it *(10 seconds)*. And, release. Let your eyes float back to the center of their sockets. Notice the sensations in your eyes when you let go. Now roll your eyes downward as though to look at your toes. Roll them down as far as you can. Hold them *(10 seconds)* before you release. Let your eyes float to the center of their sockets and relax. Notice the sensations that flow in the muscles around your eyes.

Continue with the muscles to the sides of your eyes. Shift your eyes to the right. Move them as far right as you can. Hold them there *(10 seconds)*. Feel the tension there, and release. Notice what happens to the muscles around your eyes as they float to the center. Enjoy the change from tensed to relaxed. Now tighten the muscles to the left of the eye. Shift your eyes to the left as far as they will go. Hold them *(10 seconds)*. Notice the tension, and release. Just let your eyes float to their centers. Enjoy the sensations around your eyes. Then continue to let go and relax.

Now imagine that you are looking at a huge clock that goes from the ceiling to the floor. Look up at the twelve and begin to rotate your eyes clockwise ... looking at the one, then the two, then the three, downward to the four, to the five and to the six, rotating up the other side of the clock to the seven, to the eight, to the nine, to the ten, up to the eleven, and back up to the twelve. Then let your eyes float back to the center and relax. Shift your eyes back up to the twelve and proceed counterclockwise. Looking at the eleven, down to the ten, to the nine, to the eight, to the seven, and all the way to the bottom of the clock to the six. Continue back up the right side to the five, looking at the four, the three, the two, the one, and back up to the twelve. Then let your eyes float back to the center of the clock. And, relax. Just let your eyes float loosely in their sockets as you enjoy the sensations of relaxation all around your eyes. Your eyes get warmer and more and more relaxed.

Moving down the face, tense the muscles around the nose and cheeks. Tense these muscles by wrinkling your nose like a rabbit. Feel the tension around your nose and cheeks. Hold it *(10 seconds)*. Relax! Let your cheeks and nose muscles smooth out. The feelings of relaxation flow down your face. Just let the sensations happen. Enjoy what you feel.

Proceeding down the face, tense the muscles around the lips. Either press your lips tightly together or purse them as though you were sucking on a lemon. Tense them. Hold it *(10 seconds)*, and release! Just let your lips smooth out and relax. Enjoy the sensations around your mouth. Your lips may feel heavier, warmer, or tingly. Just flow with the sensations, and relax. The wave of warmth and relaxation flows further down your face.

Now, while you tense the next muscle group, attempt to keep the previous muscle groups relaxed. Tense the muscles under your chin. Tuck your chin down and into your chest. Tighten all the muscles under your chin and in the front of your neck. Hold it *(10 seconds)*. And release! Just let these muscles smooth out as the sensations of relaxation flow down your face, down to your chin and neck. Breathe deeply and evenly and appreciate the sensations of relaxation flowing more and more down the front of your face.

After 20 seconds, continue:

Now that you have relaxed the muscles across the outside of your face, go inside. Tense the muscles of your tongue. Tighten your tongue by pushing up against the back of your upper front teeth. Feel the tension through your tongue. Hold it *(10 seconds)*. Relax! Let your tongue just lie easily in your mouth. Breathe deeply and evenly, and notice the sensations of warmth and heaviness that come inside to your tongue. Tighten this group again. Hold it. Feel the tension there. *After 10 seconds:* Relax. Let your tongue just float in your mouth. Enjoy the sensations there.

After 20 seconds, continue:

Continuing inside your mouth, tense the back of your tongue and your throat. Tense the muscles in the back of the tongue and in the throat by beginning to swallow. Don't complete the swallow. Just hold it after you begin. Notice the tension in your throat. Feel the tightness there and hold it *(10 seconds)*. Then release it. Let your tongue smooth out and your throat relax. Feel the sensations of warmth travel down to the back of your tongue and into your throat. Notice how your throat begins to feel more and more relaxed.

Now, completely relax your throat by tensing the muscles around your larynx (voice box). To tense these muscles, hum a high-pitched note without making any sounds. As you hum this silent note, notice the tension in your neck. And as you focus on this tension, begin humming silently down the scale. Notice the change in tension levels as you sing down the scale. A good operatic soprano can discriminate a hundred different tension levels to create a hundred different notes. Continue down the scale until you are humming a low note. Then relax. Let your larynx go and enjoy the sensations of relaxation as they flow down your throat and into your neck. Your entire face and head feel more and more relaxed. Enjoy these sensations.

After 20 seconds, continue:

Now complete your relaxation of the head region. Tilt your head back and tighten the muscles in the back of the neck. Hold it *(10 seconds)*, and release. Let the muscles in the back of the neck loosen and let the waves of relaxation float down the back of your neck. Then tilt your head to the right as though to touch your right ear to your right shoulder. Hold it *(10 seconds)*. And release! Then tighten the muscles to the left side. Tilt your head to the left as though to touch the left ear to the left shoulder. Hold it *(10 seconds)*. Notice the tension there. And, release. Let your entire neck relax. The warm and comfortable sensations of relaxation flow all around your neck. Appreciate what you experience there.

After 20 seconds, continue:

Now tense the muscles in the shoulder region. Tighten the shoulder muscles by pulling the shoulders upward as though you were going to touch your ears. Shrug your shoulders tightly. Hold them *(10 seconds)*. And, release. Just let your shoulders down and relax. Since these muscles get tense easily, tighten them again. Tense the shoulder muscles. Hold them. Notice the tension there, and, relax. Let your shoulders relax. Enjoy the feelings of warmth and heaviness as the waves of relaxation flow from your neck to your shoulders.

After 20 seconds, continue:

Now, tense the muscles of your upper back. Pull your shoulder blades back and together. Tighten the upper back muscles as though your shoulder blades are going to touch. *(Hold for 10 seconds.)* Release! Just let your upper back muscles smooth out and let go.

After 20 seconds, continue:

Then go to the muscles in your lower back. Tense the muscles in the lower back by arching your back. Your chest and stomach should protrude as your trunk arches to tense the lower back muscles. Hold them *(10 seconds)*. Now, release. Notice the change in sensations as you release the muscles in your lower back. Let the feelings of warmth flow down your back.

After 20 seconds, continue:

Now go to the front of the trunk. Tense the muscles across your chest. Pull your shoulders together in front. Feel the tension there, and hold it *(10 seconds)*. Then, release! Just let your chest muscles go and relax. Enjoy the sensations of relaxation as they flow from your back to the front. Since it is common for these muscles to get tense, do them again. Tighten the muscles across your chest. Pull your shoulders together and hold them *(10 seconds)*. And, release. Enjoy the sensations of relaxation as they flow across your chest. Your breathing becomes easier and deeper. Breathe deeply and evenly.

After 20 seconds, continue:

Continuing down the trunk, tense the muscles around your abdomen and your lower intestinal area. Tighten these groups by pulling in your stomach muscles. As you pull them inward, also push your chest downward. Hold it *(10 seconds)*. Feel the tension there, then release! Notice the change from tension to relaxation. Notice the sensations of relaxation flowing down your trunk. Your abdomen becomes more and more relaxed. Repeat this cycle. Tense the muscles across your abdomen. *(Hold them 10 seconds.)* Notice the tension there, and then release. Let your abdominal muscles relax. Breathe deeply and evenly, and notice the sensations across the abdominal cavity as you exhale. Each time you exhale, notice how your abdomen and entire trunk become more and more relaxed. Continue to observe what you experience throughout your body.

After 20 seconds, continue:

Now go to an important transition area, the area between your trunk and your legs. Tighten the muscles of your groin by pulling these muscles up into the cavity of your body. It is the same action as when

you stop urinating in the middle of a urination. Hold it *(10 seconds).*
Notice the tension there. Then, release. And notice the wave of relaxation flow from your trunk to your groin and into your legs.

After 20 seconds, continue:

Now tense the back part of this transition area. Tense the buttocks
by pulling them tightly together. These are large and powerful muscles
that help us walk, but that get a lot of tension when we sit. Pull them
together. Hold it *(10 seconds).* Release! Notice the change in sensation in
and around your buttocks. Let yourself experience the wave of relaxation as this transition area from your trunk to your legs is unblocked
and relaxed. Breathe deeply and evenly, and notice the sensations of
warmth and heaviness there.

After 20 seconds, continue:

Continuing down your body, tense the muscles in your upper legs.
Straighten your legs by locking the knees. Also, you might pull your
upper legs together by touching your knees tightly together—that is, as
though to hold a coin between your knees. Hold it *(10 seconds),* and
notice the tension in your upper legs. And, release! Also notice the sensations of warmth and relaxation flowing from your trunk down into
your upper legs.

After 20 seconds, continue:

Tense the muscles in your lower legs. Tighten the calf muscles by
pulling your toes back and up as though to touch your shins. You might
press the heels of your feet into the floor simultaneously. Hold it *(10
seconds),* and release! Notice the change there. Remember these sensations as the warmth and heaviness flow down to the muscles of the
lower leg.

After 20 seconds, continue:

Now, go to the last muscle group, the feet. Curl your toes and arch
your feet downward. Notice the tension there, but release if they begin
to cramp. Hold it *(10 seconds).* Release! Let your feet relax and allow the
sensations of relaxation to flow into your feet. It is as though the tension
has been pushed out of your toes as the wave of warm relaxation flows
down your legs into your feet.

Go on enjoying the sensations of warm relaxation that flow
through your entire body. With your mind, inspect all the muscle

groups again. As you think about each of these muscle groups, continue to breathe deeply and evenly. Each time you exhale, notice how the muscle group that you inspect lets go, grows warmer, and is more relaxed.

After 30 seconds, continue:

The last exercise focuses on your breathing to enhance the depth of relaxation. Take a deep breath in through your nose. Hold it to a count of four: one . . . two . . . three . . . four, and exhale slowly to a count of four. Do that several times. Now notice the tension in your chest. Then, as you exhale, notice what occurs throughout your body. Your muscles let go further and relax very deeply. Go on breathing, holding, and noticing the tension; and releasing and noticing the waves of relaxation flowing through your body. Breathe deeply and evenly, and enjoy the sensations of warm, full relaxation. Remember these feelings.

After 30 seconds, continue:

To end this relaxation exercise, it is best to go through a four-step transition exercise. One, move your hands and arms about. Two, move your feet and legs about. Three, rotate your head. Four, open your eyes, sit up, and let yourself feel awake and calm.

Although the process of progressive muscle relaxation can be shortened considerably, it is better to practice the full form first. When you practice the tension–release cycles for each muscle group, you increase your awareness of when a particular muscle group is tense. Once you are sensitive to subtle tensions, you can then make better use of your body's signals. When you are aware of these tensions, then you can consciously decide whether or not you want to unwind. The enhanced awareness achieved through progressive relaxation is one of its advantages over other relaxation techniques. You can finely tune your recognition of the signals of stress as they are registered in your muscles.

Assuming that you are now skilled in the long form of progressive relaxation, you can learn to do a shortened version. Instead of tensing each muscle group individually, you can tense several muscle groups simultaneously, as follows:

1. Tense the muscles of your hands, arms, and shoulders. Hold the tension for 15 seconds. Notice how you feel there, and then release. And be aware of the changes. Let yourself appreciate the sensations of relaxation flowing into your hands, arms, and shoulders.

Wait and focus on the relaxation for 20 seconds.

2. Tense the muscles of your face, in your mouth and throat, and around your neck. Tighten them as tightly as you can and hold for 15 seconds before your release. Let your facial muscles smooth out, your neck release, and your throat relax. Notice the changes in sensations from tension to relaxation. Feelings of warmth and heaviness flow throughout your head region.

Focus on sensations of relaxation in your head area for 20 seconds.

3. Now tense the muscles of the upper back and lower back. While tensing these muscles, also tense the abdominal muscles and chest muscles. Tighten the entire trunk and hold it tensed for 15 seconds. Be aware of the tense sensations, and then relax. And be aware of the sensations of warm relaxation flowing from your head into your trunk. Appreciate these warm, relaxing feelings. Remember these feelings.

Focus on sensations of relaxation in your trunk area for 20 seconds.

4. Now tense the muscles in the groin, buttocks, upper legs, lower legs, and feet. Tighten all these muscle groups simultaneously. Hold them 15 seconds, and release. And notice the change in the sensations from tension to relaxation. Appreciate this change and enjoy the warm, heavy, relaxed sensations as they flow from your trunk to your legs and feet. Go on appreciating what you feel there.

Focus on sensations of relaxation in your lower limbs for 20 seconds.

5. Now deepen your level of relaxation by focusing on your breathing. Breathe in deeply through your nose and hold your breath. Hold it to a count of four and notice the tension in your chest. Now exhale slowly. Blow out the air to a count of four and observe what happens throughout your body. Notice how your muscles continue to let go even more. They grow warmer, heavier, and more relaxed. Go on breathing deeply and evenly for a minute.

After a minute of deep breathing, continue:

6. Return to the awakened state by going through a four-step procedure: One, move your hands and arms about. Two, move your feet

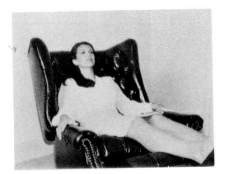

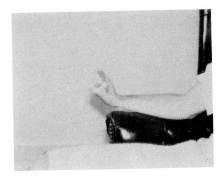

1 and 2. Assume a comfortable position.

3. Tense hand and forearm.

4. Tense both hands and forearms.

5. Tense biceps.

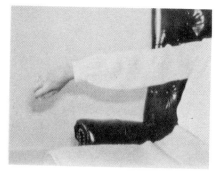

6. Tense triceps.

7. Wrinkle forehead.

8. Close eyelids tightly; rotate eyes far right; rotate eyes far left; rotate eyes upward; rotate eyes downward.

9. Wrinkle nose and cheeks.

10. Press lips together.

11. Clench jaws.

12. Tighten muscles under chin.

13. Press tongue against roof of mouth.

14. Begin to swallow, and hold. Tense throat.

15. Shrug shoulders.

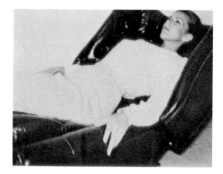

16. Arch lower back.

17. Pull shoulders back.

18. Tighten chest muscles.

19. Tighten stomach muscles.

20. Tense upper leg.

21. Tense both upper legs.

22. Tense calf muscles.

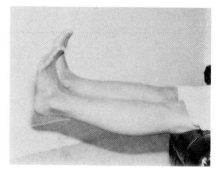

23. Tense both calves.

24. Tense foot and toes.

and legs about. Three, rotate your head. Four, open your eyes and sit up, feeling calm and refreshed.

The shortened version of progressive relaxation can be performed in a few minutes. When you do it this way, be sure to spend a full minute breathing deeply and evenly to deepen and enhance the level of relaxation. The shortened version can easily be done in the office, at home, or in the privacy of your car. And if you will stop and think for a moment, you can easily think of many other situations where this can be done. Several minutes of deep relaxation can get you through an hour or two of work when you are run down and tired.

Deep muscle relaxation is an excellent method to induce a relaxed state when a person is ready to sleep. Therefore, practicing progressive relaxation just prior to going to sleep is highly recommended. Some people, when they become skilled at progressive relaxation, even fall asleep at the end of the cycle. You can learn to sleep more soundly when you relax before retiring. This means that you can awaken fully rested.

For other people, the practice sessions are best done in the morning before leaving for work. Some people awaken rested, but become nervous and tense when they think of the impending day at work. Relaxing in the morning can be an excellent way to reduce this anticipatory tension.

If you can allow yourself to be creative, there are countless ways in which you can apply progressive relaxation. Remember that you can do it completely or partially. So, for example, if while you are at work your shoulders become tense and feel tight, you can go through several applications of the tension–release cycles with your shoulder muscles. You can even indulge in this limited application while performing a task. You can carry a briefcase in one hand and practice tension–release cycles with the other hand.

Just let your mind go and apply this technique creatively.

Autogenic Relaxation

Autogenic relaxation is a form of self-hypnosis. *Autogenic* means to apply some process to yourself by yourself. The format of autogenic relaxation is to repeat some self-instructions (e.g., "My arms are warm") several times while you observe the sensations in the area of the body that is described by the instruction. What is termed *autogenic relaxation* is a slight variation of a process called *autogenic training*. Autogenic training has been described in a six-volume series by two European doctors, Drs. Schultz and Luthe. In these books, they describe the research on how autogenic training has been successful in inducing true states of relaxation in the body. They also tell of its successful medical and psychological applications to such diseases as high blood pressure, headaches, chronic pain, allergies, ulcers, and general anxiety. Autogenic relaxation is a well-researched method for inducing a state of relaxation. Research has shown that when our bodies have an opportunity to fully relax, and hence to release tension, we stimulate a built-in mechanism for self-healing.

The idea of autogenic relaxation is incredibly simple: You repeat to yourself a series of six self-instructions. As you say the instruction in your mind, you are to observe what you experience in your body. You are only to observe; there should be *no* attempt to make it happen. Though it may be very difficult to take a passive, observing attitude, it must be understood that any other attitude may not be successful.

In fact, if you try to make something happen, the paradoxical effect often occurs. For example, if we monitor a person on a biofeedback machine that measures finger temperature and tell the person, "Make your temperature go up" while reciting the instruction "My hand is warm," the opposite will occur—the temperature will go down. In contrast, when the person repeats the self-instruction while maintaining a passive, observing attitude, the temperature will go in the direction of the instruction. With autogenic relaxation, we must give up control in order to exercise control.

The rules for practicing autogenic relaxation are similar to those for other methods. First, assume a comfortable position in which the body is not strained and is well supported. Then, loosen any tight garments or jewelry. Third, be in a quiet, subdued atmosphere. Fourth, prepare yourself to passively observe the sensations that occur when you give the instruction. Fifth, breathe deeply and evenly as you give the instruction. Sixth, end each session with some movements of the body to reestablish a state of alertness. Finally, end a session with a positive suggestion (e.g., "When I open my eyes I will feel refreshed, relaxed, and recharged").

After assuming a comfortable, supportive position, close your eyes and slowly recite the following self-instructions:

1. My hands and arms are heavy and warm. (5 times)
2. My feet and legs are heavy and warm. (5 times)
3. My abdomen is warm and comfortable. *(Omit if you have ulcers.)* (5 times)
4. My breathing is deep and even. (10 times)
5. My heartbeat is calm and regular. (10 times)
6. My forehead is cool. (5 times)
7. When I open my eyes, I will remain relaxed and refreshed. (3 times)
8. Perform the following sequence of body movements:
   a. Move hand and arms about.
   b. Move feet and legs about.
   c. Rotate head.
   d. Open eyes and sit up.

As you recite a self-instruction, breathe deeply and evenly. Synchronize your instructions with slow exhalations, and observe what you experience. Some of the sensations you might experience, such as tingling, twitching, and itching, may be uncomfortable at first. For some people, the feelings of warmth, heaviness, and occasional numbness may be disturbing. All these sensations are signs that tension is being released and relaxation is flowing. Feelings of heaviness, warmth, or lightness are the key signs of relaxation. As you repeat the experience with the sensations of relaxation, you will become accustomed to the sensations.

Be prepared to allow yourself time to adjust to becoming relaxed. Most of us are not really familiar with the sensations of deep relaxation; they are foreign experiences. If you are psychologically prepared to flow with unfamiliar sensations, then you will prevent a fear response. If you allow yourself to become afraid, you will obviously interfere with a relaxation response. Deep, full relaxation will happen as you practice. At first, you will find that your sensations of relaxation are light, but you will find that they become more intense with each self-instruction session.

Although autogenic relaxation is simple, it is not so completely benign as one might think. One contraindication is the third exercise, "My abdomen is warm and comfortable." People who have gastritis and ulcers should not use this exercise. The instruction of warmth can induce the secretion of stomach acids, which will aggravate the condition. Persons with gastric disorders might replace the third exercise with the following: "My stomach is cool and calm." This instruction should quiet stomach activity.

Another difficulty can be that the sensations stimulated by an instruction can be overwhelming and can trigger unwanted experiences. For example, some people, when they give themselves the fifth instruction ("My heartbeat is calm and regular"), experience the opposite: Their heart rate increases or they experience tachycardia, which feels like a twitching, pulsing, irregular heartbeat. This opposite reaction often occurs when a person has fears about his heart and his physical condition. Thus, for example, if he is afraid of dying of a heart attack, that anxiety might show itself when he gives himself the heartbeat instruction. One way to deal with this difficulty is to modify the instruction to include the word "slightly." The fifth instruction can be changed to read: "My heartbeat is slightly calm." To increase blood flow to the heart in such a way that one won't be overwhelmed, one can say, "My chest is slightly warm." Then, once that instruction can be recited without any adverse reactions, the original instruction ("My heartbeat is calm and regular") can be used.

Achievement of a full relaxation response may require a matter of days or a matter of months. Ideally, you should practice two times per day. The more adept you become at relaxing with autogenic relaxation, the more quickly you can induce a state of relaxation. And the more efficient you become, the easier and more accessible this method is for application to work situations.

For people who lead a fast-paced life, it can be crucial that they be efficient in their ways of relaxing.

Because the autogenic relaxation process is simple and internal, and hence easily applied, you can practice it without attracting much notice. You can practice while performing other tasks. You can pause briefly between tasks to practice. You can practice to prepare for sleep. You can practice to prepare for work in the morning before leaving for work. Although you will achieve greater relaxation with your eyes closed, you can practice autogenic relaxation with your eyes open or closed. Therefore, you can sit in a dull meeting and practice without anybody's being the wiser. The situations wherein the autogenic process can be applied are unlimited. Once you become skilled, make a list of potential situations and experiment.

Visualization for Relaxation

The process of visualization is our minds' ability to create pictures of what our bodies do. Whenever our bodies move, our minds are producing pictures of what is about to happen and what is happening. Most of these images are not conscious. When we "see" things, through any of our sense organs, our minds are creating pictures that record some memory of the event. Each time we have some experience, our bodies and minds record the happening.

The pendulum phenomenon illustrates the connection between images in our minds and movements in our bodies. To demonstrate this phenomenon, make a pendulum by tying a pebble or other light weight to the end of a foot-long string. Hold the other end of the string between your thumb and index fingers with the weight suspended. Now close your eyes and picture in your mind the pendulum swinging clockwise while you keep your hand and arm perfectly still. After picturing this for a minute, open your eyes, look down, and see what the pendulum is doing. Usually, the pendulum is swinging in the clockwise direction, just as you have pictured. The image in your mind is translated into micromovements in your hand.

Just as we have the power to use images to create movement, we can use images to create a state of relaxation. When we go into a state of consciousness where we are clearly picturing some experience or event, we also stimulate our entire bodies to recall the feelings of that experience. When we recollect a fearful or angry event, our hearts can race just as they did when we actually had the experience. Similarly, when we recollect a positive, relaxing moment, we can recreate in our bodies the relaxing mood that we had at the time.

The process of using imagery to relax is simple. Simply assume a comfortable position, close your eyes, and create an image in your mind of some place where you felt truly relaxed, calm, and happy. In this picture, observe what is happening there. Notice the colors of the scenery. Notice the quiet atmosphere, or the freshness of the air. Notice the shapes of familiar objects, and be aware of any movement that occurred. Just let yourself recall the positive feelings in that scene. Enjoy what you remember and what you see in your mind's eye. Breathe deeply, and relax.

If you feel that you need someone to guide you, the description above can be translated as follows into a narrative that another person can read to you:

Prepare to relax by breathing deeply and evenly. Breathe in slowly to a count of four. Hold your breath to a count of four. And exhale slowly. As you continue to breathe deeply and evenly, in your mind's eye create a picture of a pleasant scene. Imagine yourself doing something relaxing—maybe walking on the beach while listening to the sound of the waves with the cool fresh breeze blowing across your face and through your hair, or maybe walking in the woods with the warm sun shining on you and the birds singing in the trees—imagine some experience that you personally found relaxing.

Pause 15 seconds, then continue:

Go on imagining this scene. Continue to breathe deeply and evenly. Allow yourself to recall the details of the experience—remember the sights, the sounds, the smells, the feelings, and the mood. Just let yourself reexperience the moments. Breathe deeply and evenly. Just relax and enjoy the memory.

Pause 30 seconds, then continue:

You may now return to your waking state and remain calm now that your body has reexperienced the pleasant feelings that you had. Open your eyes, feeling refreshed and calm.

As you can see now, visualization is simple and straightforward. Most of us use visualization in our daily life, but few of us consciously use this process specifically to relax. We may daydream about some wish, and we may dream about our accomplishments or about impending events, but relatively few people know about using this method to relax.

Visualization can be used as an efficient method to relax and to create a positive frame of mind. It is quick, and it can be used easily in the most trying situations to lessen anxiety.

The power of this method was demonstrated to me by an attorney many years ago. Just before I was to enter a courtroom to testify in a trial as an expert witness, the defense attorney asked me how I felt. I told him that I was nervous and afraid of saying the wrong thing. He first told me to be honest so that I could always repeat my position at any time. He then instructed me on how to relax when I felt scared. He wanted me to relax enough to be able to smile and remain confident. Whenever I felt too overwhelmed to smile, I was to visualize the lawyers, the judge, and the members of the jury sitting there in their Jockey shorts and panties. I did just as he instructed. And sure enough, I relaxed, I smiled, and I even chuckled to myself.

So visualization can be a quick and efficient method of relaxation. Just remember to let your imagination go, discover a restful or calming scene, and picture it vividly and pleasurably. Enjoy the positive feelings you associate with that scene—and relax!

You have now been introduced to four different methods that can help you to relax more deeply and effectively: deep diaphragmatic breathing, deep muscle relaxation, autogenic relaxation, and visualization. You may wish to experiment with each of these until you find the method, or combination of methods, that best suits your needs. Once you have decided upon the relaxation technique that works best for you, practice it until you can use it efficiently and quickly. Then use your imagination to help you discover a variety of ways in which you can introduce relaxation, and its beneficial stress reduction, into your everyday life.

CHAPTER 5

RESISTING STRESS

SLEEP, EXERCISE, AND NUTRITION

Up to this point, you have been gathering a variety of powerful weapons that you can use in your battle with stress. These weapons include: (1) knowledge of stressors and the stress reaction, (2) awareness of common signs or symptoms of stress, (3) techniques for undertaking your own ongoing stress analysis, and (4) relaxation methods to help you cope better with your present stressful experiences. In this chapter, you will begin to go on the offensive against stress.

To cope effectively with stress—and maybe even eliminate it from parts of our lives—it is first necessary to build resistance. You will recall from our earlier discussion of the general adaptation syndrome (GAS) that the initial alarm reaction soon subsides and is replaced by a stage of resistance. During that second, resistant stage, the body more or less returns to normal and fights vigorously against the stressor. Eventually, should the stressor persist, the resistance stage may slowly collapse into the final stage of the GAS, exhaustion.

Normally this final collapse of resistance is brought about, as we have seen earlier, because the body's reserves of energy have been drawn down too low. With no reserve energy available, the body cannot resist effectively, and exhaustion sets in, often accompanied by disease when the organism can no longer resist. This scenario suggests an important principle for stress management and control: The stronger the body's reserves, the better able the body will be to resist the ravages of stress, without falling into the stage of exhaustion.

But how does one strengthen the body's reserves? What sort of activities do that? The answer is straightforward. Maximum bodily strength and efficiency depend upon three factors: sleep, exercise, and nutrition. Only a body that is well rested, properly exercised, and correctly fed will be able to maintain its energy reserves in the face of serious stress. Even more, such a healthy, well-maintained body will actually experience less stress because of its strong resistance and its ability to avoid exhaustion and the cycle of low energy, fatigue, and depression that exhaustion normally brings.

STRESS, SLEEP, AND REST

Let us begin the offensive against stress with an examination of sleep and rest. Other factors, such as excellent nutrition and effective exercise, promote well-being at cellular and systemic levels, but they are not enough. The brain, which controls biological survival, needs rest to maintain its equilibrium. A great part of this maintenance is accomplished through sleep. If sleep is too brief, fitful, or disrupted, then we awaken irritable, tired, cranky, and less able to cope. The reason is that the brain, without adequate rest and sleep, cannot maintain the biochemical and electrical balances needed for effective functioning. Furthermore, when the brain is in such a state of disequilibrium, a person cannot cope effectively. As a result, chronic sleep disturbances can lead to physical and psychological exhaustion, depression, and a general feeling of anxiety.

During the course of a night's sleep, we pass through different cycles in which our brains show different electrical wave patterns. One important cycle is rapid eye movement (REM) sleep. It is during REM sleep that dreams occur. If REM cycles are repeatedly interrupted, people show marked irritability, anxiety, distractibility, inability to concentrate, and depressed moods. Biological equilibrium depends upon completion of these cycles.

The completion of dreams is also vital for psychological well-being. Dreams appear to serve several purposes. They allow people to symbolically complete the unfinished business of the day as well as keep them asleep. Thus, for example, a person might dream of war scenes when anger has not been expressed during the day. Also, dreaming can compensate for a lack of fulfillment in some aspect of life. If one is not sexually active and fulfilled, then one might sublimate the sex drive through dreams. Often, external stimulation (e.g., sounds of a fire engine in the night) will cause the dreamer to incorporate the intrusion in a dream to allow him to remain asleep. The overall function, though, is the maintenance of psychic equilibrium.

For sleep to be functional, it must be full, relaxed, continuous, and long enough. Most people need from 6 to 8 hours of full sleep to function optimally. Some can function on less, and some need slightly more. The amount of sleep that each person needs is influenced by many factors. The degree of relaxation vs. tension, what we ate, what we did physically, what we did to achieve resolution of psychological conflicts, and the events we are about to face the next day, as well as the type of bed and the room temperature, can influence the depth of sleep.

Sleep must be integrative. It must not be disturbed by nightmares, by extraneous stimulation, or by unresolved conflicts. Fitful and incomplete rest leads to an energy drain and biological disequilibrium. Difficulty falling asleep, insomnia, and early-morning awakening can be signs of anxiety, depression, and psychological disturbance. They may also be signals of stressful life-style habits, such as overeating. At the very least, they are signals of tension. But more often than not, tension is related to psychological distress.

Prolonged sleep is another sign of depression, or possibly of a neurological problem. People who seem to "need" 9, 10, and more hours of sleep are often depressed. Coming home and falling asleep after work without energy may also signal depression, physical exhaustion, or a desire to withdraw from the pressure and responsibilities of the day. To "sleep perchance to dream" is a psychological defense. When stress is beyond our coping skills, withdrawal through sleep is frequently used.

Withdrawal through sleep has its origins in infancy. Go to any hospital nursery. The lights are glaring in the infants' eyes and the sound level is often high. The infants automatically protect themselves through sleep. They came from the dark environment of the womb into the well-lit atmosphere of the delivery room, and they cope with the stress of the change through sleep. In contrast, compare infants allowed to room in with their mothers in subdued lighting and sound. These infants remain awake longer.

Beginning in infancy, people have individual sleep patterns and needs. As people age, they need less sleep. It is not uncommon to hear of families complaining that grandma or grandpa awakens in the early morning. These same people may also be found to nap during the daytime. Sleep cycles may be shorter but more frequent.

Throughout life, the lack of adequate rest can be compensated for in many ways. People who regularly relax through meditation, deep muscle relaxation, or autogenic training can often get along well on fewer hours of nighttime sleep. Similarly, people who jog and exercise vigorously often find that they need less sleep. Also, self-hypnosis has been known to give a person a feeling of well-being despite having had only a few hours of sleep the previous night. Each of these compensatory actions has a positive impact upon brain equilibrium.

Most people do not want to compensate systematically for lack of rest, but would rather be able to rest fully and regularly. Before you begin a program to develop sound sleep habits, it might be useful to analyze your sleep patterns. The following question-analysis might prove helpful:

1. Observe yourself. Are you able to fall asleep readily? Do you awaken feeling rested and well? Was your sleep fitful or interrupted by nightmares? Did you awaken needing to eliminate? Were you awakened by light or sounds?

2. Can you identify *patterns?* Is your insomnia frequent, or does it coincide with specific events (e.g., rejection by spouse, following arguments, after overeating and drinking)? When did it begin? Were there specific stresses occurring in your life? What

were they? Do you lie in bed worrying and ruminating over troublesome events? Do you have aches, pains, and specific discomforts as you attempt to fall asleep?

3. *How* have you coped with these sleep problems? What worked? Were you consistent in your method? Were you haphazard? Did the successful method remain successful?

4. What specifically can you *learn* from these sleep patterns? What do your dreams tell you? Do you simply dismiss them as nuisances, or can you allow yourself to learn from them? Even the terror of nightmares offers a message. Does your pattern of sleep indicate that you are a worrier, a relaxed person, a chronically tense person, a person who overindulges himself, or a person who is depressed?

Observation and analysis of sequences and patterns can illuminate not only problems but also their solutions. For example, a family consulted me when their 8-year-old son was fatigued from early-morning awakening. Analysis of the environment and of the child's sensitivity to different types of stimulation indicated that he was photosensitive. The solution was to install dark window shades. Thereafter, he slept soundly until the alarm went off.

People who lead stressful lives are often tense, and this tension often results in more frequent urination and acid stomach. It is common for these people to experience interrupted sleep. They are awakened by stomach pain, indigestion, and the need to urinate. Practical solutions to these sleep patterns are to limit fluids prior to sleep and to eat a small, nonspicy evening meal. Also, elimination of or moderation in drinking alcoholic beverages is important. Alcohol consumption is usually accompanied by dehydration and more frequent need to urinate.

The development of viable sleep patterns is vital to the maintenance of energy reserves. It is important to develop reliable habits so that there is the expectation of sound sleep. Some of the more common contributors to insomnia are the *expectations* of having difficulty falling asleep, nightmares, and feeling poorly in the morning. The expectation of negative events typically generates anxiety and tension. These in turn create a self-fulfilling prophecy. Once sound sleep habits have been established, the expectation of full sleep facilitates that event.

There are a number of guidelines that encourage sound sleep habits. The suggestions that follow are categorized according to phenomena that have been found to encourage improved sleep.

Food Consumption

1. Do NOT overeat at dinner. Stop when you begin to feel full. Eating requires the stomach to work, and sleeping is a time for rest, not work. Overeating can cause the stomach to splash acid up into the esophagus, thereby creating indigestion and discomfort. A small meal at dinner is highly recommended.

2. Avoid late evening snacks.

3. Limit fluid intake during the 2 hours prior to retiring. The need to urinate in the middle of the night can stimulate disturbing dreams as well as cause early awakening.

4. Do NOT consume large amounts of alcoholic beverages in the evening. Alcohol is dehydrating and stimulates the need for frequent urination. Stomach acidity and abdominal cramps are also common consequences of too much alcohol ingestion. Certain liqueurs have been known to cause tachycardia, in which the heart feels as though it is skipping beats or beating in flutters. These internal sensations can disturb attempts to fall asleep, as well as disturb sleep and cause awakening.

If you must drink, many people can tolerate a small glass of wine. It is advisable to eat a small amount of food prior to or with the alcoholic drink. Foods that are high in glucose or some form of sugar are recommended. Honey is especially effective. All sugars are metabolized into sucrose which facilitates the metabolism of the alcohol. In addition to the dehydration, when the liver metabolizes the alcohol, it leaves the by-product ethylaldehyde, which is toxic. The body must then work to filter the ethylaldehyde from the bloodstream. This filtering process is a stressor that can interfere with full sleep.

Environment

1. The place of rest should be adequately supportive. Some mattresses are too soft and do not provide effective support for the musculature. Firm support is usually most effective.

2. If a person is sensitive to sound, then the resting environment needs to be quiet. Noise from clocks, heaters, neighbors, and the street can be intrusive. Thick carpeting and heavy drapery often aid in quieting the atmosphere. It is sometimes necessary to oil creaking door hinges.

3. If a person is sensitive to light, then dark window shades or drapery will shield the room from morning and night lights. Also, those who are extraordinarily photosensitive may need shielding from light that reflects from other rooms through cracks around doorways.

4. Extreme temperatures can interfere with soundness of sleep. Most people are comfortable at around 68°F. Many people find that they sleep fitfully or that their sleep is disturbed by shivering or sweating when temperatures are too hot or too cold. Sleep is often deeper when the room temperature is on the cool side (65–68°F).

Attitudes

1. To enjoy sleep, a person must accept it as a normal and desirable aspect of life. People with a sense of time urgency, who resent not having enough hours in the day to accomplish what they wish, often have difficulty falling asleep. They tend to ruminate about unfinished business. Acceptance of sleep as a desirable event is important.

2. It is important to approach bedtime with a positive attitude, with a feeling of closure to today's events and a positive expectation of tomorrow. When business is left unsettled, anxiety results. A dreaded expectation of tomorrow's activities also generates feelings of anxiety.

3. It is easier to go to sleep when you are psychologically

and physically ready. To go to sleep when you feel awake can lead to tossing and turning. Rather than spend hours of fitful tossing about the bed, it is better to flow with one's mood. Quiet activities (e.g., reading, a warm bath) often prepare a person to get in the mood for a night's rest. For many people, a relaxing routine just prior to retiring enables them to feel calm.

Relaxing Routines

1. Develop some routines that are calming prior to retiring. These include: a warm bath, a small glass of warm milk, a massage, lovemaking, a quiet talk with spouse or mate, reading relaxing materials, listening to calming music, visualizing pleasant scenes, meditation, practicing deep muscle relaxation, autogenic training, or yoga breathing. Spending a few minutes visualizing and planning something positive about the next day is often relaxing. Whatever routine you choose, select one that is calming, not arousing.

Similarly, upon completion of a relaxation technique, it is helpful to give oneself positive self-instructions. For example, as you drift to sleep, you might repeat the instruction, "When I wake up, I will feel fresh, alert, and relaxed." If one's health is of concern, the following instruction is useful: "Every day in every way I grow stronger and healthier." Drifting to sleep with a positive self-instruction can encourage peaceful, full sleep.

2. Avoid watching television programs that are arousing or frightening.

3. Avoid reading materials that are arousing or frightening.

Rest

Whereas sleep is an essential component of revitalizing our bodies and minds, it is also useful to rest during the daytime. Research has indicated that people who rest during the day have fewer illnesses. Most union contracts compel employers to give workers at least one rest break for each half day of work. Without periods of rest to change pace and pause, efficiency and quality are sacrificed. People need time to pause, to let go and unwind.

The quality of the rest period is vital for optimal benefits. At work, many people take "coffee breaks" during which they drink coffee and eat doughnuts. Some take the time to smoke. As we saw in the last chapter, the coffee and cigarettes give a boost by putting stimulants into the bloodstream, and the doughnuts or snacks give a boost by increasing the amount of sugar in the blood. Unfortunately, such a pick-me-up is temporary, and is frequently followed by a letdown. A period of low energy, fatigue, or sluggishness is common as the blood sugar level drops again, or as the nicotine and caffeine are filtered from the blood. Besides creating swings in energy, these pausing strategies drain vital nutrients. In the long run, they are more draining than energizing.

Effective resting and pausing are characterized by stability in energy level. When a person relaxes in a viable way, he experiences increased energy, a positive frame of mind, a positive attitude toward coping, and a general sense of well-being. Many people find that a change in the environment (such as going outdoors during a rest break at work) facilitates the ease and depth of relaxation. Relaxing in a quieter place with fewer people around is often useful. More energy can be gained through 5 minutes of meditation, self-hypnosis, deep muscle relaxation, or deep breathing than through drinking coffee and eating doughnuts.

To maintain high levels of efficiency and coping, it is helpful to make relaxation processes part of one's daily routine. Taking 15 minutes of one's lunch break for relaxation will restore a sense of calm and vitality for most people. Pausing and resting should be a regular routine, just as exercise and good nutrition should be a consistent part of one's life-style.

STRESS AND EXERCISE

Exercise can be as valuable to the body as sleep and rest are to the brain. High physical arousal through exercise releases tension; yet, like sleep, it can also restore energy reserves. True physical fitness, in turn, acts to reduce or even prevent stress and disease by cardiovascular and respiratory conditioning and the maintenance of muscle tone. Such fitness encourages a positive self-image and an attitude of active control over one's life. This feeling of personal control leads to a greater likelihood of respecting and liking oneself. Perhaps this is one of the reasons that active exercise counters depression and anxiety. People who jog or swim or otherwise engage in healthful exercise like themselves more—and they also have less time to worry!

The question is not, to paraphrase Hamlet, to exercise or not to exercise. Instead, the real question concerning exercise is whether we like and care for ourselves or whether we do not. Each person must ask, "Do I want to like and respect myself?" If the answer is "Yes," if there is a desire to admire and care for yourself, then physical well-being is a personal necessity. This is the case because human beings do not need to exercise to exist; even an overweight, out-of-shape body can manage to get by for a time. But most if not all of us do require high physical arousal in order to maintain the body physiology necessary for optimal survival.

The question then becomes this: Do you want to live a full life? Do you want to enjoy your body and your activities? Or are you content to merely exist—and fall victim to the forces of stress? If you want to enjoy life and live it to the fullest, then exercise is a must. The same is true if you want to endure the destructive impact of stress in your life.

Many people wonder whether or not they are physically fit. As noted earlier, our bodies will signal whether or not we are physically fit. For those who are not clear concerning what signals suggest fitness or being out-of-shape, the following indications imply a need for a program of active exercise:

Being out-of-breath after walking up a flight of stairs
Long recovery time after walking up a flight of stairs
Generally feeling "exhausted" after short periods of physical exertion
Poor, fitful sleep

Depression, anxiety

General muscle tension

Obesity

Poor muscle tone; loose, flabby skin

Winded after a round of golf or a half hour of tennis

Muscles cramped and aching for days after participating in
sports

Poor recoverability of energy at end of work day

General tiredness, fatigue, boredom

Frequent irritability

Little joie de vivre

Fear and discomfort with sensations under conditions of
high arousal states; increases in heart rate and respiration
rate occurring during sex, anger, fear, physical strain, and
exercise (If you feel afraid of or overwhelmed by these
body sensations, then you are probably out of shape.)

Inability to jog a mile in 8 minutes and recover breath
within 5 minutes

This list of experiences is not all-inclusive. It merely gives
some of the major indicators that a person may not be in optimal
physical condition. Once you are aware that there is room for
improvement, then you can decide whether you want to become
physically fit. Assuming that you want to improve your physical
condition through exercise, the next question is how to go about
selecting appropriate exercise regimes.

Choosing an Exercise Program

"Jog yourself into total fitness." "Fifteen minutes to complete health." "If you are over sixty, don't strain; walking is
enough." The myths of physical fitness continue ad nauseam. In
the area of selecting the best exercise program, there is a great
deal of confusion and fear.

As the interest in exercise has grown, there has been an
increase in the number of written articles cautioning against
every sort of exercise. Joggers are warned of pseudonephritis, or

"jogger's kidney." Prolonged running may cause the kidneys to spill blood, protein, and other substances into the urine. Most of the time, though, the condition clears in 48 hours. Tennis buffs are warned of "tennis elbow" and possible arthritis. And walkers? Beware of the neighbor's dog!

How do you decide which form of exercise is beneficial and which is harmful? There are many issues that need to be considered to answer this question adequately. First, you need to review the purposes of the exercise.

Exercise and high arousal states serve many purposes. A person's flexibility, muscle tone, strength, and general state of well-being can be improved. Exercise can relieve tension and facilitate weight loss while improving the body's general physiological condition. Improvement in the cardiovascular and respiratory systems can lead to a greater oxygen supply to body tissue. As noted in earlier chapters, these improvements enhance a person's ability to adapt to stressful life events.

First, decide your reasons for exercising—that is, which of the following you want:

1. Skill development?
2. Cardiovascular and respiratory conditioning?
3. Improved body image through muscle tone and strength development?
4. To be outdoors or socialize through some leisure-time activity?
5. General improvement in health?
6. To lose or maintain weight?
7. To have greater energy and less tension?
8. To dissipate aggression and competitive striving?

Your goals will directly determine your choice of exercises to achieve these goals. Little weight will be lost as the result of a leisurely stroll. Whereas jogging promotes cardiovascular conditioning, sprinting does not; in fact, sprinting could be harmful when a person has heart disease. Golf may risk a strained back for lack of flexibility, but may provide an excellent sense of achievement through skill development. The benefits and potential dangers of each form of exercise need to be assessed.

There are other factors to consider when choosing an exercise. Entry level is important. It is unwise to attempt to jog an 8-minute mile the first time out. Each person needs to consider age, general level of fitness, history of exercise, limitations of active disease processes, limitations of strength, physical structure, and injuries.

Repeated broken legs on the slopes might suggest that skiing is no longer advisable. Back injuries might warn against jogging, but would recommend swimming. Active heart disease would discourage engaging in isometric forms of exercise, which involve tight contracture or clamping of muscles, and include weight-lifting, water skiing, arm wrestling, and doing push-ups. Such stop-and-go movements could be a strain on the heart. Your history of exercise will also offer some clues as to which exercises are fun and which have kept you fit in the past.

The best advice if you are in doubt is to seek a consultation from an expert.

Once goals and forms of exercise have been selected, the next phase is actually exercising. Carrying out a regime of exercise on a regular basis is easier said than done. Many people begin some exercise program only to stop after a brief period. Some find the exercise "boring," "a struggle to get going," as well as "painful." They are unprepared for what happens and are easily discouraged when they do not feel fit immediately. Long-distance runners do not run 5 miles the first time out; they may take a year or longer to build up to that distance.

A first rule for beginning a new exercise program is: Be realistic by setting limited goals. Approach the exercise gradually. Build up to greater demands and skill levels in small increments. Allow some time, perhaps a month, to begin to feel differently. It takes time to become fit, just as it took time to get out of shape.

Next, expect some discomfort initially. You may find yourself using muscles that you have long been unaware of. Don't overfocus on your discomforts. They will pass as strength builds and flexibility grows through repeated use of the muscles. A warm bath, a massage, and a good night's sleep will heal the aches, pains, and minor bruises and calluses that result initially.

Increasing the pace and vigor of exercise gradually will also minimize these discomforts.

Once you go beyond the initial discomforts, it will be easier to relax while exercising. A relaxed attitude of enjoyment of the process during exercise will affect not only performance but also the degree of pleasure. The "inner game" of any sport involves awareness of the processes and experiences during movements. A focus on the end product, such as winning, will detract from relaxation. In fact, overfocusing on the performance of the skill can create tension and actually lower performance.

How does a person "enjoy" exercise? Experiment! Change rhythm, tempo, pace, intensity, and duration of movements. Alter your style of breathing (e.g., deep diaphragmatic breathing vs. shallow chest breathing) and speed of movement. Use imagery and be playful while exercising. One favorite mind game is to imagine being some animal during the exercise. A gazelle, a lion, and a cheetah all run at different speeds with varying rhythm and gait. When you imagine being that animal, attempt to capture its grace, speed, form, and breathing.

Another mode of enjoyment of process is through focused awareness. Be aware of your surroundings, your heartbeat, your breathing, your skin temperature, your excitement, your mood, your rhythms, and your smile. Be aware of any pleasurable sensations. Getting fit can be fun!

People are more likely to stick to exercise they enjoy. The sensations of arousal, the pleasure, and the expectation of good health and improved self-esteem, as well as the achievements in skill development, all contribute to continuation of the exercise. These are the rewards of exercise. They reinforce people to continue. Without them, exercise will be viewed and experienced as drudgery and as a "have-to." Once people begin to think in terms of "I *must* do this," they no longer view the process as voluntary. And as soon as that sense of control is gone, people tend to resist and lose interest.

As noted earlier, to prevent early loss of interest in a new activity, a trial month or two is often useful. Also, reviewing your exercise history will give you some perspective about likes and dislikes. Some people delight in group sports, while others cringe at the prospect. If you have an aversion to organized sports, then isolated activities such as walking and jogging might be enjoyable. There is no "best" exercise for everyone. Each person must discover what "fits" in with getting fit.

Another factor that will influence exercise selection is the amount of time allotted. Organized sports are often more time-consuming and must be planned. Individual activities are more readily scheduled, but limit social interaction. Busy schedules often dictate which forms of exercise will match a person's life-style. Reserving courts, locating partners, making sure a locker room is available, and toting equipment around can all be cumbersome within the confines of a busy work schedule. On the other hand, planning can handle these restrictions.

It is advisable to decide the frequency of exercise and the amount of time to be allotted. To gain health benefits, vigorous exercise needs to be done regularly at least three to four times per week. Most exercises require 15 to 30 minutes of activity to promote the type of physiological arousal needed for cardiovascular and respiratory conditioning. The necessity for consistent and regular exercise cannot be overemphasized. To exercise for 2 hours once a week can actually do physical damage and will frequently cause strains, aches, and pains. It would be more beneficial to spend 15 minutes four times a week and keep up muscle tone as well as major life-support systems.

A major aspect of learning to enjoy exercise is developing a habit. Through practice and continuity, people can develop the level of skill and stamina at which they are free to focus on pleasurable sensations and variations. Make a commitment to include exercise in your life-style. It is easier to adhere to daily routines than to sporadic activities.

The cost and convenience of exercise are another factor. Whereas most people can afford a jump rope, the price of a bicycle may be prohibitive for others. Skiing, tennis, and golf equipment may be too expensive for some, but most people own a bathing suit. Accessibility to pools, tennis or racquet ball courts, or golf courses will influence decisions to participate in these sports. For most people, sex is a convenient and inexpensive exercise (assuming there isn't an accidental pregnancy). It burns many calories, but achievement of a cardiovascular conditioning effect would require at least 15 minutes of preorgasmic activity.

Even though execution of an exercise program might include the aforementioned considerations, a person could find it difficult to maintain continuity. When people have spent many years leading sedentary lives, there will be a pull to return to inactivity. It is not easy to give up old habits, and it is not easy to maintain new ones.

A major part of establishing a new habit is attending to the events that reward or punish the activity. If a spouse or friend is unsupportive, critical, or mocking of the exercise, then there will be a greater likelihood of giving up. On the other hand, if these people are supportive, then the activities are more likely to be maintained. Enlisting the support of mate, friend, or children may prove facilitative and encouraging.

Similarly, sharing exercise activities can create a built-in support system. Exercising as a family or with mate, friend, or child can stimulate a positive sense of community and a group joie de vivre. Thus, in addition to the rewards and pleasures intrinsic to the exercise, creating a system of social supports will enhance the experience and maintain motivation to continue.

Although it is an added benefit to have a social system support your exercise program, the ultimate responsibility is yours. Exercise is not "good" or "bad"; those terms refer to morality. Exercise may be beneficial, however, in building your ability to adapt in a highly stressful world. If getting fit fits, then you will discover all the motivation you need to set up an exercise program that suits your liking, age, and general physical status.

High Arousal States and Aerobic Conditioning

There is a large body of research that suggests that aerobic conditioning increases the capacity of the heart and lungs. An *aerobic* process promotes the use of oxygen in the body. Cardiovascular conditioning must be aerobic; that is, the exercise must be one that facilitates the use and distribution of oxygen and can be sustained for at least 2 minutes at a time without getting out of breath. Running, swimming, cycling, and walking are aerobic exercises, but sprinting is not. Exercises that require frequent starting and stopping are not sustained long enough to achieve a conditioning effect.

Cardiovascular conditioning is important to a total stress-management life-style, especially if you live a life of high pressure and demand. When fit, your body and mind can respond to and recover from stress reactions more readily. Cardiovascular conditioning is part of prevention.

A conditioning effect can be achieved through exercise performed at least three times a week for 20 minutes at a time, during which time your heart rate should be within your "target zone." This zone is from 70 to 85% of the maximum rate your heart can beat. You can estimate your average target zone by multiplying your standing heart rate (the number of beats per minute while you are standing) by 2½. You can also estimate the zone by subtracting your age in years from 220 and multiplying that number by 70% to obtain the lower limit and by 85% to obtain the upper limit of the target range. Your heartbeat rate should be within this range during the 20-minute period of exercise to achieve aerobic conditioning.

Conditioning can be achieved only through regular exercise. Do not attempt aerobic conditioning unless you have decided to be consistent and regular. A sporadic approach can be destructive.

For some people, a warm-up period often facilitates getting rid of stiffness while getting the heart pumping. Others find warm-up periods unnecessary and just begin their exercises, slowly at first, then with increasing speed. Do what suits you.

Aerobic conditioning is based upon a natural phenomenon that typically stimulates a sense of well-being. The phenomenon is that of arousal-to-relaxation cycles. People can be aroused through anger, fear, conflict, sex, joy, sadness, and exercise. Arousal states that are continuous and prolonged to the point where tensions are dissipated and relaxation follows are usually aerobic. If tension remains and relaxation does not follow, muscles remain tense, and irritability, fatigue, anxiety, and depression may result.

When emotions are evoked but not completely discharged, the arousal-to-relaxation cycle is blocked. Blocked grief can lead to depression and even sinus difficulties. Undischarged sexual tensions can lead to irritability and fatigue. On the other hand, a fight that ends in resolution leads conflicting sides to feel calm and closer emotionally. Aerobic conditioning usually leads to increased energy, a feeling of well-being and calm, and improved adaptability. Decreased appetite is another common by-product. A person's recovery time from a stress reaction is shortened.

There are several common exercises that can achieve cardio-vascular conditioning. Walking at least 3.5 miles per hour is dynamic, beneficial, and aerobic. Cycling usually needs to be at least 8 miles per hour. Jogging at 5 miles per hour is dynamic, aerobic, and endurance-building. An eventual target zone is the 8-minute mile, but an 8- to 12-minute range should ensure a conditioning effect. Cycling at 12 miles per hour also builds endurance, while even faster speeds offer superb conditioning. Swimming is a good conditioning exercise and can be aerobic if it is continuous. Persons with joint diseases or weight-bearing injuries may find swimming the most viable exercise. Tennis and racquet ball may have a conditioning effect, but you must keep moving for at least 20 to 30 minutes.

There are several signals that indicate that a conditioning effect is being achieved. When you have done an aerobic exercise long enough to feel winded—that is, when you feel as though you are slowing down and breathing is labored—that is the point to *continue past* for several minutes. When you go beyond to a "second wind," then you are achieving a conditioning effect. It is vital to press on when you begin to feel strained and winded. At the point of achieving a second wind, there will be a surge of energy. Beyond the second wind, people often feel as though they could continue indefinitely. At this time, heart rate will stabilize and breathing will be fuller.

Some people even report an experience that parallels orgasmic relief. At the point of feeling winded, there are sensations of tension in breathing and musculature. Pressing beyond this point increases the tension until there is a momentary and sudden discharge of tension. Relaxation follows the discharge, and cardiovascular and respiratory systems stabilize. The point of the second wind often produces an altered state of consciousness wherein the person feels powerful and self-confident, yet calm. Long-distance jogging and running often produce a mental and physical "high." Joggers and runners achieve "enlightenment" through exercise.

Above all, be creative. The joys of physical fitness will emerge from regular practice. Preventive stress management through cardiovascular conditioning as well as through tension dissipation is a by-product of viable exercise programs. Select what fits you. Experiment, and hang in there long enough to reap the benefits. Eventually, the rewards will be immediate. Fitness can be functional and fun.

STRESS AND NUTRITION

In addition to both proper rest and adequate exercise, effective stress resistance also depends upon your personal nutrition. As trite as it may seem, "you are what you eat," and the ability of your body to maintain adequate reserves of energy against stress depends to a large extent upon a well-balanced and appropriate diet. This having been said, it is necessary to acknowledge that such a healthy, stress-thwarting diet is more the exception than the rule. This seems to be the case largely because of our present-day life-style.

We live in a self-indulgent culture that tends to place an emphasis upon the product and pays correspondingly less attention to the process by which that product came into being. Our children, for instance, grow up with clear ideas of *what* they want—cars, houses, clothes, and fine sports equipment. But few of them grow up with correspondingly clear ideas of *how* they are supposed to live while they pursue these goals. The emphasis is on the end, the final accomplishment, and little attention is given to habits or ways of living that will best enable them to attain these goals.

A telling example of this is our national disregard of our

diet. All parents want their children to grow up healthy and strong, but they give their children few guidelines, if any, for nutritionally sound eating habits. Part of the problem is that our society as a whole has emphasized speedy food preparation in the home, often using highly processed foods. The rice, for instance, may cook in a minute, but that quick cooking is possible because the rice has been denuded of its essential vitamins and minerals before being packaged and sold. The same is true of white bread and of many canned or frozen vegetables. Convenience has been achieved, but at a nutritional cost.

The same trade-off can be seen at the local fast-food restaurant where you take the kids for a quick and inexpensive meal of hamburgers and fries. Here, too, the nutrition is questionable: high in fats and lacking in many essential nutrients. Here, too, we tend to focus upon the results—getting the kids fed—rather than upon the process by which that end was achieved.

This product-oriented syndrome has its effects. On the one hand, few of our children grow up with an understanding of how to eat properly. If people begin to think about nutrition at all, they usually do so as adults. Perhaps it is because they find that their clothes do not fit any longer, or that they are less attractive because of those growing bulges and unwanted pounds. It might even be because they find themselves increasingly unable to cope with stress, for poor diet can contribute to stress in several ways. Simply eating too fast, for instance, while downing too many calories can result in indigestion, bloating, discomfort, and stress on the intestinal tract. When food is not chewed well, the stomach and intestines must work harder. When food contains too much fat, too many preservatives, and too many by-products from processing, the stomach, gallbladder, liver, intestines, and kidneys are overtaxed. The gallbladder works to break down the fats from frying, and the kidneys labor at filtering all the various toxins. Eating becomes stressful rather than relaxing.

A major characteristic of Western habits is *excess*. People drink too much, smoke too much, and eat too much. There is a great sense of time urgency. People attempt to cram more and more events into the same time span. Excess of most anything can be stressful.

Research has clearly demonstrated that exposure to an excess of many chemicals can cause cancer in rats. One wonders, though, whether it is the exposure to the specific substance or the exposure to large quantity that causes the disease. Excessive amounts of the chemicals may have stimulated stress reactions that then lower resistance.

Whereas too much alcohol can cause cirrhosis of the liver and brain damage, moderate drinking may in fact be beneficial. Recent research collected from the National Institute of Alcohol Abuse and Alcoholism suggests that if you drink reasonably, you may have a sounder heart, a better night's sleep, and more fun with your friends. In 1974, the Federal government's "Second Report on Alcohol and Health" disclosed that moderate drinkers live longer than abstainers. In a Kaiser-Permanente Medical Center study in Oakland, California, people who drank moderately had 30% fewer heart attacks. Other studies confirm these findings.

The key word is "moderation." Any diet that emphasizes excess excludes, by its design, a broad range of nutriments. Alcoholics drink too much and, more often than not, do not eat well. They are often malnourished. People who diet to lose weight by emphasizing carbohydrates to the exclusion of fats, or proteins to the exclusion of carbohydrates, can easily become malnourished.

About ten years ago in California, some people were attempting to live on a "macrobiotic" diet, which was vegetarian. Many were misinformed and lived on brown rice and raw vegetables. The goal was to achieve enlightenment and inner peace through this diet. Hospitals began to report cases of malnourishment, which killed some and permanently impaired others. A well-informed person can live adequately on a macrobiotic diet, but an inadequately informed and faddish person is less likely to benefit.

Another aspect of excessive eating habits is weight gain. In cultures with high average life-span (80s to 90s), total caloric intake of adults typically averages between 1500 and 1800 calories a day. There is evidence that at least in rats, fasting can increase average life-span by up to 50%. The actuarial charts of insurance companies clearly indicate that lightweight people live longer.

In general, people who eat too much also weigh too much. The body needs only so many calories for survival. Any calories above that level are stored as fatty tissue. When fat develops, the body accommodates by developing new blood vessels to feed that tissue. Thus, as weight increases, the heart must pump blood farther and thereby must work harder. Extra pounds act as an internal stressor.

The other end of the continuum from excess is insufficiency, that is, eating too little of some substances. Recently, research has suggested that insufficient bulk fiber in diets has led to the growing incidence of cancer of the lower bowel in the United States. Too little vitamin D can cause rickets, which impairs bones, and an excess can damage the liver. Similarly, too little vitamin C can cause bleeding of the gums and a disease called scurvy.

What a person eats is also central to stress management. Many products are "empty" nutritionally; that is, they may provide calories, but they drain nutrients from the body. Many processed foods have been robbed of vitamins, minerals, and bulk fiber. Such foods actually drain our stores of nutrients when we eat them. As a result, there is less energy available to us when the body is stressed.

Processed cane sugar is one such example. It not only provides empty calories but also drains reserves. It does not contain the vitamins and minerals needed to digest and absorb it, and therefore the body is robbed of these substances each time we eat sugar. Little publicized, also, is the fact that substances that are used to process sugar are known causes of cancer, and sugar contains residues from such processing. Furthermore, a recent study indicates that sugar may decrease by 50% the white cells' ability to destroy bacteria. Thus, sugar can lower our resistance to disease as well.

Another substance found in high quantities in Western diets is salt. Hypertension, a known stress-related disease and a major killer, is also linked to high consumption of salt. Salt causes water retention, which in turn increases blood volume. The increased blood volume creates more pressure in the blood vessels. An executive of the American Heart Association recently stated that if people would cut salt consumption to below 5 grams per day, hypertension would disappear entirely. It would certainly be reduced.

The evidence is clear. Excess, even of the most common nutriments, can be stressful and harmful. At times, it can be lethal. Excess often leads to exclusion, and exclusion and over-emphasis prevent balance.

Moderation and balance go hand in hand. Eating a broad range of foods leads to a balanced diet. The variety of nutrients then keeps the body in top operating condition.

The exception to the rule of moderation and balance occurs with conditions of high stress. I advocate eating, under conditions of high stress, *less*, but *selectively*.

This principle derives from my personal experiences, from research, and from the analogy of illness. When a person contracts the flu, a virus has taken hold in the body. The virus is an invading organism, and the body reacts to the invader as a stressor. There is a mobilization response that leads to an increase in the production of white blood cells. The white blood cells then attempt to surround the virus and filter it out through the kidneys.

During a mobilization response, there is a redistribution of the blood to the muscles away from the surface of the skin. During the mobilization response and when a person becomes ill, there is an initial loss of appetite while the body copes. The loss of appetite suggests that the stomach shuts down while the body defenses are mobilized. Since the stomach is deactivated while resistance is promoted, it follows logically that during times of high stress, the stomach is not ready to handle more food. In fact, it would be stressful to eat a lot at that time. It is no accident that when people attempt to eat while they have a cold, they often become nauseated. The nausea is a signal that the stomach cannot cope.

Under stress, the mobilization response draws upon certain stores of nutrients. The liver releases sucrose for energy, while there are simultaneous demands upon the reserves of vitamin C, B-complex vitamins, and pantothenic acid. Each time a stress response occurs, these substances are used. When they are depleted, the body is subject to deterioration and destruction.

Under stress, it is important to *increase* our intake of vitamin C, B-complex vitamins, pantothenic acid, and foods that are easily converted to sucrose. To eat "heavy" foods such as meats, cheeses, and fatty products under stress is counterproductive. (A heavy food is one that requires a long and complex process to metabolize and assimilate.)

This information helps us to understand the plight of the executive. To go for a business lunch and eat large amounts of meats, fried foods, alcohol, and heavy sauces is an invitation to *more* tension, indigestion, and strain on all vital systems. Most of the time, the body does not assimilate all the protein from an 8- or 12-ounce steak; much is stored as fat or excreted. Under stress, even less is used. The resulting internal strain will leave the person feeling sluggish, irritable, and inefficient. Inefficiency and sluggish thinking are counterproductive for the executive who is doing business over lunch.

Dietary Habits

When pressure, problems, and life changes cause distress, each person's body responds differently. Some get indigestion, while others' hearts skip beats. Anxiety and stress can cause nausea, vomiting, diarrhea, constipation, headaches, backaches, and abdominal pains, just to mention a few reactions. What we eat can also cause these symptoms of distress.

It is no surprise that people get diarrhea when they are anxious. In fact, it is a logical and natural consequence of excessive eating. Diarrhea is the body's way of clearing the intestines to minimize internal activity. As outlined earlier, when a stress reaction occurs, certain body functions slow down while others speed up. There is a redistribution of the blood supply away from the intestinal tract toward the muscles so that action can take place. Thus, clearing the intestines allows other systems to function optimally.

The body has clear ways of signaling nutritional problems

and poor dietary habits. Indigestion, nausea, diarrhea, constipation, stomach cramps, intestinal cramps, stomach pains, and gas are the body's chief distress signals. These symptoms may be signaling nutritional inadequacy, destructive dietary habits, organ destruction, or active disease process.

Listen to these signals. Do not ignore them. They are your body's wisdom. Rather than simply relieving distress, *observe* it and *learn* from it. Merely to seek relief and do nothing else is shortsighted.

There are many common symptoms, behaviors, and habits that signal potential problems with your nutritional status. The list in Fig. 7 identifies the more common ones. Rate yourself by checking the appropriate frequency for each statement. Your responses should give you some indication of whether or not you need to attend to your dietary habits.

Items marked "very frequently" and "often" should signal an alert. They can signal dietary and systemic difficulties. It is common that when people have a craving for some foodstuffs, rather than decide that they "need" the food, they should actually eat *less*. The craving may indicate a type of addiction. People with hypertension usually have a high salt intake and an imbalance in the ratio of sodium to potassium in their blood. Their electrolyte balance, or their body's ability to conduct electrical signals, is out of kilter. The craving for salt is in fact an indication that their bodies are accustomed to a high level of salt.

This is also true of sweets. High levels of sugar intake may indicate hypoglycemia. In hypoglycemia, the body has difficulty maintaining a constant level of sugar in the blood. There are large shifts and swings in energy level. When energy level drops, a person may feel sluggish, faint, dizzy, fatigued, irritable, and foggy in thinking. When the blood sugar drops dramatically, the person may begin to crave sugars to compensate for the drop. Midmorning coffee breaks were probably created by someone with hypoglycemia. People down large quantities of coffee (a stimulant) and doughnuts or sweets in a vain attempt to keep their energy levels up and to break the sluggish, fatigued mood.

Although this may seem illogical, the solution is to eat *less* sugar. Large shifts in energy level and in blood sugar can be

	Very frequently 50-90%	Daily or every other day	Often 20-50%	1-3 times a week	Occasionally 10-20%	2-3 times a month	Seldom 1-10%	6 times a year	Never 0%
1. Feel fatigued or "wiped out."	☐		☐		☐		☐		☐
2. Have uncontrollable hunger urges.	☐		☐		☐		☐		☐
3. Have cravings for sweets.	☐		☐		☐		☐		☐
4. Eat when not hungry.	☐		☐		☐		☐		☐
5. Eat excessively when "bored."	☐		☐		☐		☐		☐
6. Have insomnia.	☐		☐		☐		☐		☐
7. Have indigestion.	☐		☐		☐		☐		☐
8. Get diarrhea.	☐		☐		☐		☐		☐
9. Get constipation.	☐		☐		☐		☐		☐
10. Urinate often.	☐		☐		☐		☐		☐
11. Have thoughts of "to hell with it all" before indulging.	☐		☐		☐		☐		☐
12. Feel in conflict about eating; a struggle.	☐		☐		☐		☐		☐
13. Feel self-conscious about how your body looks.	☐		☐		☐		☐		☐
14. Eat to abuse self.	☐		☐		☐		☐		☐
15. Have waves of anger or hostility.	☐		☐		☐		☐		☐
16. Energy comes in waves at different times of day.	☐		☐		☐		☐		☐
17. Feel sluggish after eating.	☐		☐		☐		☐		☐
18. Feel compelled to eat meats.	☐		☐		☐		☐		☐
19. Feel compelled to use salt.	☐		☐		☐		☐		☐
20. Crave coffee, tea.	☐		☐		☐		☐		☐
21. Use antacids.	☐		☐		☐		☐		☐
22. Use laxatives.	☐		☐		☐		☐		☐

FIGURE 7. Rating chart for dietary habits.

dealt with by eating less food more frequently. The large swings in energy may signal that your diet is too high in carbohydrates, that you ingest too many calories, that your metabolism is faulty, or that some organ system (e.g., the pancreas, which secretes insulin to help digest carbohydrates) is malfunctioning. If you reduce sugar intake and still experience energy swings, you should consider consulting your physician.

The irritability–fatigue syndrome may also be related to food allergies. Allergic people often crave the very foods to which they are allergic. If a person is allergic to a food, the body reacts to the food as though it were a poison. The body's defenses are mobilized and antibodies are formed to attack the invaders. This reaction, an allergic reaction, is a stress reaction. Allergies to foods can be signaled by bloating after eating, the fatigue–irritability syndrome, hives (little swellings on the skin), unexplained rashes, eye secretions, nasal discharges, mucus in throat and lungs, hot flashes after eating, abdominal cramps, and energy swings. Only an analysis of the time sequence and a professional consultation can clarify the existence of food allergies.

Eating Habits

Once you have determined that you show signs of possible nutritional inadequacy, the next step is to review your eating habits. How you eat may cause some of the symptoms of distress. Rate yourself on the chart for eating habits (Fig. 8).

Most of the items in the chart are self-evident in their intent. Thus, for example, when people eat and feel rushed, gulp their food, and stuff themselves, they create a state of tension by the way they eat. Eating is physiologically relaxing, but eating hurriedly and under pressure produces a state of biological conflict. The result is indigestion, gas, and abdominal distress. The entire gastrointestinal tract must work harder! Relaxation is prevented.

Similarly, eating alone and hiding or sneaking foods may indicate embarrassment. Shame and guilt generate tension and are obviously counterproductive. Eating a large dinner or having a snack before retiring is a sure way to ensure indigestion, phys-

	Very frequently 50–90% Daily or every other day	Often 20–50% 1–3 times a week	Occasionally 10–20% 2–3 times a month	Seldom 1–10% 6 times a year	Never 0%
Negative habits					
1. Feel rushed while eating; have a sense of time urgency.	☐	☐	☐	☐	☐
2. Hide or sneak foods.	☐	☐	☐	☐	☐
3. Prefer eating alone.	☐	☐	☐	☐	☐
4. Gulp your food; chew only a few times before swallowing.	☐	☐	☐	☐	☐
5. Stuff yourself.	☐	☐	☐	☐	☐
6. Eat and run.	☐	☐	☐	☐	☐
7. Eat heavy snacks or meals after 7 P.M.	☐	☐	☐	☐	☐
8. Eat within an hour before retiring.	☐	☐	☐	☐	☐
9. Go on eating binges.	☐	☐	☐	☐	☐
10. Engage in other activities while eating.	☐	☐	☐	☐	☐
11. Continuously fill mouth without putting down utensils.	☐	☐	☐	☐	☐
12. Gulp fluids while eating.	☐	☐	☐	☐	☐
13. Eat sparingly in morning and heavily in evening.	☐	☐	☐	☐	☐
Positive habits					
1. Read and appreciate labels.	☐	☐	☐	☐	☐
2. Chew thoroughly.	☐	☐	☐	☐	☐
3. Avoid "contrived" foods (e.g., instant breakfasts, cereals).	☐	☐	☐	☐	☐

	Very frequently 50–90%	Daily or every other day	Often 20–50% 1–3 times a week	Occasionally 10–20% 2–3 times a month	Seldom 1–10% 6 times a year	Never 0%
4. Eat smaller, more frequent meals.	☐		☐	☐	☐	☐
5. Avoid hidden sugars in processed foods.	☐		☐	☐	☐	☐
6. Educate self about nutrition.	☐		☐	☐	☐	☐
7. Fast occasionally.	☐		☐	☐	☐	☐
8. Eat *fresh* vegetables and fruits.	☐		☐	☐	☐	☐
9. Attempt to balance diet, and supplement where necessary.	☐		☐	☐	☐	☐

FIGURE 8. Rating chart for eating habits.

ical discomfort, and poor sleep. Sleep may be interrupted by a need to urinate or by discomfort. Attempting to engage in other activities while eating, eating and running, and continuous mouth-filling can indicate a personality style characterized by a sense of time urgency. These behaviors distract one from possible relaxing processes during eating, as well as generate tension.

Gulping food precludes complete chewing. Chewing not only is important for grinding the food into small particles, but also is a major method for releasing tension. Chewing and biting are aggressive actions, and minimizing these actions removes this outlet for dissipating aggressive feelings. Poor dietary habits may preclude relaxation and easy digestion and may actually increase tension states.

On the other hand, there are a series of behaviors and habits that maximize relaxation and aid digestion. Eating slowly, chewing fully, enjoying aromas and tastes, eating fresh and minimally processed foods, and enjoying one's surroundings during eating all promote a relaxed atmosphere. Digestion is improved by full and lengthy chewing. Waiting until after the meal to drink also aids digestion. Making ourselves aware of what and how we eat by reading labels, educating ourselves on nutrition, and participating actively in the preparation of foods also promotes active participation in our nutritional lives.

A sense of full responsibility in dietary habits, a relaxed atmosphere while eating, and a process-oriented approach to eating will facilitate relaxation. A process-oriented approach involves focusing on the process of eating: enjoyment of aromas, tastes, textures, and temperatures. Enjoyment and relaxation are closely tied to the manner in which we approach eating.

What to Eat

In doing a nutritional analysis, determining what to eat is a more difficult question to answer. There are some clear guidelines for what NOT to eat, and there are some broad guidelines for what to eat. The determination of how much to eat is an individual matter, but observation of one's body weight and sensations will give clues as to whether or not your selections fit for you.

To clarify this last point, let's say that you eat a large spaghetti dinner and feel bloated afterward. Your first impulse might be to get some Alka Seltzer. If you take the seltzer and forget about your discomfort, then you have created a state of distress and have not learned from it. Instead, you might evaluate your body's reaction. Reflect for a moment. Did you have the same reaction when you last had spaghetti? Did you stuff yourself that time too? The discomfort could be from having eaten too much, from eating something to which you are allergic, or from having gulped your food. Eating less and stopping when you begin to feel full will test whether the amount eaten is the cause. Next, try eating less and chewing more thoroughly. Finally, observe similar reactions to other dishes and determine what patterns exist. For example, do you get bloated when you eat other dishes in which tomatoes are an ingredient? You may have an allergy.

In addition to an individual analysis, there are some specific guidelines to indicate what foods are nutritionally unsound. Evaluate how often you eat them, using the chart (Fig. 9).

Although, according to the principle of moderation, we can probably tolerate these items in small amounts, most of them have been shown to be liabilities. Coffee, tea, and cola drinks contain caffeine, a central nervous system (CNS) stimulant. Alcoholic beverages contain ethyl alcohol, which is a CNS depressant. Stimulants and depressants cause undue strain on our biochemistry, especially when overdone. One or two drinks per day

	Very frequently 50–90% Daily or every other day	Often 20–50% 1–3 times a week	Occasionally 10–20% 2–3 times a month	Seldom 1–10% 6 times a year	Never 0%
1. Pastries, candy, soft drinks, ice cream, etc.	☐	☐	☐	☐	☐
2. Processed meats (e.g., bologna, sausage, bacon)	☐	☐	☐	☐	☐
3. Canned or processed foods	☐	☐	☐	☐	☐
4. Commercial seasonings (catsup, imitation syrups)	☐	☐	☐	☐	☐
5. Sugar in tea, coffee, cereal	☐	☐	☐	☐	☐
6. Salty foods (chips, crackers)	☐	☐	☐	☐	☐
7. Fried foods	☐	☐	☐	☐	☐
8. Alcohol	☐	☐	☐	☐	☐
9. Coffee, tea, cola drinks (caffeine in drink)	☐	☐	☐	☐	☐
10. Instant breakfasts	☐	☐	☐	☐	☐
11. Cold cereals, quick desserts (Jell-O®, puddings)	☐	☐	☐	☐	☐
12. Beef products	☐	☐	☐	☐	☐

FIGURE 9. Rating chart for consumption of nutritionally unsound foods.

might be tolerated, but much more can be harmful. Swings in energy level and intestinal or stomach distress will signal whether or not you can tolerate these.

Sugar offers empty calories and drains stored nutrients. Most cold cereals contain anywhere from 15 to as much as 65% sugar. To make sugar the mainstay of our morning diets is to commit nutritional suicide. Ice cream, puddings, cakes, processed foods, and commercially prepared seasonings usually have large quantities of sugar (read the labels!). Ask yourself whether you want your teeth to be bathed in sugar daily. The dentist's bill will give you a clue to the answer. Ingestion of large amounts of sugar may also produce dramatic swings in energy and produce fatigue.

Processed meats usually have large amounts of salt and preservatives. The most common preservatives are compounds of nitrates and nitrites. During digestion, nitrites are converted into nitrosamines, which are known to cause cancer. Also, large quantities of salt can contribute to water retention and to elevation of blood pressure. Some people develop high blood pressure in direct proportion to their salt intake. Why strain your heart and vascular system unnecessarily? Once we eliminate the salt habit, the craving disappears, and our sensitivity to taste increases.

Eating large quantities of beef products, either processed or fresh, has recently been identified as potentially harmful. In addition to the large amounts of fat and salt in beef products, they are saturated with growth hormones (the same as in birth control pills) and antibiotics. The meat of most cattle raised in the United States contains these chemicals. Some researchers believe that long-term ingestion of antibiotics will lessen the usefulness of these antibiotics when they are needed to treat diseases. We are probably being desensitized to the drugs needed to fight disease. The recent rise in newer and more virulent forms of venereal diseases, which no longer respond to common antibiotics, may be partially attributable to unnecessary exposure of the population to antibiotics.

If the foods discussed above are nutritionally unsound, then what *beneficial* nutriments are left? Evaluate the list (Fig. 10) to get a feeling for what offers sound nutritional value.

	Very frequently 50–90%	Daily or every other day	Often 20–50%	1–3 times a week	Occasionally 10–20%	2–3 times a month	Seldom 1–10%	6 times a year	Never 0%
1. Fresh fruits		☐		☐		☐		☐	☐
2. Fresh or lightly cooked vegetables		☐		☐		☐		☐	☐
3. Eight glasses of water daily		☐		☐		☐		☐	☐
4. Milk, eggs, cheese, flesh foods (chicken, fish)		☐		☐		☐		☐	☐
5. Whole grains (e.g., rice, millet), whole grain bread		☐		☐		☐		☐	☐
6. Wheat germ, yeast, protein supplement (e.g., soy-based)		☐		☐		☐		☐	☐
7. Herbs (fresh or dried)		☐		☐		☐		☐	☐
8. Vitamin supplements		☐		☐		☐		☐	☐
9. Balanced meals from different classes of foods		☐		☐		☐		☐	☐
10. Snack of nuts (unsalted), dried fruits, beans (soy)		☐		☐		☐		☐	☐
11. Small quantities of different types of foods		☐		☐		☐		☐	☐

FIGURE 10. Rating chart for consumption of beneficial nutriments.

In determining what to eat, *moderation* and *variety* are key principles. Each day, a "balanced" diet would include fresh fruits, raw or minimally cooked vegetables, milk or cheese products, flesh products (e.g., chicken or fish), whole grains, vitamin supplements, and possibly some protein supplements. Foods that contain proteins (vegetable or animal), carbohydrates (fruits, grains), fats (cheese, meats), minerals (vegetables), and vitamins (all categories) must be sampled for optimal nutrition. Shortages in any category can contribute to low energy, biological break-down, low resistance to disease, and even psychological and per-ceptual problems (e.g., you need vitamin A for adequate night vision).

The question of vitamin supplements is controversial. Research has demonstrated that too much vitamin A and D can be toxic, while not enough can cause disease. Milk products have high levels of these vitamins, and consuming these products should suffice. If you have poor skin, poor night vision, high sus-ceptibility to infections, or dry, brittle hair, then you may have a vitamin A deficiency. Bleeding gums may signal a vitamin C deficiency. Under conditions of high stress, the body uses huge amounts of vitamin C, pantothenic acid, and B-complex vita-mins. Insufficiency of folic acid and B vitamins can contribute to irritability and disruption of the CNS. If your diet includes sugar and alcohol consumption, you probably have a vitamin B_1 defi-ciency. Lack of it can contribute to depression, fatigue, moodi-ness, and loss of memory and concentration.

Many people do not know that exposure to various chemi-cals contributes to vitamin deficiency. Oral contraceptives reduce blood levels of thiamine, riboflavin, B_6, B_{12}, folic acid, and vita-min C. People who smoke, take aspirin, or eat foods containing nitrates have lowered blood levels of vitamin C. Exposure to environmental chemicals [e.g., DDT, polyvinylchloride (PVC)] has been shown to reduce the blood levels of vitamin A and nia-cin. Vitamin supplementation is essential for most urban dwellers.

In summary, sound nutrition is necessary for successful cop-ing and maintenance of energy levels. Ultimately, survival and quality of life are at stake. For sound nutritional living:

1. *Listen* to and *learn* from your body's signals.
2. Attend to *how* you eat. Eat slowly, chew fully, and enjoy the process of eating. Relax while you eat.
3. Stop eating when you begin to feel full, yet are still comfortable.
4. Avoid large meals in the evening, and avoid late eve-ning snacks.
5. Eat in *moderation*.

6. Sample a *variety* of *fresh* foods. A daily diet should include items from all categories.
7. Take *vitamin supplements* according to your life-style.
8. *Limit daily caloric intake* to maintain a trim body. Few adults over the age of 40 need more than 1800 calories a day. From 30 to 40, few need more than 1800 to 2500, the amount depending upon activity level. An active 20- to 30-year-old might need 2000 to 3000. You do not really need a scale. Look in the mirror.
9. *Vary* the amount you eat according to conditions. Under stressful conditions, including illness, eat *less* but *selectively*. Increase vitamin supplements of vitamin C, pantothenic acid, folic acid, and B-complex vitamins. Listen to your body and be flexible; nutritional demands are not static.
10. Eat to *live* and to *laugh*. Enjoyment and energy will follow.

The first real step toward stress control, then, is to build your energy reserves as a bulwark against the forces of stress. The three fundamental steps in erecting such an energy barrier are simple and direct: (1) Get adequate sleep and rest; (2) develop an exercise program that will keep you in optimal physical condition; and (3) learn to eat a well-balanced, moderate, and healthful diet. Taken together, these direct actions will provide a solid foundation from which you can continue to confront the forces of stress in your life. If you follow these three simple steps, your resistance to stress will grow and your ability to cope in other, even more effective ways will be increased. Sleep right, exercise properly, and eat well—and you will be ready to undertake the next step in developing mastery over stress in your life. This step, as you will shortly see, examines the pace of your life and the nature of your personal relationships.

CHAPTER 6

STRESS REDUCTION AT WORK

PACING YOURSELF

Although rest, exercise, and proper diet can increase resistance and enhance the body's tolerance for stress, such coping tactics cannot eliminate or even dramatically reduce many of the stress-producing situations that each of us encounters every day. Take Art, for example. The sales manager for a large carpet firm, Art has found his work increasingly stressful. Recently, he has begun a jogging program and feels great. He is sleeping better, eating a better-balanced diet, and smoking and drinking less. At work, however, Art still feels stressed much of the time. He has even begun to keep a stress journal in an effort to uncover the roots of his stress problems, but so far he has not made much progress toward that goal. All that seems clear so far is that whenever he comes to work and settles into his usual routine, he begins to feel the specific symptoms of stress.

A more careful look at Art's routine reveals, however, that there is a distinct pattern behind his stress. Art is ambitious and highly competitive, and he has extremely high expectations for himself. As a result of these attitudes, Art sets unrealistic goals, trying to do far too much in too little time. When he attempts to perform the tasks he has set himself, he discovers that there is not enough time to complete them. Instead of stopping at this point to reevaluate his priorities and amend his schedule, Art now drives himself harder to get everything done. Under such unrealistic pressure, his efficiency drops, the quality of his work suffers, and he soon begins to have negative feelings about both his job and himself. By this time, his usual stress symptoms have reappeared as well, and Art is harried and miserable—caught in a vicious and self-defeating cycle.

Art's experience is not unusual. Like him, many of us are victims of poor *pacing* at work. Because of unrealistic expectations or impractical arrangement of tasks, we actually create stressful situations for ourselves. By becoming aware of the times that we ask too much of ourselves, or the occasions when we arrange tasks in a more difficult way, we can begin to explore other ways of pacing our work—effective, practical changes in efficiency and job satisfaction—and actually eliminate job-related stress.

To understand the effects of poor pacing in the workplace, we need to examine "Parkinson's Law": "Work expands to fill the time available." That is to say, if you have 8 hours in which to do ten assignments, then you will finish those ten assignments in 8 hours. Yet if your boss gives you the same ten assignments the next day, and adds two more so that you have twelve, then somehow you manage to finish all twelve in that 8 hours. Conversely, if you had only eight assignments to do, then you would probably somehow *expand* the time needed to finish the eight tasks in the 8 hours. The law says that *efficiency* is defined by the situational demands of *time* and the *number of tasks* to be finished within that particular time span.

The law also says that we can be more efficient, or less efficient, depending upon the demands made on us. Thus, we can take a long time to finish some assignment, or a brief time. For example, if I tell our secretary that I want a letter written, in final form, and handed back to me in 15 minutes, then I get the letter returned in 15 minutes (assuming there are not too many interruptions). On the other hand, if I tell her that I do not need that letter until several hours later, then somehow she takes that long to get it finished. The demand will help the secretary define her priorities and her pacing.

With 3 hours to complete the letter, she may place the paper in the typewriter, but spend more time on telephone calls or chatting with other workers. If she has only 15 minutes in which to finish the letter, then she will be brief with intruding tasks.

She will be brisk and efficient with phone calls, she will either engage very briefly in or ignore other staff activities, and she will focus on typing the letter. Thus, time constraints help to define the focus of our priorities and activities.

Now you can see how Parkinson's Law operates. This law does not operate in a vacuum, but is in fact influenced by the quality of work demanded, by a person's state of mind and body (e.g., is the person well rested or tired? angry or content? assertive or passive?), by environmental input (e.g., is the office noisy? how often is the worker interrupted? are supplies immediately available?), and by how the person paces himself. We who do the work can have direct control over our efficiency—and effective pacing is one important variable to explore and be aware of.

Pacing refers to the *flow* of work through the course of time. Here, pacing refers to the scheduling of units of work (e.g., an appointment, a letter to be written, phone calls to be made, hems to be stitched) through the course of some time span allotted for the work and the resultant flow from event to event. Each day we have "X" number of tasks to complete (either our boss directly tells us *what* is to be done or we decide ourselves *what* tasks have to be done that day), and we decide the *order* in which the work is to be done, how *fast* we will do each task, how *well* each one is completed, and *when* each one singly and all together are to be completed. The secretary might say to herself, for example, "This pile of letters is to be completed by the morning break time, and this other pile of reports can wait until the afternoon." Somehow, the piles of work get done during those times.

Many variables interact to determine the pace and effectiveness of our work. The most important of these variables include: (1) Time demands—How much time is allotted for the completion of work tasks? (2) Sequencing and priority setting—How much work, and what type of work must you do? (3) Personality style—Do you work slow or fast? Enjoy many tasks at once or prefer to stick with one? Prefer details or seek a broad perspective? (4) Quality demands—What levels of quality do your various work tasks require? (5) Tension level—How tense are you? (6) Level of resistance—How healthy and well rested are you? (7) Emotional state—Are you positive or negative, optimistic or

pessimistic, relaxed or perfectionistic? (8) Environmental problems—What about lighting, ventilation, or noise at work? Is your
work area comfortable and convenient? (9) Rhythm and timing
of others—How do your co-workers affect your pace and style of
working?

Obviously, the issue of pacing yourself effectively at work
is complex. But you can begin here as you did earlier in the stress
self-analysis: Your body, your behavior, and your feelings are all
sources of valuable information about how well you are pacing
yourself at work. By observing your work situation, and how you
behave in it, you can begin the process of analysis and understanding that will lead to constructive changes in the ways you
function at work. To help you with this analysis of your work
pace and style, let us explore each of the nine variables described
above.

1. TIME DEMANDS

Let's begin with time demands. If you want to be maximally
efficient and make use of Parkinson's Law, then look at the time
demands of each work unit and at the time constraints in relation
to each type of work to be done. An essential part of this process
also has to do with setting priorities. To give yourself a frame of
reference of your own style of working with and within time
demands, ask yourself the following questions:

Does your boss typically expect a job done within a certain
time?

How much time is permitted to finish the job? A few minutes? Several hours? Or longer?

How do you respond emotionally to these time demands?
Do you take them as a challenge? Or get flustered? Or become
angry? Or can you relax under pressure?

What happens to the quality of your work when you feel
under time pressure?

If your boss is generous or vague about his time demands,
do you create your own deadlines?

Now that you have answered these questions, can you let yourself see any *patterns* in the way you handle or set up time schedules? Are there any patterns that characterize your particular office setting (e.g., no one takes the initiative, and everyone—or particular people—waits for the boss to set the schedules)? Simply seeing such a pattern and, hence, the possible stressful *consequences* of the patterns may provide sufficient motivation to make a change for the better. If you wait for a time constraint to be demanded by your superiors, then a consequence of your lack of initiative in this area is to give up an element of *control* over the scheduling of time units. In contrast, if you actively set your own time limits, you exert control and hence avoid some external pressures. One very common stressor at work is the experiencing of time demands as pressure. People who can arrange to set their own time limits to match their own *rhythms* for that particular day are in a better position to flow from task to task and to relax while working.

2. SEQUENCING AND PRIORITY SETTING

The number and type of work units will also influence one's efficiency and flow. Sequencing and priority setting for work units are crucial to the pacing of your work day. It is very common for a person to cram too many units of work into a period of time, only to find that he resents what he has to do, and also finds that there is a loss of energy and interest. Part of what may be happening is that unimportant and low-priority tasks get sandwiched in with the more important tasks, and the person feels rushed, flustered, and irritable.

Let's say you find yourself in such a situation. So now you ask, what can I do about it?

The first thing to do when you feel rushed and flustered is to look at the sequence and flow of events and go through a *review* of your priorities. Review your priorities at least twice a day, and you can do this by asking a series of basic questions. You may find it helpful to close your eyes and visualize the answers as you ask yourself these questions:

What *tasks* are to be done today?

What *must* be done today, and what can wait? and until when?

In addition, what do I *want* done today?

And then, what do I want done by *when*?

After asking these questions, you know *what* you are to do, and you have separated what you *want* done from what you *must* do (or think you have to). This is a very important issue: separating what is voluntary from what is involuntary. If every task is viewed as a "have-to," the person who has to do the work will surely resent doing it. It should be possible for most of us to view some tasks as voluntary.

Our next task is to select the *order* or *sequence* in which the tasks are to be done. I have discovered that my day is more pleasant if I start by doing a task that I must do, or do not really care to do, and then follow it with a task that I enjoy and want to do. This way, I have something to look forward to as I march through the not-so-pleasant assignments. Another strategy that I have found useful is to march through a series of brief but tedious tasks first, and then go on to the larger, more important ones. That way, I don't have the tedious ones to look forward to upon finishing the large task, which would happen were I to reverse the sequence. Whatever your style, select some sequence for doing the assignments that ends with positive feelings.

With this picture in mind of what task follows what task, we also need to program in our *breaks*, that is, our rest periods, fruit juice breaks, lunch hours, and little pauses. You would be surprised how many people forget to include time to pause or rest during the course of a normal work day. And how many people do you know who work even while they eat? It is no wonder so many of us feel frazzled or worn out by midday and get indigestion too!

Now that you have the frame of reference for *reviewing* what there is to do, and setting up the *order* of doing the tasks, and spacing in the *rest* periods, it might be helpful to look at a sample outline of a schedule for a typical work day:

8:45   Enter work. Greet secretary and available staff.
       Pick up mail and telephone messages.

8:50   *Review what* I am to do. Review how I feel about the tasks.
       Phone calls (sometimes enjoy). Whom to call first? Who can
          wait?
       Scheduled appointments (enjoy). "Have to" and "want to."
       Consultations (enjoy sometimes). "Have to" and "want to."
       Supervision (enjoy). "Want to."
       Meetings (do not enjoy). "Should" attend, sometimes can avoid.
       Report-writing (do not enjoy). "Have to"; decide on deadlines
          and delay where possible.
       Visualize the sequence in my mind.

9:00   Meeting (neutral to positive feeling).

9:50   Return phone calls (neutral).

10:00 Appointment (enjoyed).

10:55 *Pause.* Relax on couch (enjoyed).

11:00 Review materials for consultation (mild negative feeling).

11:30 Phone calls (negative feeling).

11:40 *Pause.* Call a friend to chat and relax (enjoyed).

11:50 Report-writing (negative feeling).

12:00 *Review* afternoon schedule (positive).

12:05 Lunch (enjoyed).

12:30 Meeting (positive and negative; high performance demands—
          stressful).

1:30   Reports, miscellaneous (negative task).

2:00   Consultation (enjoyed, even though high demands).

3:00   Appointment (enjoyed, but tired).

3:55   *Pause,* meditate, and/or snack (enjoyed).

4:00   Appointment (enjoyed).

4:50   *Pause*. Leave for other office. Relax in car before driving away.

5:30–8:00   Other appointments.

As you can see, upon entering the office, I review what is to be done for the morning and day, and then just before lunch I review the work for the afternoon. At the beginning of the day I also assess which tasks do NOT need to be done immediately, and shelve them either for specific times later in the week or for times when I have a cancellation or other time that is freed.

Since jobs also require scheduling unplanned tasks throughout each day, we must plan for the unplanned. Some people experience dealing with the unplanned as stressful, and may react by saying, "How can I fit this in? I need 36 hours in a day to do this job!" If this is the case, then your survival and sense of well-being are being threatened, and you need to analyze the issues related to your distress. You may be doing the job of two people, and you need to request (maybe demand) more help. Or maybe you are not as efficient as you could be and are overwhelmed because of your inefficiency. Think about it and decide what you want to do.

3. PERSONALITY STYLE

One variable that strongly affects the flow of our work is our personal styles of *how* we do the work and how we approach work. Some people are fast workers, some are slow, and some are methodical. Some people demand perfection in even the minutest details, whereas others are not concerned about the specifics of a situation. There are people who thrive on doing several tasks at once, whereas others grow frantic when they must do several tasks simultaneously. Then there are the people who focus only on the details of a situation, while others can take a broader perspective. Some people are driven when they work, and others are more easygoing about working. We all have some qualities that characterize our *attitudes* about how we approach work. And it is these attitudes that govern how efficient we are and how we *feel* about what we do. It is also important to recognize that these styles not only govern our flow of work but also have a direct influence on those who work closely with us. Some examples might give you a better feel for this issue.

Can you imagine, for a moment, a director of some service agency who is perfectionistic and who likes to sift through all the details of a situation? She cannot seem to find enough time to complete all the organizational tasks in order to plan ahead for meetings. The subordinates look to the leader for direction, but instead of giving them the broad perspective of what they are to do (e.g., plan policies), the director gives them details of a situation. The subordinates feel frustrated and are angry at the director for not doing her job and for not giving them the guidance they want. The subordinates want to be given some direction in order to plan ahead, but instead find themselves constantly making last-minute decisions (which is stressful) because of the lack of a broader policy. After some months, the staff finds that they cannot "communicate," and the system is full of tension. The subordinates may take on some of the work of the director just to get things done, but they resent the extra work. In this situation, the director's personality style is incompatible with her being an effective director and has a direct influence on the overall degree of tension among workers. Here, everyone is under stress!

Or can you imagine a director of another agency who has a passive style—always waiting for others to make the decisions or letting the situation deteriorate until it demands decision-making at the last minute. Typically, the passivity of a leader will lead to low morale, slow production, the frequent occurrence of crises, confusion, and disorganization. The personality characteristics of the leader (director, supervisor) have a ripple effect on the workers in his or her charge. So, if there is low morale, confusion, disorganization, poor and slow production, and so on at your work, begin your analysis with the supervisory personnel and their styles for work.

Then there is always the person who is overly serious about his or her work. This type of person behaves as though work performance were a life-and-death situation. People who take their work too seriously frequently get depressed and are a drag to be around. If one fails to discover and enjoy the humor of life, then one tends to generate an air of tension in one's work space. And this type of tension contributes to lowered efficiency and to low morale.

Generally, I have found that in systems where workers share the humor of their work experiences, there is also a relaxed mood and high morale. Stop and think for a moment. What do you feel like when you are around someone who is typically serious about his work? These people tend to be overly self-critical (and probably critical of others) and do not smile much. It is almost as though this type of person is surrounded by a gray cloud. And this is the type of mood created—a gloomy one.

At this point, you may find it useful to stop and reflect about yourself. Just what are your *attitudes* toward work and what *style* do those attitudes generate? How does this style influence your mood, accuracy, and efficiency? And how does it affect the workers around you?

In terms of *attitudes* and beliefs, for example, do you look at life and work as a grave and serious matter?

Or do you believe that your work must be perfect and exact in order for you to feel worthwhile?

Or do you care little about what you do and how it reflects on you?

Or do you believe that the first person to finish a task is the best worker? And hence, do you rush about finishing your work as fast as you can to prove that you are superior by doing so?

Or do you believe that being neat and meticulous is a virtue and should be the standard at all times?

Now that you have looked at some of your attitudes about how work should be done, also take a look at your *style* that comes from these attitudes:

Are you a fast or a slow worker?

Are you methodical or haphazard in your approach?

Do you focus mostly on the details, or do you see the larger perspective when you approach a task?

Are you the type who is single-minded and can do only one

task at a time, or can you easily flow with many tasks simultaneously?

Are you a leader or a follower? Do you initiate your pace?

Do you like to create projects, or to carry your projects, or to do both?

Do you tend to be passive, or are you assertive?

Answers to these and other questions (you can make your own additions to the list) will give you clues to whether or not your personal style is lowering your efficiency, morale, and organization, and whether or not you are suited for the particular job that you are now doing.

Now that you have some idea about your personal style of approaching your work and about how this style affects both your efficiency and morale, you may be asking: "So what do I do now?"

1. First, given this awareness, are you really willing to change your personal approach to work just to improve your efficiency and your feeling about the work?

2. If your answer is "No," accept the inefficiency and enjoy your suffering. No one can take that away from you.

3. If your answer is "Yes," then:

a. Get a consultation on how to change, from either an efficiency expert or a trained psychotherapist. Behavior therapists are your best bet here.

b. But if you are a do-it-yourselfer, then list *alternative* behavior styles and *practice* them. It is only through practice that you can effect any real changes in efficiency and experience the feeling that goes with the new style.

c. Then, if you are not sure about what to do for an alternative work style, *observe* your peers. Find someone who is relaxed, happy, and efficient, and observe what that person does and how he or she does it. After you observe, ask the person what goes on inside his or her head in the course of working.

d. Finally, if none of the steps above has worked for you, call a group of your co-workers together and begin a group discussion of the issues to *discover* and *share* your observations and ideas. In the course of many consultations, I have found that

workers are constantly amazed at how others have similar difficulties and concerns about how they approach work.

Changing one's personal styles and attitudes is one of the
most difficult areas to tackle, for it is threatening to most people
to question their own beliefs, especially in public. Just remember, you can change if you *want* to, but only when you think the
possible benefits are worth the risk of self-confrontation. It will
take a lot of courage and practice to make the shift.

4. QUALITY DEMANDS

This is perhaps one of the simplest variables affecting your
efficiency and flow. A common theme that hangs people up is
the mistaken *assumption that all work requires equal quality*. It is surprising how many people waste time and energy attempting to
be neat, methodical, and perfect in situations that do not call for
high quality. The amount of time needed to complete a simple
task can be increased by demanding a quality of work beyond
what the situation demands. For example, worrying about typo-
graphical errors in a rough draft will tend to increase errors and
waste time and energy.

There are several points to keep in mind here:

1. Quality demands *vary* according to the *nature* of the task
and according to the context (e.g., are the notes to be private or
public?).

2. For *each* situation, you should decide what quality standards are *necessary* and which are *desired*. *Do not assume* that all
situations demand equal quality. If you cannot decide, then
request a clarification of the standards from your superiors.

3. Evaluate your own *personal* standards. Do these match
what is expected of you? You may be projecting your own standards onto the situation and may be overlooking what is really
needed and warranted in that situation.

Remember these points and discover how your standards of
quality are either interfering with or facilitating your flow and
efficiency.

5. TENSION LEVEL

One's level of muscular tension is a most essential issue that powerfully affects one's flow, speed, efficiency, and enjoyment of work. Many events happen when our bodies are tense. There follows a partial list of possible events that each of us has experienced at some time or another and that are signals of tension:

1. The mind wanders and the ability to focus on a task decreases.
2. Errors increase in frequency.
3. Memory is worse.
4. Disorganization of thinking, planning, and working increases.
5. Tiredness is experienced more frequently.
6. Accidents happen.
7. Speech is less fluent.
8. The body aches (e.g., indigestion, headaches, lower backache).
9. Irritability increases.
10. Enjoyment of work decreases.
11. Humor decreases.
12. The desire to smoke increases.
13. The desire to drink alcoholic beverages increases.
14. The desire to eat increases for some and decreases for others.
15. The desire to escape and leave work increases, etc., etc.

When we experience these events, we continue a vicious cycle that leads to increased tension and to a compounding of the tension level. Review this list several times and remember: Each of these events is a SIGNAL to you that you are tense. Once you recognize the signals, and you decide that you want to step out of the cycle, then you had better review the sources of the tensions and relax (see Chapter 4 for relaxation exercises). It is surprising how few people are actually *aware* of the tensions at the time they occur. If we learn to pay attention to these signals, then we are in a good position to change, and hence improve, our flow, efficiency, and enjoyment of work.

Now that you are more attuned to the signals of tension, you might want to consider just what causes tension in the body. Unfortunately, an entire book could be written about the myriad of life experiences that create tensions for human beings. The following list must be considered as only a sample of the experiences, and will at least get you started on the track of the causes of your tension states:

1. Noisy environment
2. Inadequate lighting
3. Poor ventilation
4. People working too close to each other
5. Stagnant positions (e.g., sitting, standing in one place too long)
6. Doing what you *have* to do more than what you *want* to do
7. Time pressures
8. Pressures (internal or external) for exceptional performance
9. Constant pressure to make important and high-risk decisions
10. Lengthy time between vacations
11. Frequent demands for overtime (and hence less leisure time)
12. Working with clients who have many personal problems
13. Working with people who are always serious
14. Doing work that involves mostly fine motor coordination
15. Doing tasks that require a lot of close visual work
16. Working with tense people or people who are always in a rush
17. Inadequate sleep
18. Inadequate diet
19. Cigarette smoking
20. Too much drinking of alcoholic beverages
21. Lack of exercise to release tensions
22. Marital conflict

23. Psychological conflicts (e.g., unresolved historical conflict—your boss reminds you of your father, whom you hate)
24. Economic insecurity
25. Continuing low self-esteem (e.g., you persistently remind yourself of your faults and errors)
26. Major life changes (e.g., job change, move to new geographic location, death or severe illness of someone close, change in marital status, other losses)
27. Unexpressed feelings (How many times have you had a headache when you were angry with someone?)
28. Lack of recognition for work performance (Too often after leaving school, people go to work only to find no one consistently praising them any longer, and they find themselves getting depressed at work. This points to one of life's major and most difficult tasks—learning to praise oneself.)

Some of these events and experiences are discussed in depth elsewhere in this book. But simply becoming *aware* of the causes of your tensions is often enough to aid you in deciding on alternatives that will eliminate or deal with the causes.

Reread the list. Then add other possible causes of your tensions to the list. Finally, creatively figure out your own solutions to the issues. When you do this successfully, praise yourself and enjoy the ensuing relaxation. If you are unsuccessful, then get yourself a consultation. Or if you are not terribly interested in understanding and analyzing the causes of your tensions at work, then you might simply read Chapter 4 on how to relax. Finally, if you do not want to deal with this issue at all, then just be tense!

6. LEVEL OF RESISTANCE

The states of being healthy and well rested are most important for most people in order to maintain a sense of well-being. When we are ill or not rested, we also tend to be in a state of tension. And we already know how tension interferes with the flow of our working. It is true that there are some people who can function on little sleep or when they are ill, but most people seem to require a good night's rest and that they be well in order to feel well balanced. The condition of your health and the degree to which you are rested can affect not only your tension level but also your ability to flow from situation to situation. They also affect your sense of equanimity and vulnerability, your outlook on events, and your efficiency.

This issue is mentioned here simply to point to these as variables to be aware of that influence our ability to flow and pace our work. (See Chapter 5 for an in-depth review of the issues of nutrition and rest, and for recommendations for how to deal with sleep and health problems.)

7. EMOTIONAL STATE

Whether we set our own time schedules or have them imposed on us, we all must set our own pace. And how we handle the flow *emotionally* will influence our performance. When we become angry, sad, distracted, discouraged, disappointed, or tense, we tend to make more errors and be less efficient. On the other hand, when we are relaxed and in a positive state of mind, we tend to flow more fluidly from task to task and to be more efficient. The issues that influence our emotional state of being are infinite. They can range from *biological* (Are our enzymes in balance? Is our blood sugar level up or down?), to *social* (Are we getting along with our spouses, friends, relatives, and boss?), to *personal* (Are we engaging in the activities that give us pleasure, or are we being too inactive?), to *environmental* (Is the office too hot, noisy or stuffy? Have we been sitting too long in a static position?), to *psychological* (Do we worry about job performance? Can we feel okay about taking orders? Do we feel in conflict about what we do at work, home, or play?).

What is important here is to *acknowledge* that our emotional state of being is a factor that influences how we flow with work. Only after we recognize and accept this can we be in a position to deal with our emotional life. Unfortunately, most people either do not recognize the importance of their feelings or do not want to deal with the issue. It is remarkable how many people walk around in fear—of others, life, and even of themselves!

An example might help to give you a better feeling of the complexity and relevance of this factor.

A secretary once consulted me about her problem with report-writing. When she was under pressure to finish assignments within designated short time periods, she would become tense, and she would make more typing errors. And once she became tense, a vicious cycle ensued. She became aware of her tension and would get angry at herself for being tense and for making more errors. And the more critical and demanding she became of herself, the more errors she made. In sum, she was in a negative frame of mind that fed on itself.

Analysis of the situation revealed a psychological problem and a mind–body problem. Psychologically, this woman resented some authority giving her orders and placing demands on her. She felt like a little girl when this happened. Physically, she did not have adequate separation or differentiation of body parts. That is to say, when she was typing with her fingers and hands, she would tense the muscles in her neck and shoulders, which in turn interfered with her fingers typing.

To remedy this problem, we dealt with the last part first. I taught her deep muscle relaxation so that she could relax one part of her body at a time and relearn to type with her hands, fingers, and arms, but without tensing the shoulders and neck muscles. (These deep muscle relaxation techniques are discussed in Chapter 4.) Learning to separate and differentiate these muscle groups alone improved her typing performance.

To deal with the psychological issues, I recommended that she go into psychotherapy to resolve the long-standing authority problems. I also suggested that she ask herself the following questions:

"Are time demands part of the job description?" If so, and you resent such demands, remember, nobody forced you to take this job.

"Is there any way to view the situation differently?" If you can view the situation in a more positive way, then you can defuse and destress the situation. For example, it is helpful for some people to view a time demand as a *challenge* rather than a burden and as an opportunity to test their ability to flow with events. On the other hand, for others a challenge may produce anxiety and hence be a burden.

Tension, anxiety, or conflict, or a combination, derives from how we *label* and *view* a situation. We can just as easily assign a positive meaning to a task as a negative one, but only if we are free of our personal psychological conflicts.

There was an interpersonal issue that also contributed to the secretary's tension state. Her boss was very abrupt when he made requests, and his abrupt manner stimulated her to feel angry and unappreciated. I suggested that she might express her feelings to him in as nonthreatening a way as possible. Specifically, she said to him: "Dr. J., I find myself getting tense when you ask me to do certain things. When you appear to be in a hurry and seem brusque, I do not know how to take it. I get tense when I think you do not appreciate my work. I would really appreciate it if you would explain what you are feeling so that I don't feel bad when you ask me for a job in a rush." Her boss was very apologetic and agreed to be calmer or at least explain the demand so she wouldn't personalize his seeming indifference.

If you are not interested in, or unwilling to seek, a consultation, as the secretary did, to figure out why you get into emotional states at work, then begin by thinking about the factors that contribute to your emotional state of being: the psychological, social, environmental, biological, and personal factors. Then, read the chapters in this book that deal with these factors in more depth. In each chapter, you will find some suggestions for solutions and alternatives to your dilemmas.

8. ENVIRONMENTAL PROBLEMS

Although it is easy to blame the environment for our problems, there are environmental conditions that will definitely influence our ability to flow from task to task and from situation to situation. The conditions most frequently associated with difficulties in flowing have to do with office layout, availability of materials, lighting facilities, ventilation, noise level, and structures that help limit interruptions.

The way you have your work area set up can be crucial to your either being able to continue the stream of your work or being halted or interrupted. If the desks or work benches are too close together or staggered in such a way as to limit or block the flow of traffic, then the act of walking from one area to another could take more time than necessary and could cause traffic congestion. If the work areas are too close together, then the noise factor increases and interruptions increase. Sometimes simply partitioning areas can improve the flow of traffic and significantly lower the frequency of intrusions.

Take a look at your work space and consider the following:

Do you find areas of traffic congestion that block your path to other areas?

Do you find that the voices of others intrude into your work and your conversations?

Do you ever find that the movement of people by your work space distracts your concentration?

Do you ever find that people standing in or walking by your area cast shadows that interfere with your lighting?

If the answers to these questions are "Yes," then office layout is probably contributing to lowered efficiency and creating difficulty in maintaining your flow of work. If this is the case, then creatively think of other ways to restructure the *layout of your work space.*

Another obvious yet often overlooked condition is the *availability of materials.* I have seen many office areas in which frequently used materials are out of reach and personnel must get up and walk to another area many times a day to obtain them. Although there is something to be said for walking and stretching to relieve tensions, there is also a loss of work time that goes into getting materials that might easily be closer at hand. If you find yourself getting annoyed because you have to interrupt tasks to get materials to maintain your flow of work, then you might assess the availability of your materials.

The materials that you keep in your desk or immediate work area should be easily reachable and available according to the *frequency* of use. To set the priorities for materials, begin by observing for a period of a week or two just what materials you use and how often you use them. Also, make a *list* of the materials so that you get an accurate sample of the frequencies of usage. Using this list, you are in a clear position to set your priorities empirically and realistically arrange these materials in your immediate work space for easy access. You will be surprised how much the flow of your work can be improved by easy access to materials.

Another variable that directly influences not only the flow of the work, but also the mood of workers, is *lighting*. Effective lighting can boost morale and relax eyes while minimizing or preventing eyestrain. In a setting where there are no windows that let in natural ultraviolet light from outside, the staff often feels gloomy, has low energy, and seems lethargic. In such closed settings without ultraviolet light, fluorescent lights are usually used for illumination. Unfortunately, most fluorescent lights do not radiate the entire spectrum of light. This means that such lighting prevents certain colors of light rays (particularly ultraviolet) from hitting our retinas. There are some people whose biological systems require that a full spectrum of light hit their visual systems for them to experience a feeling of well-being and to be in equilibrium. When these people are not exposed to a full spectrum, including ultraviolet light, their systems may get out of balance—which in turn means that they are subject to more frequent mood swings, lowered energy levels, and stress.

The solution is simple: Install *full-spectrum* fluorescent light in offices that do not have windows that let in natural ultraviolet light. These lights cost a little more, but the improvement in morale and work output will more than make up the cost.

Once you have rearranged your work space for easy access and improved traffic flow and have corrected your lighting, then it is important to consider the *quality of the air* that you breathe. Do you attend meetings in rooms with inadequate ventilation where you have to sit near someone who smokes? Do you find yourself resenting those who subject you to smoke and other noxious odors?

We are talking about air pollution. The solutions and alternatives are obvious—provide adequate ventilation, adequate circulation of fresh air, and filtration of stale, pollen-filled, smoke-filled, polluted air.

Part of dealing with the issue of polluted air has to do with our first *believing* that we have a *right* to clean air and then *asserting* our rights. You would be amazed at how many people will sit by and quietly suffer assaults on their noses and lungs, all the while resenting their situation!

Polluted air not only interferes with easy breathing but also smells up our clothing, assaults our sense of smell, and leaves a grimy film on hair, skin, and other surfaces. Furthermore, noxious smells and foul air interfere with the smooth operation of our bodies and interrupt the flow of our work.

On the issue of smokers vs. nonsmokers, one solution is that used by the major airlines—have sections of the office separated according to where smokers and nonsmokers work. Another set of solutions has to do with setting the *rules* at your office. In many doctor's offices today, for example, you will find signs requesting that you not smoke. In the offices where the rules are followed consistently, you will not find ashtrays either.

In your own office spaces, it would be best first to survey your personnel to find out how they feel about smoking and then make the rules to benefit as many as possible. Some offices have now set up rules whereby there is no smoking allowed at one's desk and, if someone wants to smoke, he or she must go to a designated area (e.g., break room, washroom, outdoors). I've even seen one office where the solution was simply to open a door to the outside. If you do not survey the feelings of the personnel first, then you might find the resentments greater than before, and such harbored resentments about working conditions and rules of the office interfere with the smooth flow of work.

If you respect your body and your sense of well-being, then you will demand some solution to pollution! But if you don't assert yourself, then you deserve what your environment gives you.

It is to be hoped that by now you have cleaned up your air and are ready to deal with the assault on your ears. Irrelevant, abrupt, and noxious noises constantly bombard our ears, yet few people take the time to deal with the problem. Noisy interruptions commonly disrupt the flow of work in many offices and work spaces.

Stop and reflect for a moment about the noises in your work area: Are there loud noises of machines going constantly? Are there voices that continually intrude on the flow of your work? Are there noises from outside your work space that interrupt you? Do you ever feel a bit disoriented, dizzy, or irritable and find yourself seeking the quiet refuge of the toilet (what a place to seek peace!) or find yourself sighing in relief as you walk out of the office?

If the answers to any of these questions are "Yes," then you are experiencing the consequences of noise pollution.

Each of us is different in the way he uses his senses to learn and understand the world around him. Some of us emphasize our ears, some our eyes, some our touch or smell. People who use hearing as their primary mode for dealing with incoming events are often auditorily sensitive. That is to say, noise pollution bothers these people much more than others who depend upon other senses such as vision or touch.

An example of this condition involves my personal experience with driving. I am more auditory than visual and am very sensitive to sounds. Several years ago, I held several different jobs and was required to drive many miles between them daily. At the time, I drove a small, noisy car, and I felt disoriented, irritable, and tired when I drove on the freeway for more than 10 minutes at a stretch. I found it very stressful just driving to work!

One day, I finally paid attention to the ringing in my ears and actually listened to what my body was saying: "It's too noisy in here." I experimented with the difficulty by noticing how I felt when I drove with cotton in my ears and how I felt when I drove in larger, more insulated cars. And to my surprise and delight, I discovered a pattern—when I was more insulated from noise, I felt more relaxed and less disoriented. Several months later, I purchased a slightly heavier car, which I had specially insulated. The happy result was that I felt much more relaxed while driving because I had reduced the stressing agent—noise. This illustrates a common principle of stress reduction: Once we discover the pattern, the solution is often obvious.

Review whether you experience the symptoms of noise pollution in your own office or work space. Then, if this is a problem for you and your staff, make a list of your options and alternatives. The size of rooms, closeness to machines, insulation in walls, on ceilings, and in windows, barriers between work spaces, and rules about loud talking—all of these can contribute to a relaxed and nonstressful atmosphere for our ears. Sometimes such simple solutions as hanging drapery or laying carpet, or installing insulated vinyl floor material, can cut down the noise factor tremendously.

Go through the following steps:

1. Listen to what your ears and body tell you. Is it too noisy at work?
2. Listen to the sources of the noise.
3. Explore the possibilities for limiting and attenuating the noise sources.
4. Review possible solutions to quieting the environment.
5. Change your environment to a quiet and less stressful one.
6. Enjoy the improved flow and ease of your work.

9. RHYTHM AND TIMING OF OTHERS

The last factor that influences our flow of work is the rhythm and timing of others around us. As a rule, when someone lives and works with people who are tense, that person tends to pick up the tension of others around him. Similarly, if a person is a slow or easygoing worker and works with several people who work fast and furiously, then he or she might feel tensions or conflict simply from being near them.

In addition to physical proximity, there is the psychological factor. Some people will compare themselves to those around them; for example, a slow, easygoing person might start won-

dering whether he is doing an adequate job in the face of someone who constantly completes tasks before him. Also, just the
sound of someone working (e.g., typing) faster or at a different
pace can throw one off the rhythm of one's own pace and speed.

People who have a low self-esteem, or who tend to look outside themselves for the answers to questions in their lives, or
who have difficulty in concentrating are all prime targets for
being distracted and thrown off their own pace and flow. In the
case of low self-esteem, such persons tend to evaluate themselves
negatively in most situations, and their sense of a disparity in
work rhythms may stimulate self-disparagement (e.g., "Gosh,
she's fast, there must be something wrong with me!").

For those who tend to look outside themselves for answers
to life questions (e.g., blaming others for what happens to them
and taking little responsibility for their own lives), such a disparity of rhythms invites comparison and often leads to
distraction.

Those who concentrate poorly need to practice attending to
various tasks until they cultivate and develop adequate focusing
skills.

Each of us is vulnerable to having his or her own pace, flow,
and rhythms thrown off by being near others with differing
rhythms simply because each of us experiences different moods
each day, is more or less distractible, and is vulnerable to looking
at what others are doing.

Some people find it difficult to regain their composure when
they are influenced by the rhythms of others. As a solution, some
try to copy the rhythms of those who are providing the distraction. That tactic is usually disastrous and often creates more tension and worse performance. An example would be the professional golfer, new to the tour, who is paired with a famous player
and attempts to keep up with that great player's pace. That usually throws off the less-experienced golfer's rhythm. That is why
there is an unwritten rule in tournament play: Play the course,
not the golfers! In your own line of work, set your own rhythms
and do not copy those around you.

You might be wondering what to do if you are distracted
from your own rhythms. Several possibilities come to mind:

1. Stop your work for a moment. Pause and relax.

2. If a pause is not enough to regain your focus, then reflect on your own psychological state. Ask yourself how your mood, tension level, and peace of mind (are you in conflict about events that day?) are affecting your ability to remain focused.

3. If that is not enough to refocus, then pick up a new rhythm and practice that one. Try one that is faster, slower, or varied. Focus on the feelings that you have as you take on this new pace.

4. If none of these suggestions works, maybe it is time to take a longer break from work. Maybe you are ready for a vacation or long weekend. Or maybe you need a well-day off from work to regain your psychological equanimity.

5. Finally, if there is a pattern of repeatedly being distracted from your own pace by the differing rhythms of others, then maybe you need some psychotherapy to learn to like yourself and to learn to focus.

In all the preceding sections on issues that influence your flow and your pace at work, there are many suggestions as to how to deal with the issues. These are in no way intended to be definitive. So be creative and come up with your own solutions. In general, the formula remains the same:

1. Recognize that an issue exists.
2. Be aware of the factors that contribute to flowing.
3. Observe any patterns to the events.
4. Review possible alternatives and solutions to difficulties.
5. Be responsible for your flow—risk some change.
6. Assuming you have done all this: *Enjoy* the flow and rhythm of your work.

CHAPTER 7

STRESS PREVENTION AT WORK

CREATING A POSITIVE ATMOSPHERE

Adjusting the rhythm and pace of your work can lead to effective and long-lasting stress reduction on the job. There is, however, another aspect of the work environment that even proper pacing cannot correct: the emotional atmosphere in the workplace. When people are happy and enjoy working together, the positive emotional climate generated by their interaction makes work pleasurable and satisfying. On the other hand, if there is an air of tension on the job, people sense it and begin to reflect that tension in their work or in their relationships with co-workers. Similarly, if there is dissatisfaction, discord, or even chaos in the workplace, those negative feelings permeate the atmosphere and create a pernicious climate that workers want to avoid or escape. After all, who wants to be tense or miserable five days a week?

To get some sense of just how poisonous a negative emotional environment can be at work, imagine that the following situations prevail at your job. Try to experience the feelings you would have in the situations described: Imagine what you would see, how your body would feel, what sounds you would hear. The more vividly you can imagine your responses, the more accurately you may sense the power of the emotional environment in generating stressful feelings at work.

Picture, if you will, a state of tension at work. You can hear it in the tone of your co-workers' voices. You can feel the tension filling the work area like radiation. Experience that feeling for a few moments, as strongly and vividly as you can. Then turn your attention to your body and your mood. How does the thought of such tension make you feel? Do you notice any symptoms of stress? How about your mood? Would you like to feel like that all day? If you did feel like that at work, what would it be like when you got home? Would you be relaxed and happy, or would the irritation and other remnants of the tension accompany you? Would your family enjoy dealing with you when you were in such a mood? Might you want to kick the family dog?

Tension or bad feelings can poison the working environment, but stronger, even more negative feelings can do even worse damage. Consider, for example, how you might feel if the tension you previously imagined was increased. How would you feel if your superiors were not supportive or did not appreciate your hard work? Imagine them obtusely demanding more output, all the while belittling or even overlooking your efforts. How would you feel now? Bitter? Angry? Some people react to such pressure in these ways. Others become unmotivated and lethargic toward their work. Still others feel bored or unexcited. All such reactions are responses to strongly negative emotions in the workplace.

Finally, imagine the strength of your emotional reaction to even stronger emotional pressures on the job. Imagine that your bosses not only ignore your efforts or achievements, but also find opportunities to criticize you. Now blame is added to disregard and the general sense of tension. How would you feel if this final insult were added? Many people react to such abuse by feeling bad about themselves. Lowered self-esteem then becomes added to the sense of tension and the negative feelings of anger or withdrawal. Taken together, these reactions indicate the possible range of effects that emotional difficulties on the job can cause. Clearly, the emotional environment in your workplace can have a profound effect upon your personal experience of stress. A congenial, cooperative atmosphere can alleviate stress and make working attractive and pleasurable. In such a working situation, people look forward to work and enjoy, or at least tolerate well, the tasks they have to do. In a more negative emotional environment, however, the tone changes, and employees find themselves bored, uncomfortable, or irritated. In powerfully negative situations, people feel even more strongly: hostile, resentful, bored, trapped, bitter, lethargic, or dull.

It is important to stress the profound differences between an emotionally healthy environment and a negative and destructive one. Such a comparison will enable you to evaluate the extent to which emotional considerations may—or may not—be a factor in producing stress at your work. If you suspect that the emotional environment at your job may be stress-producing, then just ask yourself the following questions. Your answers should help to make apparent whether the atmosphere at your work is positive or negative.

Do you and your co-workers want to work?

Do people at work talk about leaving?

Do workers at your job make a large number of errors?
(A high rate of errors is often a sign of a negatively charged emotional atmosphere. People respond to the pressure by making more mistakes than usual.)

Do you or your co-workers miss work frequently?
(A high rate of absenteeism is another indicator of tension or other negative aspects at work. People often escape unpleasant situations by becoming ill.)

Do people seem lethargic or gloomy?

Does the atmosphere seem tense—or even critical or hostile?

Do you or co-workers feel unappreciated or disregarded?

Is the turnover rate high?

If you are not sure how to answer some of these questions, you might ask your co-workers. If you answer "Yes" to many of these questions, then it is probable that your work situation is suffering from negative emotions—the more "Yes" answers, the greater the negative atmosphere. If you want to reduce or even eliminate stress, such stress-producing situations must be dealt with.

Assume for the moment that the climate at work is at least on the negative side. If it is, what can you do to change that atmosphere into something more positive and gratifying, both for yourself and for others? The answer lies in two simple but sharply opposed principles. Understanding these two principles will provide you with the necessary foundation for beginning to reshape the emotional environment at your job.

The first principle is this: Praise, affection, appreciation, compliments, and supportive messages all act like boomerangs— they return to the person who sent them just as positive and constructive as when they were first uttered. This happens because genuine statements of support make others feel positive about themselves and about the person who made the supporting comment. People appreciate being praised for good work, and they like themselves when others notice and comment about positive qualities in them. In turn, people who have been made to feel good about themselves tend to feel good about others. We respect and appreciate others if we feel respected and appreciate ourselves. You can test this principle by simply asking yourself whether you like to be recognized and praised if you have done a good job. If your answer is "Yes," then the point of this first principle should be clear.

The second principle is quite different: Criticism, disdain, arrogance, hostility, and disrespect all echo in our minds. They linger and haunt us, and it is difficult to erase the negative feelings that result. The reason is that when people are criticized, they tend to question their competency and self-worth. Sometimes this negative self-view leads to defensiveness and hostility. For example, a secretary whose boss continually criticized her took revenge upon his arrogance and contempt by making subtle errors in the letters she sent out. The hostility need not always be overt. However, whether overtly or not, people cannot help but react to those who treat them unfairly or with disdain. The price of being hostile or petty toward others can be very great indeed.

These two principles provide the basis for understanding how to achieve a positive and healthy atmosphere at work. The first principle illustrates what you need to do to create such an atmosphere. The second is a warning about what not to do. Criticism and hostility are the best ways to make people feel terrible about themselves and their work.

Creating a positive atmosphere generates a desire to work

and can also prevent severe stress reactions; it is easier for a person to resist and recover from a stressor when the atmosphere and surrounding emotional climate is positive and supportive. A warm, happy working environment makes it easier to overcome stress. Similarly, such a supportive and relaxed emotional atmosphere actually diminishes the body's response to minor stressors. When people feel good about themselves and their work, they are less likely to experience the alarm reaction when confronted with insignificant difficulties—and even less likely to proceed to the further stages of the general adaptation syndrome (GAS).

This means that a positive working climate can actually serve as a bulwark against stress. Every day, each of us has to deal with a variety of demands—assignments, responsibilities, time and production schedules, conferences, deadlines, and many others. On one day, a particular demand or responsibility may be read as a stressor by the mind, and a full-blown stress response may ensue. It might take a day or even several days to recover. On another occasion, however, the same situation may produce a very different result. The demand or responsibility might be interpreted as harmless or insignificant, and little or no stress response might be triggered. The difference in bodily response is due to a combination of many factors, but one of the most significant is the nature of the emotional environment that one is experiencing. Positive, pleasant feelings toward one's job and co-workers can actually reduce or even eliminate what otherwise would be interpreted as stressful. The emotional climate can really make a difference.

If the climate is negative, however, what can you do to change it? The answer is that specific behaviors can often enhance, or even transform, what otherwise would be negative and unproductive work situations. These affirmative, emotionally enhancing behaviors can be summarized in six simple rules for straightforward communication on the job. If you want the atmosphere at your job to become supportive and nurturing, it is essential that you follow these six rules:

RULE 1. Give feedback *immediately.*

When you feel positive about something that an employee

or co-worker has done, share your feeling with him or her as soon as possible. All of us appreciate genuine messages of appreciation, but if such a message is to have its maximum positive effect, it must be delivered as promptly as possible. If a compliment or positive judgment is delayed too long, the person we wish to commend may already have begun to feel discouraged or disappointed before our belated feedback arrives. By then, our praise may sound hollow and produce an effect opposite to that which we had intended.

Several years ago, I worked with a researcher whose staff felt unappreciated by him. As part of my consultation, I became aware of this attitude among his employees and relayed the information to him. He was stunned and perplexed. He thought of himself as a good and beneficent boss, and he was quite unprepared to view himself as thoughtless or uncaring. As a result, he dismissed the possibility that he could be anything less than a perfect boss and continued to behave as he had in the past.

Eventually, his workers summoned the courage to tell him about their dissatisfactions. They pointed out very specifically (and accurately!) that he usually failed to recognize a job well done and that he habitually offered appropriate praise or thanks days or even weeks after the fact. Given their boss's unappreciative and ill-timed behavior, his staff regarded him as a strange and often hostile person. Unfortunately, this researcher was not prepared to accept such criticism, even though it was offered forthrightly and without animosity. He continued to behave much as he always had, remaining obtuse to the needs of his employees for prompt and direct feedback about their work. The final result was that, several months after their unsuccessful conference with him, his entire research staff resigned en masse—a vivid testimonial to the cost of clumsy, ill-timed communication.

As illustrated by this example of the researcher who ignored the signs of poor communication and its consequences on the job, if you want to improve the emotional climate at work, you must do what he refused to do: Respond promptly whenever you have something positive to say to someone. For instance, if a secretary has completed typing a letter and brought it to you for your signature, now is the time to thank the secretary for completing the task on schedule. Should you later read the letter and find it especially well done, the best time to say so is immediately. Take the extra moment to go to the secretary's desk and state your appreciation. The closer your positive comments are to the work that you are praising, the better is the chance your employee or co-worker will benefit from your genuine praise. Remember, a rapid positive response will produce the best results!

RULE 2. Make your feedback *concrete* and *specific*.

When you feel good about something that someone else has done, your praise is most likely to be accepted and appreciated if it refers to a specific behavior or piece of work. For example, it would be much more effective to say "That report you gave me was really well organized" than to make some vague compliment such as "You're really a good worker." Being specific about what you liked makes it easier for the person to repeat the work or behavior that you admired. The employee who learns that you appreciate clear, easy-to-follow organization in reports is far more likely to emphasize such clear structure in future assignments. The worker who has received a nice but unspecific compliment such as "You did a terrific job" has little idea what to concentrate on in future assignments. There are many, many aspects to most jobs. The more specific you are about what you like or want, the easier it will be for others to figure out exactly what you expect. Clear, precise feedback offers an excellent guide to others.

A good example of how *not* to give feedback is that of the boss who approached his secretary at noon and murmured, "You did a great job. See you after lunch." As he disappeared out the door, the secretary was left wondering what he was talking about. Was it the letter typed on short notice earlier that morning? Or the efficient rescheduling of tomorrow's meeting on short notice? Or perhaps the obtaining of tickets for the exact flight he wanted next week? Without more precise indications from the boss, the secretary simply could not know what the boss thought had been done so well. The end result was that a genuine compliment failed to achieve its purpose. Instead of feeling competent and pleased, the secretary was left confused and uncertain. Had the boss paid a little more attention to being specific in his praise, identifying exactly what it was that he liked so much, this vagueness could have been prevented. And the boss's pride could have created a similar sense of pleasure in the secretary's mind as well.

RULE 3. Make positive messages *congruent* with your feelings.

Another way to phrase this rule is to say that "phony messages don't work." To contribute to an improvement in the emotional atmosphere, a compliment must be genuine. Inauthentic praise rings hollow and usually produces a negative effect. Only a genuine positive feeling, honestly and directly stated, can really make others feel better about themselves.

The reason behind this principle of communication is that when we speak our listeners perceive both the *content* of our message and its verbal and nonverbal *context*. If the message is to be received and accepted, both content and context must be congruent—that is, they must match. The nicest, most flattering words, uttered in a harsh or sarcastic voice, will fool few, if any. In fact, when what one says does not match up with how one says it, the listener is more likely to attend to the context, rather than to the specific words that are spoken.

A superior may, for instance, say all the right kinds of things about his employees and their work, but his tone of voice and his nonverbal gestures give him away. He talks about the fine work done in a particular section while his head wags from side to side, denying his very words. He describes his workers as equals and waxes eloquent about their common efforts to help the company, but his tone and his hand gestures suggest that he holds his employees in contempt. Such contradictory messages register, even though people may not always be conscious of what is going on. Have you ever met a person, for example, and left feeling that you could not trust him or her? That vague sense of distrust is an example of how each of us reacts to incongruity between the content of what people say to us and the context within which that utterance is made.

The point is clear: Don't try to fake it. False compliments are counterproductive and only undermine the sense of trust and mutual respect that is necessary as a foundation for effective, personally enhancing communication. If you have nothing good to say, avoid trying to cover your negative feelings with fraudulent positive ones. It is honestly better to say nothing than to make up compliments when they are not deserved.

RULE 4. *Encourage* others to perform well.

The last rule suggested that it is counterproductive to "fake" a feeling. If you cannot say something positive, it is better to remain silent than to try to fabricate a compliment. This does not mean, however, that we need to be dishonest about our feelings. There is nothing to be gained by denying our beliefs or acting as though we do not hold them. Negative comments are most effective when they are quite specific, however, and when they are not dwelt upon. Criticisms can certainly be given, but if you really want to change behavior in others, such change is best accomplished by accentuating the positive rather than criticizing the negative.

Put another way, this means that it is unproductive to dwell upon failure or poor performance. Certainly, errors and short-comings must be acknowledged (how else would someone know that he or she had done the wrong thing?). But real behavioral change occurs only when people are encouraged to repeat and improve upon positive behaviors. Part of the reason for this is that positive feedback ("You really did this well") serves as a reward and reinforces positive behavior. Another factor is that affirmative comments about our work make us feel more able and encouraged about ourselves. Specific and legitimate praise enhances our self-esteem and helps us to perform up to our best capability. Criticism, on the other hand, tends to discourage us. Our self-esteem drops, and our rate of error on the job (or our disinterest) increases dramatically. If you want to create a positive emotional atmosphere at your work, emphasize communications that focus upon the strengths of others. Accentuate positive, useful accomplishments. Praise them immediately in specific terms.

RULE 5. If you want others to side with you, *be on their side.*

The essence of this rule lies in the notion of recognition. All of us feel the need to belong. If we are treated with disrespect, disdain, and criticism, then we feel that we are not wanted and do not belong. (Remember the people who worked for the researcher who would not admit his personal failures as a boss? His negative attitudes literally drove them away.) On the other hand, whenever we feel genuinely appreciated and understood, then we feel comfortable and safe. We belong.

The significance of this notion for creating a positive emotional atmosphere at work is this: If you want your employees or co-workers to be on your side, be on their side first. Recognize their strengths and tell them specifically what you recognize and value in them. This does not mean, of course, that you always agree with them, or even that you share their goals. Such recognition simply makes clear that you understand their perspective and respect it. When a group of workers feel on each other's side, they experience an emotional sense of harmony. This sense of common value and purpose will, in turn, bring about improved performance, relaxation, and effective stress reduction.

RULE 6. To feel positive toward others, *recognize your own strengths.*

This is perhaps the most fundamental rule: If you do not like yourself, you will have difficulty making others feel good about themselves. People who dislike themselves tend to be critical, hostile, disdainful, arrogant, and negative in general. Those who feel better about themselves sense their own strengths and accomplishments—and are more likely to recognize and affirm those capacities in others. Truly, the creation of a positive emotional atmosphere at work begins with you. Liking and respecting yourself can be major steps toward transforming the behavior of others.

These ideas translate into specific actions. When you do a job well, then praise yourself. For example, when I finish a section of this book within the allotted time, I say to myself, "Martin, you're efficient. You are really good at letting the ideas flow." This statement of praise to myself is my way of recognizing a positive action and functions as a personal reward. In sum, I am acting as my own best friend.

As an exercise in praising yourself, select each day for the next week two instances of a job well done. After noticing that you did the job well, tell yourself something positive and notice how you feel. At the end of the week, see whether you find that you have been recognizing your strengths more frequently. Assuming that you are successful, continue the exercise for one month. Keep a journal of all the instances where you recognize your jobs as well done. At the end of the month, read the journal and ask the following questions:

At this point, do I feel positive or negative about myself?

As I recognize my good performance, is it easier to do my work?

When I acknowledge my strengths, do I feel more competent?

As I praise myself, do I have more energy and enthusiasm?

When I have recognized my strengths, have I found it easier to see the assets and good jobs of others?

After you have completed this exercise, the impact of focusing on your positive achievement and behaviors should be apparent. You may find this task difficult if you have been the type of person who dwells on mistakes. Some people seem to get stuck worrying about their errors; when they are stuck, they find it difficult to appreciate their positive actions. If you do this, you will need to act to break this cycle by telling yourself repeatedly about your specific accomplishments.

In addition to retraining yourself to focus on your positive actions, one of the best methods for getting out of a negative cycle of rumination is to reframe or reinterpret the meaning of errors. Beneath the self-denigrating comments that people make when they make mistakes (e.g., "Oh, how could I be so dumb!"), there is often a hidden demand or desire to be perfect. If we assume in our minds that we must be perfect, then we set ourselves up to feel miserable and get stuck in the rut of self-laceration. If you can give up the luxury of punishing yourself when you make mistakes (which is to say, give up hating yourself and proving that you are worthless or incompetent), then begin by reframing the meaning of making errors.

The key to doing this is to gain a perspective on the nature of reality. You do *not* have to be the only one to be "right." In fact, what is "right" is often relative or even arbitrary. Try this experiment: Take a coin and hold it upright so that the edge is pointing toward one person and one face of the coin is pointing toward another person. (The two people are to be standing at right angles to the coin.) Then ask the two persons to state what they see. One will see a straight line (the edge of the coin), while the other will see a circle (the face of the coin). Yet both people are looking at the same coin! So who is "right"? The answer is that reality is defined by each viewer. What is "right" depends upon one's perspective. This insight makes it possible to look at errors in a new, positive way.

Since two people can look at the same coin and see something quite different, what, then, does it mean to "make a mistake"? At the most basic level, making a mistake means that you have simply done something that you or someone else might not want to do. Some other response would have been preferable. This means that error-making is a matter of giving incorrect or undesired responses, nothing more. Given this perspective, it is possible to escape a negative cycle based upon your perception of your own errors. All you have to do is to practice thinking about your mistakes in a new way. Instead of seeing an error as an absolute failure or a sign of total incompetence, think instead that the error is an *opportunity* to learn something about yourself or about the context in which the error occurred.

For example, suppose you notice that your mind is wandering as you perform a particular task and that you are making mistakes as a result. Instead of berating yourself or trying to coerce yourself into a more careful performance (neither of which will probably work—and may even make the situation worse), try this instead: Recognize that your mistakes are a positive and informative message that you are sending to yourself. These mistakes are a way of telling yourself that something is not right, and until whatever is wrong is corrected, the mistakes will continue to occur. Once you recognize the mistakes for the messages that they are, then turn your attention to possible causes. Here, the kind of information about sources of stress you have gained earlier may come in handy. Are you too tired, for example? Or is there something about your work environment that interferes with your work? Poor lighting? Noise? Interruptions? Or could there be psychological factors behind these errors? Are you angry or resentful about your work? Are you in conflict with your boss or co-workers? Or could difficulties at home be affecting your ability to perform on the job? By analyzing such possibilities, and making use of the techniques described in earlier chapters, you may well be able to discover the causes that have led you to make errors in your work. You can then focus on correcting the real source of the difficulty, rather than waste time and energy putting yourself down for making mistakes.

Regarding mistakes as an opportunity to learn about yourself can help you deal more realistically with issues in your life, but it has other advantages as well. Being fair and open-minded toward yourself and your own actions will also make it easier for you to act that way toward others. You will find yourself giving feedback that is *immediate, concrete* and *specific,* and *congruent* with the nonverbal aspects of your messages. You will also find that you are better able to *encourage* and *side with others* and at the same time *recognize your own strengths.* In so doing, you will be taking important steps toward generating a positive work atmosphere that will minimize or even prevent stress for yourself and your co-workers.

CHAPTER 8

STRESS REDUCTION IN THE FAMILY

IMPROVING COMMUNICATION

Understanding how to overcome stress on the job is important, but there is also another area of our lives in which stress often plays a crucial role. Indeed, for many the tensions and stresses produced within the family can be just as strong as, if not stronger than, those produced at work. In fact, family problems often spill over into the workplace, creating stressful situations that neither job pacing nor creation of a more positive atmosphere at work can overcome.

Dealing with such sources of stress within the family can be complex and may require the assistance of a professional. In many cases, however, stressful family situations can be alleviated or even eliminated entirely. The first step in learning to identify and control such stress problems within the family is to learn more about the family itself and how it functions.

FUNCTIONS OF FAMILIES

The family is the basic unit of society. Traditionally, the family has been defined as a group consisting of mother, father, and child or children. In a broader sense, the family has been described as a group of intimates with a history and a future. The three most common family groups are the nuclear, the single-parental, and the communal. Each group has its own types of problems and ways of coping.

During the last several hundred years, technological advances have replaced many essential family functions, such as the production of food and clothing. Whereas families used to cooperate and focus on basic survival needs, industrialization has led to greater concern for emotional and social development within the family. Industrialization has led to an overfocus on job security, which has created more pressures for the breadwinner of the family. No longer can other members readily pitch in when the breadwinner is ill or incapacitated. Thus, the breadwinner has come to rely on other family members more for emotional support to shore him or her up under the weight of economic pressures and responsibilities.

Traditionally, family systems have five major functions: economic, reproductive, sexual, educational, and emotional. Division of labor will often occur to ensure best use of individual skills. Adults fulfill sexual drives through a stable family group, while also reproducing as part of survival needs. Parents educate their children to pass on cultural and personal values, thereby preparing them for interaction in society. Emotionally, the family group provides social and emotional interaction and support.

Beyond the perpetuation of society, the family is the major source of emotional support in times of stress. When this support is replaced by family conflict, individual family members are exposed to some of the most significant stresses imaginable.

A large body of research indicates that when there is stress within the family, there is a greater chance of disease. For example, people who have streptococcal infections are four times more likely to have had some family crisis prior to the onset of the infection than are people with other types of infections. One study found that 76% of the heart attack victims seen in the emergency room had a major family crisis immediately preceding the heart attack. This does not mean that the family stress "caused" the heart attack or that there was no heart disease before the attack. It does mean that a family crisis can be overwhelming and can push a person beyond coping.

Chapter 2 discussed the Life Events Survey created by Drs. Holmes and Rahe (see Fig. 2). If you will look at this list again, you will see that "death of a spouse" is the first item, and hence is the most stressful of events. In fact, of the first ten events, six involve family crises: death of a spouse, divorce, marital separation, death of a close family member, marriage, and marital reconciliation. Family arguments, trouble with in-laws, sexual difficulties, and a child leaving home are also stressful events.

With each family crisis, there is tension, conflict, and the greater likelihood of disease. A researcher named LeShan found that about 75% of patients with cancer reported the death of a close family member in the 2-year period prior to the discovery of cancer. The importance of depending on another family member is dramatically revealed by the fact that when one spouse of a couple who have been married for 20 years or more dies, the surviving spouse frequently dies or becomes seriously ill within 15 months of the death of the first. Losses create profound stress.

STAGES OF FAMILY DEVELOPMENT

Throughout the evolution of a family unit, there are significant stages of development. Each stage brings changes in roles, rules, amount of affection received and given, amount of time spent together, and amount and type of pressures and demands. Thus, each stage becomes a prime time for stress and family crisis. The major stages include:

Stage 1. Union
     a. Courtship
     b. Marriage

Stage 2. Expansion
     a. Birth of first child
     b. Birth of second to last child
     c. First child goes to school
     d. Onset of puberty

Stage 3. Dispersion
    a. Children leave home
    b. Middle age—empty nest, being a couple again

Stage 4. Ending
    a. Retirement
    b. Death

The roles people assume change in each stage. Couples often have sex very differently before marriage than after, and differently again following the birth of their first child. Sex becomes less spontaneous and is planned more. The addition of each new family member demands more sharing of time, affection, interest, and contact. As children go to school or begin challenging society in adolescence, they bring new information and experience to the family group. The family may attempt to protect itself from this new input, or it may attempt to integrate it. Pressures from outside the family can easily create tension within a family. For example, a family argument and crisis may well follow when a 9-year-old comes home and says: "Johnny's allowance is five dollars a week. How come I only get one dollar?"

Middle age brings on concerns about potency, about being loved or worthwhile in the eyes of one's mate, and about having led a significant and meaningful life. Retirement and death of spouse and friends bring on increased isolation. In old age, it is more difficult to find emotional supports.

Throughout the natural evolution of a family unit, the family as a system may function well under stress, may falter, or may dissolve. The loss of a job, the onset of alcoholism, prolonged sickness, or the birth of a handicapped child can profoundly influence the family's operation and communication. The ability to cope with different life changes varies from family to family.

Coping refers to the adjustments that a family makes to the stresses within and outside the family. One researcher found that families that made successful adjustments to serious illness—that is, that coped well—had the following characteristics:

1. Effective, open, and constant communication
2. Clear separation of generations

3. Tolerance of individuality
4. Flexibility in roles.

Effective coping during crises demands flexibility. If the breadwinner is sick for extended periods of time, the economic survival of the family unit depends upon other members temporarily becoming breadwinners. During adolescence, when children are likely to want to be different and to taste the forbidden fruits (called "vices" by some) of drink, smoke, sex, and drugs, family conflict is likely to occur. Parents may overreact to the adolescent's attempt to find identity and may severely punish or restrict the child. The child wants to be an individual who is free to choose his own life-style. If the family is to remain intact, there must be some tolerance for individuality and difference. When parents are preoccupied with the child's differences and challenges to their values and power, they are tense and may have difficulty in coping with everyday matters at work and at home. The breadwinner may fly into irrational rages, while the spouse may become depressed. The family interactions are thick with tension, and all members have a rough time coping. The likelihood of illness is high.

It is interesting that a clear separation of generations is characteristic of effective family coping. Although many children of the 1960s complained of a so-called "generation gap," its very existence may be a sign of health. Differences in values and ideas have a useful purpose; they offer children some standards for comparison. A parent is always a parent to a child. The parent may be friendly and an effective listener, but can never be a friend like a peer. In fact, when parents proclaim to their children that they are really their friend, while pushing aside the role of a parent, they create confusion and tension. Children feel safer when the parents hold on to their power, yet are friendly and supportive. To deny a role that is natural and defined by one's biology, age, and relationship is to act in an unreal manner.

Finally, effective coping within the family is accomplished through open and constant communication. Most families who come for family therapy during a crisis complain that they just "can't communicate." Interestingly, most sexual problems seem to solve themselves once a couple learn to express their likes and dislikes clearly and learn to listen to each other. Effective communication involves sending clear messages, having them received as they were intended, listening actively, and offering continuous feedback until both parties are satisfied.

When families run into trouble, tensions build, illnesses become more frequent, and the effects of stress are compounded. Some automobile companies have hired counselors to provide someone for their employees to talk to, especially on Monday morning. The weekend is the time when families spend the most time together. Most conflicts arise during this time. The employee who comes to the plant angry may get rid of his or her tension through acts of sabotage. A loose bolt here, an overtight connection there, and a defective machine is produced. The worker has lessened tension at the expense of the consumer and the company.

SIGNS OF FAMILY TENSION

The first step to an analysis of how effective your family unit is in coping and communicating is to look at *signals* of distress in the family. The following events suggest that the family system has some difficulty in coping and communicating:

1. The children have frequent tension-related symptoms such as nail-biting, prolonged stuttering, bed-wetting beyond the age of six, frequent unresolvable school difficulties, and years of tantrum behavior.

2. Parents and children have escalating arguments that seldom end in resolution.

3. Parents and children "never" argue and fight.

4. The family cannot seem to talk about certain topics. Topics such as sex, violence, drugs, politics, and feelings are taboo.

5. Whenever there is conflict and disagreement, there are extremely long periods of silence. The topic gets buried.

6. The family seems threatened by what outsiders think.

7. There is an unspoken understanding or rule that anger

must be controlled. Under this condition, individual family members often develop migraine headaches and backache.

8. Family members don't seem to listen to or hear what is said when there is disagreement.

9. Disagreements become battles over "who is right." There seems to be a power struggle over who will win and dominate.

10. Decisions seem never to be made by any one person.

11. Disagreements and resentments lead to continual alienation. At least one member withdraws from the conflict and may not be seen for days or years. Father and mother may silently smolder while going about their daily business.

12. Conversations seem never to stay on the topic long enough to arrive at any resolution. Ideas and feelings seem never to get communicated.

13. The household is seldom quiet. There is a sense of pandemonium.

14. Individual family members usually seem to be "doing their own thing" with minimal interaction.

15. The family must do all things as a group with little tolerance for separate and independent action.

16. Children are seldom included in decision-making.

17. Spouses are having affairs—with others, with work, or with a hobby. This isolates a family member. Other members are usually anxious, suspicious, and depressed.

18. Spouses have an unsatisfying sex life.

19. There is extreme tension and uproar at dinnertime and bedtime.

20. Affection and physical contact are seldom if ever communicated, or stop at some point in time. Some people stop hugging their children around puberty for fear of sexual arousal. Children respond to the loss of contact as a message that they are no longer loved.

21. Family members get unexplainable illnesses—e.g., stomachaches, headaches, colds, intestinal distress. Or family members seem to alternate getting ill. One month mother may have a headache, and the next month father has chest pains, each alternating going to the doctor month after month.

The preceding list includes only 21 of the more common signals of tension that reflect poor communication within family systems. If these examples do not give you enough clues as to whether your support system is having trouble coping, then consider the following:

Do you look forward to going home at the end of a day at work or after a day away from the family? If not, your family is probably not supportive.

Do you find that conflict and disagreement are affiliative—that is, that they bring you closer together? Or do you find that conflict leads to alienation, isolation, and further tension? Such negative, stress-producing conflict is nonsupportive.

Do you find yourself being frequently critical of other family members, or they of you? If so, you or they have anger that has not been expressed or resolved.

Do you find yourself continually wishing to be single again? It is normal to occasionally wish to be free again, but continual wishes reflect deep problems.

Do you find yourself or your partner fabricating "reasons" not to have sex or not to engage in some other activity initiated by you? Daily protests of "I'm too tired" may be signals of lack of viable support from other family members.

Do you feel free to say what's on your mind without fear of being put down or discounted?

Each of these questions and patterns of behaviors reflects some form of problem in communication. They are listed to give you some idea of whether or not your family is having difficulty.

SUCCESSFUL FAMILY COMMUNICATION

Once you have recognized that your family is having difficulty, the next question is: "How do I deal with the problems?" Before identifying specific steps that you can take to improve communication and coping, let's review some revealing ideas from research on family interaction.

Families that cope well under stress tend to have *open* systems of communication. An "open" system of communication is one in which all family members have the right to discuss freely any issue that is of interest or concern without fear of reprisal or punishment. In families with "closed" communication patterns, members do not usually feel they have the right to talk about what is on their minds. Also, they usually fear being criticized, discounted, or ignored if they speak up. In closed systems, independent thought and action are feared and discouraged. In an open system, people are supportive of one another, and in a closed system, people are nonsupportive and negative more frequently than they are positive toward one another.

Open families also tend to be physically healthier. Some research clarifies the differences. In one study, 83 families discussed the hypothetical situation of a gravely ill family member who is dying. Family interactions were observed while the members talked about this topic. Then the amount of illness in these families was observed over a 6-month period. The families that were comfortable discussing death in a personalized way were healthier. They had more days free of illness than families that ignored the subject of death or did not feel comfortable discussing it.

Thus, families that are "open" to talk about difficult topics in a personalized way tend to be healthier. Health is a sign of effective coping. Families that have a difficult time coping with stress often have topics that are taboo. They act as though these topics were dangerous or a threat to their survival. Families that cannot talk about topics such as death, sex, violence, drugs, religious beliefs, political ideas, and family differences typically have conflict. Families that cannot openly discuss such "hot" topics usually find their children's adolescence a time of extreme distress.

Although research to date is not definitive, there are some patterns of family interaction that relate to the types of illness that develop. For example, families of patients with ulcerative colitis (where the large bowel gets constricted and may bleed from sores) are often socially restricted. They tend to avoid interacting with people outside the immediate family, and they tend to have minimal communication within their own families.

There seems to be a great deal of tension when people talk with one another, and family members seem to walk on eggshells as though expecting to be criticized.

Similarly, research that I conducted ten years ago indicated that families with a depressed spouse had difficulty talking and responding. The depressed person received from other family members a greater amount of feedback that was negative and often hostile. The depressed person was also frequently ignored and therefore received less emotional support than other family members. A simple treatment plan was formulated from this finding. Family members were told of the findings and were encouraged to be supportive of and attentive to the depressed person. The depressions systematically resolved. When people are depressed, they are having trouble coping. They need all the support they can get from the family.

When a family network does not have effective ways to communicate and does not provide emotional support, then times of crisis become critical for survival. For many families, a crisis will lead to divorce, separation, alienation, abandonment, or illness. In 1967, one research study found that when one spouse became ill, almost 60% of the healthy spouses experienced tension severe enough to lead to their having subsequent illnesses.

Family crises test a family's survival skills. A crisis can occur when a family member is hospitalized, a child or parent dies, or there is prolonged separation. Separations are common in our mobile culture because of work or military obligations. Demoralization is another crisis time. A family can be stressed through the disgrace of alcoholism, crime, delinquency and drug addiction, infidelity, prolonged unemployment, or sudden impoverishment.

Other crises involve family expansion or change. A child may be adopted, a relative may move in, or a stepmother or stepfather may marry in. Each is a crisis that tests adaptiveness.

The last category of crises involves some combination of elements. Common crisis times occur with desertion, divorce, illegitimacy, imprisonment, institutionalization, runaway, or suicide or homicide.

If families are to survive ordinary changes as well as these extraordinary crises, they must be *flexible* and creative in their adaptiveness. The rules that govern how they communicate must be viable and growth-producing. When family rules are rigid and constricting, then the distress of crises becomes destructive. Individual family members become ill, divorce or abandonment results, or family members cannot function mentally. Breadwinners cannot cope at work, and children cannot cope with the demands of school. Even death can result.

Growth-Promoting Communication

Since change and crises are part of life, you might be wondering how one family can thrive while another cannot even survive.

In families that function well under stress, there is a clear idea of what is expected of each member. Parents clearly accept their roles as parents and do not give up their power to children. Spouses understand that each has some domain that is to be respected and consistent. The psychological and social needs of all family members must be met so that frustration and internal conflict are minimized. This translates into being able to listen to each other when a person experiences pain, conflict, frustration, and turmoil, while also being supportive even though the others may have different ideas and feelings. Finally, the family must be able to respond to change.

For individual members of a family to cope well, the entire family must be able to adapt. When mother is having conflict with grandma, or father must decide whether or not to put his mother in a nursing home, each needs the support and understanding of other family members. The stresses placed upon the individual cause shifts in mood and behavior. Mother may not be so cheerful when children come home from school, and father might seem preoccupied and unavailable for play. Husband or wife might not be easily approached for sex when weighted down with pressures. Pressures and demands on each member of the family create demands for adaptation from other family members.

Crisis and change can be opportunities for growth, non-growth, or death. When adaptation leads to nongrowth, people are tense and defensive. They tend to disregard their self-care and appear unconscious. When adaptations are not viable, people and families die, psychologically or physically. "Death" can be real or symbolic. A person dies psychologically when he or she remains depressed or anxious for years on end without resolution. Family structures "die" with divorce, separations, abandonment, or actual death of a family member.

Nongrowth and psychological death occur when family members do not talk with one another, when they seem to be struggling continually for power and domination, when they are constantly hostile and nonsupportive of one another, and when they lose their sense of community. That is, they no longer seem to be on each other's side. A family has true intimacy and caring when each member acts on his or her own behalf while also considering the needs of other members.

Families that adapt to change well are flexible and open to difference and individuality. Here, family members view differences and disagreement as valuable and exciting *opportunities for growth*. They see feedback as necessary for growth and view *disagreement* as an *opportunity for learning*. Families that do not cope well with change see disagreement as a loss and a threat.

When a family views disagreement as a threat, then changes often become crises. This viewpoint leads to communicating in accord with some restricting rules. Typical nongrowth rules would be: "When there is a disagreement, let's change the topic when things get too heated," or "Let's avoid controversial topics," or "If you must disagree, please be nice," or "Let's be reasonable, let's not argue about this." The request to be "reasonable" is a manipulation to suppress conflict and differences.

These rules come from fear that conflict will lead to greater distance and to loss. Some people worry about not being loved when there is disagreement, and others dislike the discomfort of disapproval. Whereas some relationships are so fragile that discord will lead to separation, emotional distance, and divorce, other relationships seem to thrive on discord. Some relationships have the rule, "When we fight, let's keep it going as long as we can." The prolonged fighting with its high arousal may be the way family members feel close, even though they seldom seem to resolve any conflicts.

Families that adapt successfully typically live by the following rule: "It's okay to disagree, and even to agree to disagree." President Carter was able to get Israel and Egypt, two historical enemies, to move toward a peace treaty by having both parties agree to disagree. People, because they are different, see things differently. Each person sees, hears, touches, and feels in unique ways. People cannot always view things the same way and remain real. Therefore, without the rule of agreeing to disagree, there cannot be acceptance, intimacy, and growth.

In families that cope well with change, there is an attitude and philosophy of being *responsible* for one's own well-being. Being responsible for ourselves involves accepting our own feelings, actions, and fate. A delinquent child is not the fault of mother or father. The child's actions may contribute to the tensions within the family, but it is the child who acts. No one makes us do this or that. We do what we do because we do not want to pay some price or because we do want something else to happen.

Families that do not cope well can be seen blaming each other for what happens, criticizing one another, ignoring one another, and not being supportive when others are hurting. In these families, emotional survival is seen as depending upon external factors: "If I only had more money I would be happy" or "If you hadn't done that, I wouldn't have gotten in trouble in school." These families act as though the responsibility for their well-being is beyond their control.

In contrast, families that cope well see emotional survival as stemming from oneself. There is a sense of community where each member takes care of his or her domain, while being supportive of others. You do not find such family members manipulating one another, but you will find them *encouraging* and *sharing* their experiences.

Clear Communication

Optimal family survival depends upon successful communication. Effective communication exists when the message sent is the message received. Frequently, what is said is not what is heard, nor is it what is understood. Disagreements and conflicts often arise when what we said is not what someone else heard or understood. People cannot agree or resolve differences when they do not even know what is being said.

Effective communication depends upon a series of events. First, the message sent must be *clear*. All information must be included. You can distort and mislead by omitting part of a message or by overemphasizing another part. For example, imagine a boss quickly passing by his secretary's desk and saying, "Please get that report done by noon." The secretary hands in the report on collection trends and gets yelled at for doing the "wrong" report. The boss didn't realize that he had said "that" report, which is vague. The secretary did not ask what "that" referred to, and made an assumption. A crisis resulted.

Crises can often be prevented by *checking out the intent* of the message. If there is any ambiguity, it is important to ask, "What specifically did you mean?" Or even if the message seemed clear, repeat what you heard to the sender of the message. By hearing you say what you think you heard, the sender can tell you whether you heard accurately. A complete transaction will then be accomplished.

The *"checking-out"* process is vital to human interactions. As we have seen earlier, a message has not only a content, but also a context determined by the manner of its delivery. You can say "I love you" and really communicate "I dislike you." To mean "I love you," the nonverbal parts of the message must be *congruent*; that is, they must match the idea being communicated. To frown and say "I love you" gives a different message than to smile and say the same. If you say the phrase very quickly and mumble it in a soft voice, the receiver might wonder whether you really mean it. If the receiver does not check your intent—perhaps by saying, "You mumbled quickly when you said 'I love you' and I'm scared that you're just saying that to please me. Is it true?"—you will not have the opportunity to clarify your intent by saying, "I have a hard time saying the word 'love,' but I do mean it."

Making your messages congruent requires that you say what

you mean and mean what you say. Listen carefully and check with the other person to see whether your understanding is accurate. Assumptions, mind-reading, interruptions, and premature judgments interfere with true understanding. In fact, they encourage misunderstanding and conflict. You are creating conflict by assuming you accurately know what the other person intends. When conflict and miscommunications occur, the victims are seldom innocent.

The principles of clear communication include the following:

1. *Speak clearly.*
2. Say what you mean with *complete* messages.
3. Be *specific* with regard to time, place, context, and reference.
4. Make *nonverbal* aspects of your message *congruent* with the verbal content of the message.
5. *Listen* carefully and actively, *without* mind-reading, assumptions, or judgments.
6. *Check out* and clarify that what you understand corresponds with what was intended.
7. *Complete transactions* until both parties have the same understanding of a message.

FIGHTING FOR CHANGE

When a man and a woman join together to form a family, they bring to this relationship different histories and experiences. Each person has his or her own ideas and feelings about the fundamental aspects of a relationship, including intimacy, dependency, independence, control, dominance, affection, sex, and decision-making. Each person has different expectations of what will be gained in the relationship and what will work to achieve what he or she desires. The rules of the relationship come from what people want from life and from how they have learned to deal with others in the past.

In all families, there are rules about intimacy. Usually, the rules are unspoken, but are quickly established within the first few meetings. Some people want a lot of contact and closeness, and others want less. Conflict exists when both parties do not get what they want and expect. And the conflict may simmer for years and decades without clear resolution. For example, whereas one spouse might want closeness through sex, another might want simply affectionate contact. When differences are not clarified early in the relationship, then each party may attempt to coerce the other into the desired behavior. Whatever happens, each family system will evolve a series of rules about how to conduct itself. Once these rules are established, there will be a resistance to changing them.

Imagine, for example, a 28-year-old woman who comes from a family in which people did not physically touch one another very often. Thus, she is not used to being touched and seems standoffish and cold. She marries a 30-year-old man who comes from a family whose members touched one another, but did not openly express caring and loving; rather, they expressed their caring through the giving of gifts and through actions. The wife desires to be told often that she is loved, partly because she wants reassurance, and partly because she wants to get what she missed as a child. The husband expects to be hugged when he comes home and to have his wife do things for him (e.g., make him lunch) as a way to show she cares. Basically, each is somewhat insecure about being intimate in all ways (touch, talk, sex, actions, feelings). Their relationship was established because "we fell in love at first sight." It was founded upon physical attraction, and they never openly discussed their different feelings about intimacy.

Over the years, they developed rules about how to conduct themselves. They have a rule, "Let's not touch in public," with which she is comfortable, and they have a rule, "Let's hug when husband comes home from work, and on special occasions," so he gets some of what he wants. Each has different rules for how to approach sex, she by talking and he by touching. When they shift from these rules, tension develops and "miscommunications" arise.

Once children arrive, the basic rules remain essentially the same, but tensions seem to increase. Young children require more touching than the wife is accustomed to giving, and the husband seems to have more contact with them. She is more verbal, so as they grow older and become verbal, they seem to communicate more with her. Each spouse develops different styles of relating with the children, and conflicts arise as each parent becomes jealous of the other's relationship with the children. Also, since children demand so much time and energy, the husband finds his wife doing less for him (which he equates with loss of her love), and the wife finds that her husband talks to her less (which she equates with loss of his love). Each makes assumptions about what these shifts mean and acts according to these interpretations. They may become more aloof, more critical of each other, and less interested in giving, and may begin having affairs. The affairs may be with other sexual partners, hobbies, or work, and may distract each partner from the basic issues. When either partner attempts to make some change, little seems to happen. Dissatisfaction and distance grow. The couple may drift apart for years, and may become so bitter that change seems impossible.

Why does this entrenchment happen? Systems, by their nature and structure, operate to keep the relationship in balance. Early rules become habits, and unless the system has a rule that "it is okay to change a rule at any time," behavior patterns become fixed.

In addition to this characteristic of systems, most people do not know how to fight for change. More often than not, fighting fails to bring about changes. When there is conflict and difference, people tend to defend their positions. And when people become defensive, they tend to fight dirty. "Dirty" fighting is destructive fighting, where there is some attempt to discount or discredit the other person's thinking, feeling, or behavior. When people fight dirty, they provoke others to feel bad about themselves. And when self-esteem is threatened, people fight back, sometimes actively, as with hostile remarks; sometimes passively, through silence or uncooperativeness.

There are a number of dirty tactics that evoke defensiveness and that *prevent* change. When people use *name-calling* (e.g.,

"You're stupid," "You s.o.b.") during a fight, they provoke the other person to feel bad and ensure that the other person will retaliate.

Critical *judgments* also evoke resistance. These occur during a fight if a person says "That's bad," or "You're wrong," instead of saying what they *experience*, such as "I'm mad at you for. . . ." Critical judgments usually push feelings aside and discredit the other person's viewpoint. To say that someone is "wrong" is to say that what he or she experiences is not real. The other's viewpoint may be inaccurate, incomplete, or distorted. Giving the other person more information might change that view, but a judgment of "wrong" (which is moralistic, but not accurate) connotes a finality that generates defensiveness.

Sweeping *generalizations* also stop communication and foster defensiveness. If the wife says "You *never* tell me you care," her statement will probably stimulate the husband to justifications ("Don't you remember when . . .") or counteraccusations ("You are *always* dissatisfied, you *never* get enough attention"). Sweeping generalizations are *accusations*, which bring about defense and resistance to change.

A common and ineffective fighting tactic is *digging up the past*. To tell another person of all the "wrongs" and injustices done months and years ago will not win the person to your side. This behavior will show the other person that you hold a grudge and that you probably lie to yourself to make peace. If you are still angry or disappointed over some event in the past, then, to interact peacefully, you must pretend that you feel good, deny your feelings, or delude yourself. Holding a grudge will not settle a conflict, but will alienate you from the other person.

People who hold grudges at some level do not want resolution, are fearful of open conflict, and are uncomfortable with change and closeness. Whatever the reason for holding the grudge, digging up the past will evoke pain, anger, and resentment. Stirring up old feelings also contaminates the present. Fighting gets very confusing when a person adds the past to the present.

Another confusing tactic is *mind-reading*, where one person assumes that he knows what the other thinks and feels. The effect of mind-reading is that the other person feels left out or discounted. To assume that we know a person so well that we can predict all that person's feelings and thoughts is an act of arrogance and superiority. It is also foolishness.

Mind-reading assumes that the mind reader knows *all* the workings of the other person's mind and that the other person's reactions are so limited and fixed that they are easily predictable. Even machines are not that reliable. People's feelings, thoughts, and actions vary from situation to situation, but mind-reading assumes they do not. Thus, mind-reading is really a maneuver designed to keep a safe distance emotionally by limiting reactions and avoiding conflicts. If you assume you know what other people are thinking and feeling, then you don't have to ask them. Therefore, if they have reactions you won't like, you don't have to face them. Viable resolution of a conflict cannot be achieved through mind-reading.

There are several more common communication tactics that come under the dirty-tricks category. *Interrupting* and *finishing sentences* for another person are annoying maneuvers that provoke anger and distract the speaker. Interpreting another person's behavior will also stimulate resentment. An interpretation imputes some special motive or cause to the person's actions. For example, for the wife to say, "You hate all women, you . . . ," when she is angry at her husband's putdowns is a generalization of his behavior that goes beyond the immediate situation. *Silence*, passive *uncooperation, sabotage* of efforts, and enlisting the aid of children into *alliances* are all actions that provoke anger, resentment, and defensiveness. Even if a husband says, "Well my mother would have . . . ," he is using his mother as an ally in an attempt to control the situation.

The communication tactics outlined above are not all-inclusive; they are just the more commonly used ones. They all serve as attempts to control a situation. They provoke more defensiveness, alienate the other person(s), and ultimately have the same end—failure to achieve a satisfactory resolution.

If you really want to effect some change in your family system, then a number of rules of fair fighting are necessary. First, recognize that changing a system is a difficult job and will take some time. Second, recognize that *you control yourself and your actions*, not other people. You can change yourself directly, and others indirectly. Third, act with *integrity*. Dirty fighting discredits you even more than it does the other person. It shows that you are insecure and afraid and may not even love the person whom you attack. Think about what you want to communicate about yourself with your style. Do you want to be viewed as hostile and abusive, or as caring? If you do not care about the relationship, why bother even fighting? Why not just leave? Finally, communicate clearly and fight fair.

Fighting for change "fairly" involves a number of principles. These include:

1. Be *specific*. When you ask for some change, identify specific actions in terms of what, when, where, and how.

2. Ask for *one* change at a time. Asking for several changes at once will be confusing and distracting.

3. Talk in the *present*. Avoid digging up the past. We can behave—or change our behavior—only in the present. Learn from the past, but don't use it as a weapon.

4. When you describe the problem, do so in terms of *your side* of the interaction, *without blaming* others. Describe your *experience:* your feelings, your actions, your thoughts and patterns. For example, you talk about yourself when you say, "I feel scared that you don't love me anymore, especially when you rush out to work in the morning without giving me so much as a hug." In contrast, you blame the other person when you say, "You are such a cold s.o.b., only thinking about yourself when you leave in a hurry." To talk about yourself invites concern; to blame others invites defensiveness and attack.

5. State what *you* are willing to do about the situation. If in your talking you discover that your mate is preoccupied with some external pressures, then you may have to remind your mate of what you want. Asking doesn't make the response less valuable. It may be less romantic, but then again, romanticism is based on assumption and illusion.

6. When you ask others to do *more* for you, then indicate what you might do in return. Others are more likely to give when they are assured of receiving something. Set up an

exchange. One-sided requests seldom result in long-term change.

7. When you ask others to do *less*, you must explain the impact. If people's sarcastic remarks lead you to feel hurt, or their silence leaves you feeling left out or unloved, then it is important to tell them of your *reactions*. If people are given knowledge of your feelings and reactions to their actions, without being blamed for your reactions, then they have more information upon which to base any decision to change. Remember, others do not "make" you feel this or that.

8. Be *responsible* for your feelings and thoughts. When you feel angry, upset, disappointed, sad, happy, or tense, it is your thinking and history of experience that provoke that feeling. The other person did not "make" you angry. You *became* angry at some action of his. Another person might have become sad or anxious. It is fallacious thinking to say "You *make* me. . . ." Therefore, when introducing change and describing your experience, say "I feel . . . when. . . ."

9. Speak for yourself. Talk in the first person singular, "I." When asking for change, avoid prefacing your request with "We . . ." or "My mother and I feel . . ." in an attempt to create the illusion of power through an alliance or agreement. The implication of this illusory alliance is that the other person *must* agree. Without room for disagreement, there cannot be growth.

10. Talk about what you *like* and *dislike*. Let the other person know the specific details of what turns you on and what turns you off. Let the other person know who you are at this particular time.

11. *Update* people. People change over time, and if others operate on old impressions and information about what you like and dislike, then how will they know what to give you? The art of making a family a viable support system involves keeping other family members apprised of any changes.

12. *Clarify* communications and *complete* transactions. Many conflicts remain unresolved because people stop the conflict too soon, without completing transactions. Rather than walk off in a huff feeling victimized or resentful, stay around long enough for the transactions to be completed. Make sure the other person knows precisely what you think and feel. Remember, transac-

tions are not complete until both parties know and understand what the other person experiences.

13. View conflict as *affiliating.* It can lead to closeness. It is an opportunity to learn and to grow. Fighting for change can be constructive and creative, or destructive and deadly.

DEVELOPING A FAMILY SUPPORT SYSTEM

In a world filled with stress and change, it is vital to develop emotional support systems. Stress is easier to cope with when we feel that others are available to encourage us as we struggle. It is easier to ride out the turmoil of disappointments, conflicts, anxieties, and depressions when we know there are loved ones supporting us. Without these supports, it is usually more difficult to cope with stress. In fact, when our family is not only nonsupportive, but also discouraging, critical, hostile, or avoidant, our reactions to stress become more pronounced. Thus, it is imperative to encourage our families to be positively supportive.

The following strategies reflect the essential characteristics of families that cope well with stress:

1. Recognize the *signals* of inadequate family functioning. Once you accept the inadequacies, then you can change the way you live with your family.

2. Have a *family council.* Sit down with your entire family and talk about how you *communicate* and how you *operate.* Discuss the following and clarify your *roles* and *rules* about the roles:
   a. Decide who does what chores, and who is responsible for each aspect of running your household.
   b. Decide whether these roles are flexible.
   c. What is the process for changing roles?
   d. Decide who has the *right* to make a decision. Are decisions made by one person, or democratically, or by council?

3. Think about *how* you want to deal with *feelings.* Each family has unspoken rules about how and when feelings are

to be expressed and who has the right to express them. Under stress, emotions are evoked and must be dealt with. Stressful situations cannot be fully resolved until the feelings and tensions are discharged. Consider and discuss the following:

a. Is it okay for you to express your anger openly and directly (e.g., "I'm mad at you for embarrassing me")?

b. Is it safe to say that you are disappointed?

c. Is it legitimate to feel and express sadness? Is it okay for both male and female family members to do so?

d. Is it okay to get very excited when happy? Or must the atmosphere be subdued and "reasonable"?

e. Is it okay to be afraid or confused?

f. Is it safe to say "I love you" directly?

g. Is it safe to say "I hate you" without fear of punishment or retaliation?

h. Is it okay for men and women alike to have feelings without judgments being attached to the feelings? Some people believe that "Boys must not cry; only girls do that," or that "Little girls must be sugar and spice," which means they don't express anger. These beliefs are based upon judgments that certain feelings and their expressions are signs of "weakness," "badness," or "evil." When someone is angry to the point of hate, it means only that the person is very angry; it does not mean that he or she is possessed by the devil. Judgments and beliefs restrict experience.

Remember, feelings have a survival function—they mobilize us to cope and adapt, and they serve to release tension. If your rules restrict the expression of feelings, then you interfere with nature's way of letting go of tension—and with survival.

Families that adapt well to change express feelings directly and openly without judgments. The family members are also supportive and will tell each other that they care. Remember: Hugs don't hurt, they help.

4. Consider *growth-promoting attitudes:*
   a. Conflict can lead to *closeness.* It does not have to be a

threat or loss. Families that adapt well to change view conflict as affiliating—it leads family members to greater understanding and contact. Love and respect are enhanced when conflict is resolved.

b. Disagreement is an *opportunity* to *learn* about the unique viewpoints of other family members. Creative coping involves seeing as many options as possible. Poor coping usually results from seeing only selective options. Disagreement can offer you the chance to discover different options and solutions to problems.

c. Changes, conflicts, and crises are *opportunities* for personal *growth*. Instead of viewing life changes as only a threat of some loss, consider viewing them as chances to experiment with new situations. For example, consider the father who responds to his daughter's engagement by saying, "Terrific, I haven't lost a daughter; I've gained a son-in-law!" This father adapts well. The father who laments, "Oh, no. I've lost her to someone else. She won't want to see us any more," adapts poorly and creates more stress for himself.

To realize that we can cope effectively is to become more self-confident. Personal growth requires change and courage. It means developing individual and unique ways of adapting. Families that survive well allow room for growth and change of individual family members, even when the individual develops conflicting values, ideas, and behaviors. A family does not have to like what a member does, but if the family is to function well, there must be room for the family member to be different. A person cannot remain the same throughout life.

d. Assume full *responsibility* for your life. Don't blame others for what happens to you. No one "makes" you have the feelings and ideas that you have. They are all yours. If you are not getting the affection, attention, and encouragement you desire, then it is *your* job to ask for it. You may have to demand it so that other family members know of your wishes. Some people think: "If I have to ask for affection, then it's not real." Consider this: What if other people are assuming that you don't really want much affection because you seem so preoccupied? To say to yourself, "Well, they should know better!" is to play a mind game that shows your passivity and unwillingness to be responsible for your fate. People who actively make their wants and needs known are more likely to have them satisfied. If you are not for yourself, who will be?

e. Decide how much *intimacy* you really want. Decide how much you want to share your time, energy, and space. Decide how much you are willing to give to and care about other family members. The amount of caring you demonstrate will be closely related to how much you receive. Intimacy within a relationship takes on a unique characteristic: It is like a pie that seems to get bigger each time you take a bite. Families that cope well seem to feel more enriched each time a family member grows.

f. *Encourage* one another. Adaptive families seem to be able to encourage each family member irrespective of the turmoil and distress that must be weathered. Families that do not adapt well, that have a lot of illness, and whose members have severe emotional problems have an imbalance in the way they support one another. For example, one family member might say something supportive to another member, who is then negative in return. Functional families have a better balance in the way they are supportive.

Active encouragement and support involve active *listening*, *understanding*, and positive *expression of feelings*.

5. *Communicate clearly.*
   a. *Listen* carefully. Active listening means hearing what is said as it is intended. This means accepting a message without judging the message as "good" or "bad," "right" or "wrong."

b. Speak clearly and say what you mean. Send a message that is specific, with regard to time, place, context, and characteristics.

c. Make all parts of the message *congruent*. *What* you say should match *how* you say it. Be aware of your tone of voice, facial expressions, and physical mannerisms.

d. *Clarify* what you heard. Ask the sender of the message if what you heard was accurate.

e. Complete transactions. When a topic is broached, continue to discuss it until each of you has heard and understood what the other has said and intended and until both of you are satisfied. Letting conversations stop midstream will not accomplish resolution of conflicts—they will smolder until someone erupts from the tension.

f. *Fight fair*. Request change, ask for what you want, and act with integrity.

Creative coping and successful adaptation to stress will be enhanced when your family is with you and behind you. People can weather the worst of storms when they feel that others care. Coping and caring go hand in hand.

Developing positive, growth-promoting attitudes, then, can contribute to more healthful and honest family life—and lessen stress in the process. Similar effects can be achieved on the job as well. Successful coping can reduce the stresses in the work environment, while clearer and more positive communication can lessen tensions generated by personal interactions. Clearly, effective and appropriate coping forms a significant part of any program to reduce and control stress.

It should be emphasized, however, that coping—either at home or on the job—is not the last word as far as stress is concerned. Coping is basically a technique for stress reduction—not an instrument for control over stress. Coping alleviates the stress reaction and reduces its physical and psychological impact. Other techniques, however, can promise even more. You can gain control over the stress reaction itself, eliminating it in some cases, turning it to your own positive use in others. The key to such power over stress lies in the mind itself, particularly in the power of the mind's cognitive processes to determine what is or is not a stressor. The role of cognition in overcoming stress is the subject of the next chapter.

CHAPTER 9

COGNITIVE STYLES AND STRESS-PRONENESS

The secret of power over stress lies in your ability to think. Actually, there is nothing new about this insight. In the 17th century, Shakespeare's Hamlet said, "There is nothing good nor bad but that thinking makes it so." Fifty years later, René Descartes, the French philosopher and mathematical genius, echoed the same point when he described the source of certain knowledge in the Latin phrase *cogito, ergo sum*, "I think, therefore I am." In recent decades, however, psychologists have begun to specify the actual processes by which the mind imposes its own order upon "reality." These scientists have revealed the cognitive processes by which we experience, organize, store, and understand the information that constitutes our world.

At all times, we are constantly taking in information through our senses. Once such information is sensed, it is transmitted along sensory pathways of the nervous system to the brain (or mind), where the information is then processed. During this processing, an appraisal or evaluation of the information takes place as the incoming data are sent through a complex of neural pathways. That appraisal is, in turn, subject to an even higher level of monitoring as well. The experience is judged according to its safety or danger for the organism. As we have seen in Chapter 1, an appraisal of "danger" can trigger a full-blown stress reaction. A judgment of "safety," on the other hand, keeps your whole system in balance, or in homeostasis.

This process of appraisal is neither automatic nor arbitrary.

Instead, each person seems to develop his or her own unique pattern, or style, of judgment. The creation of this style of appraisal begins with conception and is constantly enriched by experience throughout our lives. Over the years, a complex of different experiences are woven together and form a constellation of characteristic attitudes and beliefs. These characteristic ways of thinking form, in turn, each person's cognitive styles—or patterns of mental appraisal. In a potentially stress-inducing situation, possible stressors are matched against these characteristic patterns. Events that conform with the person's cognitive expectations are judged harmless; while those that conflict are judged dangerous, and the stress reaction is subsequently triggered.

A useful way of picturing this process is to imagine the mind as a vast library, packed with volumes containing our ideas, beliefs, attitudes, and the like. These books span a vast range of subjects: self, life, family, friends, relationships, the world, the body, love, death, religion, work, play, and almost infinitely on. Indeed, the holdings of this mental library are virtually endless. When new information is brought in from the senses, it is checked against the library's holdings and then evaluated in terms of how it relates to what the mental library already contains.

A person might hold the belief, for example, that self-worth is measured by the amount of dollars earned. Past experience and observation of others have allowed the mind to create this idea, and repeated instances have confirmed it, figuratively filling volumes in the mental library with this idea. A new situation now occurs in the world outside, and the sensory networks convey to the mind the possibility of undertaking a new job. How much, the mind demands on the basis of its belief and past experience, does the new job pay? The answer is then evaluated in terms of the person's attitudes and expectations. An increase in salary conforms with the deeply held belief that self-worth is measured in dollars and cents. If the new job pays more than the present one, the appraisal would be favorable. The new data would conform to the information and beliefs previously on file. Should the newly offered post pay less, however, there would be a problem. Accepting the new job might conflict with the person's conception of self-worth because the salary is not high enough. Taking the new position might actually lower self-esteem and set off a stress reaction as well. Based upon this judgment, the person might well reject the new post and continue to search for a job that offered pay high enough to match the assumptions stored in his mental library.

This image of cognitive appraisal as comparing new input to the contents of a vast mental library also helps to explain a phenomenon of central importance for understanding stress: cognitive dissonance. Based upon the work of the psychologist Leon Festinger, this concept describes what happens when a person encounters situations that do not match the beliefs and attitudes stored in his or her mental library. Festinger has observed that any two elements we become cognizant of—beliefs, ideas, or whatever—can be described as consonant, dissonant, or irrelevant to one another. That is, the elements may match each other, disagree with each other, or simply not relate to one another. Exactly which possibility proves to be the case will depend on cognitive appraisal. Or, to put the matter another way, the way we judge the world depends on the contents of our mental libraries.

As an example, consider a situation in which what you experience agrees with what you had expected. You might, for instance, consider yourself an effective public speaker. When you think of making a speech in front of others, you typically feel confident and able, and you have had a variety of earlier experiences that have confirmed this impression. As far as this subject is concerned, your mental library is well stocked with positive volumes. Imagine further that you have just given a speech as a part of your job, and your audience has reacted enthusiastically. Because their reaction matches your own expectation, you will be able to accept and appreciate their compliments—and to praise yourself for a job well done. Furthermore, this matching between your expectation and the audience's actual reaction will be self-affirming and positive and will contribute to homeostasis, or balance, within the organism that is you. Such a positive, consonant experience will make you feel good about yourself and will not set off any kind of stress reaction.

Different expectations, however, can lead to very different—and far more stressful—results. Assume for a moment that instead of regarding yourself as a fine public speaker, you had always believed the opposite. You were a terrible speaker, you told yourself, and nobody ever liked any of your speeches. In this case, your mental library would be crammed with negative messages. Imagine further that you had to give a speech and the audience reacted enthusiastically, pressing forward afterward to offer congratulations and heartily praising you for your efforts.

At first glance, this might seem like something wonderful. After all those years of negative feelings, you have apparently just delivered a wonderful speech! Unfortunately, things are not so simple. You have that whole library of negative thoughts to contend with. As a result, you experience dissonance, or mismatch, when your mind tries to compare the previous beliefs and experiences stored in its mental library with this recent event of the successful speech. In such a mismatch, the past tends to win out. The mind, forced to choose between past belief and present reality, opts in favor of the past. The end result is *cognitive dissonance*, the rejection of authentic present experience because it does not conform to one's cognitive expectations. Thus, when the admiring members of the audience press close to murmur their compliments, you might try to explain away your apparent success as a speaker: "Oh, it wasn't anything really. Anybody could have done it. I'm not really a very good speaker."

This sort of verbal discounting is a common way of dealing with cognitive dissonance. When your mental expectation and the reality of the situation do not match, the most likely response is to try to rationalize or explain away what has just happened. In dissonant situations, the tendency is to bank upon the contents of the mental library—even to the point of denying any reality in events that, at least to others, seem very real. Some further examples of this process of explaining away dissonance are presented in Table 1, which draws examples from a variety of spheres of influences that may operate in your life. In each case,

TABLE 1

Examples of Dissonance

Sphere of influence	Belief	Feedback or experience	Negative response
The body	"I am ugly."	"You look great today."	"He's a poor judge of character."
Achievement	"I can't succeed."	"Congratulations, you're hired."	"I sure was lucky."
Self-esteem	"I can't be worthwhile."	"We really appreciate your work."	"They're new. They must have missed my mistakes."
Feelings	"Men shouldn't cry."	Eyes begin to water at the thought of parent's death.	"I'll think about work and forget about all this sentimental nonsense."
Life	"Life must be a constant struggle for survival."	You get a job with little effort.	"It must have been a fluke; it was too easy."
Play	"Only children have the luxury to play."	Your spouse starts to tickle you in an effort to have some playful contact.	"Stop that. You're so immature."
Work	"You have to keep your nose to the grindstone to get anywhere in this world."	Boss tells you to take 2 weeks off to relax.	"Well, at least I can catch up on all those projects at home. I wonder if he wants me around anymore?"

an accepted belief is compared to a dissonant, or contradictory, experience. These are then followed by a "negative response," some verbal formulation that copes with the dissonance by denying the recent experience and affirming the earlier belief.

Dissonance does not have to be positive, however. That is, your expectation may be favorable and the reality quite the opposite. You might have an unrealistic, even conceited, opinion about yourself as a speaker, for example. When you are called upon to speak, though, your audience may react with yawns, restlessness, and other signs of disapproval. Here, too, you would experience dissonance as your internal conception of yourself (your mental library's contents) fails to match with your experience. Once again, the likely response is to favor the expectation over the reality. In this case, however, your responses will be hostile and directed against the unsympathetic audience: "What's wrong with those people? Don't they know anything? Why am I wasting my time with them anyhow?"

Regardless of its exact form, dissonance always extracts an additional cost in the form of stress, because whenever the organism experiences a mismatch between its expectations and the actual reality that it experiences, the result is a stress reaction. If this dissonance is not coped with (for example, by some form of verbal denial), then the stress reaction persists. Clearly, cognitive appraisal itself can be a source of stress! Conversely, agreement between our cognitive assumptions (the ideas, beliefs, and attitudes stored in our mental libraries) and our experience is positive and maintains personal homeostasis.

These relationships are spelled out in the cognitive appraisal chart (Fig. 11). As this chart indicates, the contents of our mental libraries inform the cognitive appraisal that either triggers or rejects the stress reaction. How we think, and how we have organized our past experiences, combine to form the foundation against which future events are to be judged. Events that match up to our past appraisals of ourselves are welcomed; those that contradict are explained away—and trigger off stress responses in the meanwhile.

Another way of putting this is to say that we welcome new information that conforms to the style and content of our cog-

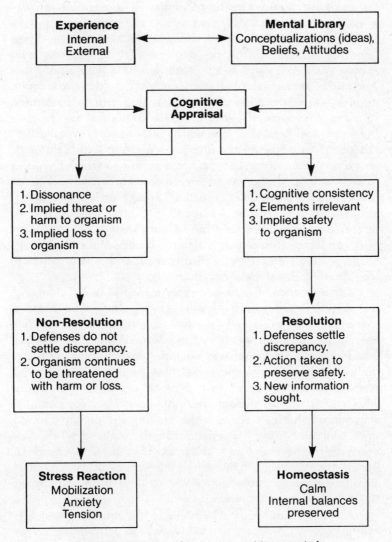

FIGURE 11. Sequence of events in cognitive appraisal.

nitive appraisal. We accept and appreciate data that confirm our vision of the world. On the other hand, we deny or actually reject information that disagrees with our previous assumptions.

This perspective has been confirmed in a fascinating experiment performed by the psychologist Richard Lazarus, who showed various groups a film dealing with rituals among the Australian aborigines. The contents of the film were quite graphic—showing adolescent circumcision rituals performed with crude implements—and generated intense stress in viewing audiences. Lazarus compared the responses of several different groups by showing the film to each group with a different sound track. By testing, Lazarus had determined which members of each viewing group would tend to defend themselves against unpleasant or dissonant information through each of two different defense mechanisms: denial and intellectualization. That is, by the time he showed the film, Lazarus knew which members of the audience would deal with stressful dissonance by simply claiming they weren't aware of it (denial) and which members would rationalize it away (intellectualization).

The brilliance of Lazarus's experiment lies in his changing the sound track for each viewing group. One group heard a sound track that explained the ritual in terms of denial, another heard a sound track that utilized intellectualization, yet another heard a sound track that was neutral. Lazarus found, interestingly enough, that people were most comfortable when the sound track matched their own personal cognitive style. Those who tended to deny dissonant or unpleasant data, for example, experienced the least stress while hearing the denying sound track. The same thing happened for intellectualizers when they heard the intellectualizing sound track. The message seems clear: People are most comfortable when the world conforms to their cognitive preconceptions as well as to their cognitive coping styles (psychological defenses).

Another factor needs to be added to this equation, however: People experience cognitive dissonance to varying degrees. This variance is due, in part, to the importance of the belief or attitude that has been called into question. If, for example, being a good public speaker is a pleasant but not terribly significant aspect of your life, then getting a negative reaction from an audience might be irritating or confusing, but little else. On the other hand, if you are a speech professor or a championship orator, then a poor audience response could be devastating.

Another factor to be considered is the number of elements that are discrepant in the situation. A vague restlessness in the audience, for example, might cause little or no concern if the speech is followed by warm congratulations and appreciative comments from a variety of persons. Such restlessness might cause far more concern, however, if it is combined with other evident signs of displeasure—yawning, people leaving early, lack of applause at the end, and the absence of friendly comments afterward.

The final element in determining the impact of cognitive dissonance is more subjective. Cognitive attitudes that are rigid and negative tend to create far more problems—and stress— than those that are more flexible and positive. A person who has a strongly negative view of himself or herself as a public speaker, for example, will tend to reject any positive feedback more strongly and absolutely than would a person who had a more moderate or ambiguous attitude toward speaking in public. Similarly, a person who found the thought of succeeding at public speaking terribly threatening would tend to react far more strongly to positive feedback than would someone who was at least willing to consider the possibility that he or she could deliver a decent speech on occasion.

Taken together, these aspects specify the kind of personality that is prone to stress because of cognitive factors. Rigid beliefs (particularly negative ones), when combined with situations that are perceived as personally important, are stress-producing. This stressful situation is increased further when the number of elements appearing in the discrepant event is large. A minor dissonance is tolerable, but a major disagreement between one's beliefs and the present reality can only lead to more stress. Clearly, differences in cognitive styles can be stress-producing.

TYPE A VS. TYPE B BEHAVIOR

The role of cognition in producing stress can be seen in many ways. One of the most revealing involves a model that has been used in research on personality styles—a model that distinguishes two extremes of behavior: "Type A" and "Type B." This model was originated by two physicians, Dr. Meyer Friedman and Dr. Ray Rosenman. The model can best be described by looking at the way in which two people with radically different cognitive styles react to the same situation. Imagine, if you will, two different drivers about to pass through the same intersection:

Ann is a sales representative for a major computer company, on her way to a very important business meeting. If she plays her cards right, Ann believes, she should close a half-million dollar sale—complete with a ten-thousand dollar commission for her! This morning, however, Ann left the office a few minutes later than she had anticipated and, as a result, found herself having to drive slightly faster to catch up. When she entered a busy intersection in the middle of the city, another car raced ahead of her and cut her off. Ann reacted instantly, slamming on the brakes and seizing the steering wheel. "You idiot!" she fumed, and pounded on the horn. As her anger boiled, her pulse began to accelerate as well—up over twenty points. Ann took a deep breath in an effort to calm herself. After all, she did not want to look frazzled or ruin her makeup. "I must regain my composure," she thought to herself.

The traffic, however, refused to cooperate. After the car in front of her had cut in, the entire lane of traffic had stopped dead in the middle of the block. It was nearly noon and the cars were moving at a snail's pace—if at all. Ann searched for a way to escape and maneuver around the traffic jam, but there was no path out. She could feel her tension building. Her heart skipped a few beats, her breathing became shallow, her entire body tensed. Finally, panic set in as she glanced at her watch, pale and frantic.

Internally, she began a frantic dialogue, and a full-blown stress reaction was already well under way: "Oh, my God," Ann thought, "I'm late." She kept looking at her watch over and over as the minutes slipped past. "This damn traffic isn't moving. What am I going to do?" Ann began to worry that she would lose the deal and its commission. She became flooded with negative thoughts as the tension mounted. Her stomach knotted up while her blood pressure rose in response to her negative thoughts about the situation.

Ann's internal dialogue continued to spiral downward, thinking of how her boss would be furious and all the problems that she—and other women salespersons—had to face without such additional traumas as this! "What will I say to him?" she thought, "What will I do?" All the while, the cars crammed in front of her moved with an agonizing slowness. The longer they took, the more stressed Ann became.

Not that this kind of stress is anything new to Ann. At the ripe old age of 39, she is already a stress veteran. She has gone from normal health several years before to recurrent problems with insomnia, indigestion, and general, free-floating anxiety attacks. Sometimes Ann simply sits at her desk, yet she still experiences severe energy and mood swings. Sometimes she even experiences cardiac arrhythmias that her doctor has told her are "stress-related." His advice of "Don't take things so seriously" was quickly lost in Ann's fears of an early death. Her cardiac symptoms are actually benign—just a warning signal—but she seems unwilling to alter her style in response to that warning. In time, the symptoms may well become pathological.

Ann's appraisal of her situation is only one way of looking at the situation, however. Consider the very different reaction of Ben, a vice-president for a major corporation also on his way to an important meeting. While not quite as much money may hang in the balance for Ben as it does for Ann, it is clearly very important for him to arrive on time as well. Should he fail to show, his job could well hang in the balance.

Ben begins his journey at about the same time as Ann does. He unlocks his car, settles into the seat, and buckles up the seat belt. Ben takes a deep breath before he turns over the ignition; unlike Ann, he has allowed himself plenty of extra time to reach his destination. Once in traffic, Ben too is cut off by someone who pulls in front of him. Like Ann, he too manages to hit the brakes and avoid a collision. Unlike Ann, however, he breathes a sigh of relief and thinks about how dangerous the other driver is. That poor guy, he thinks, is really in a hell of a hurry. He's going to get hurt if he doesn't slow down! Although Ben's body began to react stressfully when the man in front cut in, the nature of Ben's interpretation of that event has short-circuited the stress reaction. Unlike Ann, who was caught up in anger and its resultant stress, Ben has dealt with the situation effectively, and it no longer has any impact on him. He waits in traffic, listening to classical music on his car radio.

Music or not, Ben is soon confronted with the same slow, practically immobile traffic. No matter how positive his attitude, the cars in front of him simply refuse to budge. Here, too, Ben's reaction is different from Ann's. Instead of becoming increasingly frustrated, Ben examines the situation carefully and finds an appropriate course of action. Since it will obviously take him some time to reach the meeting, Ben decides to pull over at the first opportunity and make a phone call. Once he has done this, Ben is relaxed once more because the meeting has begun on schedule with the understanding that he will arrive as soon as he can.

It is well worth noting that Ben's health is excellent for a 53-year-old corporation executive. He has been rising slowly but surely toward the top of his corporation, and he has enjoyed every step along the way. Ben has managed to be successful without jeopardizing his health. Unlike Ann, who is experiencing cardiac symptoms at a relatively early age, Ben is pleased that his doctor praises him for being such an excellent specimen for his years.

Ann and Ben indicate two very different ways of reacting to a similar, potentially stressful situation. Their differences, however, are not accidental. Ann and Ben illustrate differences that arise out of profoundly diverse cognitive styles. Ann shows some of the potential consequences of being a Type A, while Ben illustrates an attitude more typical of the Type B.

The Type A cognitive style, for example, has characteristic behaviors, attitudes, and emotional reactions. Each of these is grounded in some underlying beliefs that drive these behaviors. Those who illustrate Type A manifest the following cognitive patterns and behaviors:

1. Has an intense sense of time urgency, as well as an impatience with the rate at which most events take place.

2. Has a strong *competitive* drive. He thinks that he "must" get ahead at all costs and feels driven to win.

3. Experiences easily aroused *hostility*. He tends to blame others or circumstances for what goes wrong. He places the responsibility for error outside himself.

4. Does not take quiet time to do nothing but relax. He thinks he must always be active and feels vaguely guilty when not accomplishing something.

5. Sets unrealistic deadlines. He seldom plans his time realistically.

6. Has a tendency to evaluate himself by the number of accomplishments. The number of accomplishments is viewed as

some index of self-worth. The more he accomplishes, the more he is worth.

7. Desires the *approval* of *superiors,* not peers. Criticism from a superior can be shattering.

8. Strives to get ahead *materially.* Material objects seem to "prove" or validate accomplishments and are another measure of self-esteem.

If you can imagine this constellation, then you might imagine that the Type A person is a very difficult person to live with. Type A people are hard-driving, aggressive, hostile, critical, and very demanding. They seek approval more than affection, and will sacrifice family and relationships in order to succeed. They feel frustrated when their goals are thwarted, and they will blame others or external circumstances for their frustrations and losses. Material possessions seem to demonstrate something more than a sense of accomplishment. Success, as demonstrated by rising to the top of a corporate ladder, or by having all the material goods anyone could want, seems to be some rite of passage. They strive while being driven in a vain effort to prove something to themselves. It is almost as though they must prove they are grown up or are intact. They certainly do not know how to relax. Even when there is no pressure to produce, such as on a vacation, they create their own internal pressure through guilt. Coronary artery disease, eternal frustration, and depression are the prices for this form of behavior.

But are you Type A? Do you create stress for yourself by following this particular cognitive style? The answer depends on how you respond to the following series of questions. Please note that the most prominent characteristic of the Type A personality is time urgency. If you are Type A, you will find yourself being impatient with the pace at which most events take place. This tendency may be further revealed if:

1. You find it difficult to refrain from hurrying the speech of others.

2. You attempt to finish the sentence of the other person speaking to you before he can finish.

3. You sit on the edge of your seat when you talk.

4. You become unduly irritated or enraged when a car ahead of you moves at a pace that you consider too slow.

5. You find it anguishing to wait in line or to wait your turn to be seated in a restaurant.

6. You become impatient with yourself when you are obliged to do some repetitious task (e.g., wash dishes, fill out forms). These tasks are necessary, but take you away from doing things that you really want to do.

7. You find yourself hurrying your own reading, always attempting to obtain condensations or summaries of truly interesting and worthwhile literature.

8. You find it difficult to "make the time" to take care of everyday necessities such as getting your hair cut.

The Type A's urgency about time generalizes to the issue of productivity and efficiency. The Type A person attempts to get more and more done in as little time as possible. Typically, the Type A will engage in "polyphasic" thought or action. Do you find yourself striving to do two or more things at the same time? For example, do you read while eating, or shave while driving, or read while half-listening to the stereo or television? Or do you try to listen to another person's speech while continuing to think on an irrelevant subject? If you do, you create internal tension and pressure. And if some event intrudes in this polyphasic activity, then the Type A becomes unduly frustrated and may explode at the intruder.

The Type A personality will attempt to schedule more and more in less and less time. In doing so, he will make fewer and fewer allowances for unforeseen contingencies. As in the traffic scene described earlier, Ann did not leave any extra time for traffic jams, thereby risking being late and frustrated.

The result of this striving for super efficiency and productivity leads to a preoccupation with the self. The Type A is typically egocentric and focused inward. The self-preoccupation leads to the tendency to ignore the environment. For example, you may be a Type A if you no longer observe more important, interesting, or lovely objects in your environment. Upon leaving a strange store or office, can you recall what was in it? If not, you are not observing well and may be preoccupied.

When a true Type A person meets another Type A, an interesting interaction frequently takes place. Type A's do not feel compassion for one another; instead, they compete. They tend to feel compelled to challenge each other. Each competes against the other as though they were enemies. Type A's lock horns in a deathlike struggle to win at any cost. Domination and success are foremost in their minds. Did you ever see two Type A's play tennis or racquet ball? They are not engaging in relaxing exercise; they are fighting to win. Each point becomes a serious matter. The Type A person can drop dead with a coronary while doing exercises presumed to build cardiovascular resiliency. The competitive striving (e.g., "I *must* run this mile under seven minutes, or I won't be in shape," he tells himself) can be with self or others. In either case, it creates an internal pressure that can transform a healthful activity into a destructive one.

The Type A person is clearly a stress-prone person. The matrix of behaviors, feelings, thoughts, and beliefs that characterize this personality type creates an almost continuous state of internal tension and stress. For example, the Type A person will take a vacation, but will experience guilt when doing "nothing" but relaxing. Relaxation is considered unproductive. This phenomenon was once brought home to me when a professor came back from a weekend in the woods only to exclaim: "I had a great weekend. I caught up on my reading. I read four books and eight journals." The Type A belief that "doing nothing but relaxing is a waste of time" generates tension when a person might be resting or has the opportunity to relax.

Type A's feel driven to achieve, accomplish, succeed, and, above all, win. They are driven while they strive, and typically hold the belief that "I must achieve and accomplish something worthwhile in order for me to feel worthwhile as a person." The Type A also thinks that "I am worthwhile according to how many accomplishments I complete." A single major project well done is not equivalent to several minor projects done fairly well. They are driven by the belief that "I am in control when I win." Obstacles, delays, and intrusions are experienced as major setbacks and elicit great frustration and anger. This type of thinking can drive up one's blood pressure.

The entire belief system of the Type A person restricts his

or her experience of life. The beliefs do not allow for flexibility, error, or even enjoyment without tension. It is no surprise that the Type A is most disturbed when he feels out of control. A simple traffic jam, or having to wait in a long line at a bank, can evoke intense frustration and helplessness. This perceived loss of control leads to stress reactions with no discharge of the tension. The tension is trapped in the body. Such a continuous series of stress reactions can lead to coronary artery disease for the Type A. The cardiovascular system cannot tolerate such chronic arousal without tension release.

Since this original research was published, a great deal of controversy has arisen in the medical field. Some physicians reject the Type A phenomenon as a factor in coronary artery disease, but the research has been validated in several medical research centers around the United States. The state of California has now mandated that if a fireman or policeman has a heart attack on or off the job, it is considered job-related and hence compensable under the Workers' Compensation Laws. These professions are considered stress-producing, just as the Type A personality is stress-prone. These professions force people into situations where there is time urgency and pressure to "win"; it may be a matter of life or death when a policeman or fireman makes an error. These professions create Type A thinking.

Dr. Friedman has been doing a treatment–research project with Type A's who have already had a coronary to see whether some modification of this syndrome can yield longer life and fewer repeat coronaries. In a personal interview with the author, Dr. Friedman said, "I can tell which group leader is being effective according to the cholesterol levels of the group members!" Although the research is only in its second year, he had observed that effective group therapy would lead to a lowering of cholesterol levels. The group therapy situations not only taught more adaptive behaviors, but also offered the group members the opportunity to vent their frustrations on a regular weekly basis. Bottled-up tensions can destroy us.

Unlike Type A personalities, in which the cognitive style produces a stressful and time-driven person, there is another extreme as well: Type B. As we shall see later, persons whose cognitive and personal styles fit this pattern are healthier and are psychologically more flexible than Type A's. Type B's may cope better with stress. In fact, Type B's may even seem to thrive in the face of stress!

Type B persons are free of time urgency, but can respond to time demands when realistically desired. Such people are flexible and respond to each situation without a preconceived belief about how they "should" handle it. These people enjoy vacations and are able to do "nothing but relax." They are not driven to compare themselves to peers, nor do they count the number of their achievements. Type B's derive self-worth from following up on life goals that transcend social and economic success. They do not measure their success through materialistic acquisitions as Type A's tend to do.

Since they are flexible and treat situations separately, they are more creative in their approach to coping and problem-solving. Whereas Type A's are externally governed, Type B's tend to be governed by their own internal needs. They are not rendered helpless when not in control. Therefore, Type B's are less easily frustrated, and even when frustrated, they accept the situation more realistically.

Overall, Type B persons are characterized by a relaxed demeanor. They are not driven. Their general characteristics include a facial expression of relaxation, calm, and quiet attentiveness, a gentle handshake, a moderate to slow pace of walking, and a mellow, low-volume voice. In contrast to the Type A's clipped speech, Type B's responses are often lengthy and rambling. They rarely interrupt a speaker, will not hurry the speaker or finish his or her sentences, and will sit back and listen attentively. Type B's seldom clench their fists or point a finger to emphasize their speech. Hostility or sighing is rarely observed. They are often calm to the point of speaking in a monotone. They make excellent listeners and are observant of their environment.

Type B's are less stress-prone because they are more *flexible* and *realistic*. They are not restricted by beliefs such as "I am worthwhile only when I succeed." Type B's can accept mistakes and can view them as opportunities to learn. Type A's view mistakes as defeats. Instead of operating according to a rigid set of beliefs into which they must force their experiences, Type B's live by their experience. They are often successful and live long enough to enjoy their success. They strive for accomplishment when they decide to, not because they "must." They are therefore in control even when events are not fully under their control. Life's vicissitudes, the good and the bad, are viewed as challenges and opportunities, not roadblocks. Type B's can roll with the punches and cope more creatively.

Friedman's and Rosenman's research not only revealed that Type B's have fewer heart attacks, but also implied that their quality of life was better than that of Type A's. Interestingly, a Harvard psychiatrist, Dr. George Vaillant, found that working professional men who were successful in their careers were similar to Type B's. Although his research is not a rigorously based one, Dr. Vaillant drew observations from hundreds of hours of interview data. He studied 95 Harvard men who became lawyers, doctors, teachers, businessmen, architects, bankers, and other types of professionals. The most successful were not hard-driving, competitive, and aggressive as Type A's are; instead, they were characterized by a relaxed warmth that made the interviewer glad to have known them.

A very distinctive constellation of characteristics and behaviors typified the successful professionals. They were calm and secure and possessed a basic trust in life and people in general. They enjoyed and embraced life's challenges without being driven to control the external world. These men enjoyed play without guilt, could let go on vacations, and made full commitments to relationships. They not only used relationships for expanded growth, but also enjoyed the basic functions of life (e.g., eating, sleeping, sex). Basic functions were not viewed as intrusions or a "waste of time" as Type A's are prone to see them. Successful professionals viewed conflict as a challenge and were divergent in their thinking.

Dr. Vaillant saw a different picture with the less successful men. They were driven at their work, and at the expense of family relationships. They were prone to worry about their work and life even while on vacation. These men felt conflict between work and play; while engaging in one, they thought of the other. Anxiety and depression were common among them, and they avoided conflict, which was seen as a roadblock. They often abused alcohol and medications, and they tended to isolate themselves. Men who were unsuccessful typically had a higher incidence of illness later in life, more days of hospitalization, and more failure at work. Like the Type A, they were serious and coped poorly. They seemed to engage in a life-and-death struggle in living.

Although Dr. Vaillant's research takes a form different from that of Drs. Rosenman and Friedman, a theme emerges. Certain constellations of behaviors and attitudes converge to imply that there are "personality types" that appear to be stress-prone. They are more prone to illness, and the quality of their lives seems to suffer. They adapt poorly. They strive but do not thrive.

My own observations in clinical practice confirm the observations described above. When confronted with the research, my Type A patients have typically asked: "If it's a matter of 'personality,' then how is it possible to change?" This question has often been a rationalization for not changing. It has been my clinical experience that most Type A's do not want to change their personalities, but may be willing to consider some practical ways of reducing tension. Change is viewed as a threat because they think their way to success is the "right" one. The Type A is uncomfortable in attempting relaxation exercises, but is often pragmatic in his approach to problems.

There are some practical operational changes that can help a Type A take the pressure off in everyday life. They might learn to allow more time in their scheduling to provide for unforeseen intrusions and demands. They might learn to complete all assignments before going on a vacation so they can leave the office at home. They could schedule time for recreational activities on a regular basis just as they schedule their work week. Type A's might avoid situations that involve waiting in line and simply have someone else take care of the necessary chores for them. They can develop tension-release activities through exercise, and might even change their dietary habits as suggested earlier in this book. These practical changes can help reduce tension, but they may not release the frustration and hostility that generate most of the internal pressure. One must deal with the thinking patterns, the attitudes and beliefs, that govern their behavior in order to successfully transform the Type A behavior patterns into more adaptive ones that do not lead to illness.

STRESS-PRONE PERSONALITIES

Put simply, some cognitive styles produce stress, while other styles reduce or even eliminate it. This observation leads to two questions: First, how do we tell the difference between stress-prone and stress-resistant styles? Second, if we discover that our styles are in fact stress-prone, what can we do to make ourselves more resistant to stress? Let us examine the first question here. The answer to the second question will be the subject matter of the next chapter.

Stress-prone personalities can be described in many ways. The distinction between Type A and Type B behavior, for example, is a useful way of describing a particular stress-prone style (and a stress-resistant one as well). Similarly, cognitive dissonance can serve as a measure of one's susceptibility to stress. Rigid, negative cognitive styles that generate a good deal of dissonance also create a lot of stress. There are some other ways of indicating stress-prone personality styles that may be useful. Several are discussed below.

One approach is to identify stress-proneness by the presence of stress-related illnesses. For instance, people who suffer migraine headache are usually stress-prone. They often have difficulty falling asleep, their arms and legs feel cool, they may experience nausea, and they are sensitive to light and visual aberrations. They may be rigid or narrow in their thinking and frequently have a desperate desire for approval by others so they can fend off a sense of personal inadequacy. (Interestingly, migraines tend to occur on weekends or during other leisure time; this may be due to a sense of guilt about not being productive or active.) Migraine sufferers often have trouble letting go and experiencing, and tend to contain their anger and resentments. They often even withdraw from emotional involvements—a characteristic that they share, according to some research, with unsuccessful businessmen.

Another stress-prone style is seen among those who develop ulcerative colitis, or ulcers in the intestines. Such persons tend to have "obsessive–compulsive" personality traits. These include neatness, orderliness, punctuality, conscientiousness, indecision, obstinacy, and conformity. They tend to worry and brood and are very vigilant. These people are usually easily hurt, and are constantly alert to the disapproval and criticism of others. They are typically either very dependent in relationships or avoid them altogether. The ultimate impact of these characteristics is poor coping and unsuccessful adaptation leading to disease of the bowel. The tensions created by the worry, vigilance, and rigidity of behaviors are too much for the body. Biological breakdown is inevitable.

Stress-proneness may also be signaled by a variety of other maladies, ranging from stomach ulcers to skin rash. (Many of these conditions were discussed in earlier chapters.) Illness is not the only clue, however, that your personality style might be causing you to experience stress. Behavior too can signal stress-proneness.

A straightforward example would be the depressed person who often broods or feels blue. Such a person feels helpless, and hopeless about life. He is pessimistic about the outcome of events as well. Such depressed persons do not recover quickly from pressure or tension, and they often have difficulty sleeping, which contributes to a constant state of low energy and fatigue. Some researchers even believe that such people are also cancer-prone.

Another instance would be the person who is constantly anxious or fearful. Such people seem to worry about everything, and their nervous habits (nail- or lip-biting, finger-tapping, nervous coughing, or twitches) are enough to make others feel uncomfortable too. Even when things go right, these stress-prone persons worry and fear the worst. They feel helpless and out of control, and assume that more problems are waiting "just around the corner." Such people often cope poorly and tend to have physical problems relating to the gastrointestinal tract.

There are many other ways in which stress-prone styles

	Never	Seldom	Occasionally	Frequently	Very frequently
1. Do you have self-destructive health habits (overeating, drinking, smoking, compulsive exercise)?	N	S	O	F	VF
2. Do you find yourself questioning whether you want to live?	N	S	O	F	VF
3. Are your goals for work, family, and play unidentified or not very clear?	N	S	O	F	VF
4. Do you think of yourself as not worthwhile?	N	S	O	F	VF
5. Do you feel vaguely guilty when you lie around and do nothing but relax?	N	S	O	F	VF
6. Do life changes seem like burdens or obstacles (as opposed to positive challenges)?	N	S	O	F	VF
7. Are you pessimistic about life, the world, and yourself?	N	S	O	F	VF
8. Do you feel as though you are not in control of your life?	N	S	O	F	VF
9. Do you feel conflict and tension in your work, relationships, and play?	N	S	O	F	VF
10. When things go wrong all at once, do you feel overwhelmed?	N	S	O	F	VF
11. Do you feel trapped or tense when unforeseen intrusions occur?	N	S	O	F	VF
12. Do you find yourself doggedly defending your ideas and beliefs when others present divergent ways of viewing a situation?	N	S	O	F	VF
13. Do you blame others or external phenomena for what goes wrong with your life?	N	S	O	F	VF
14. Do you avoid taking responsibility for both your successes and your failures?	N	S	O	F	VF
15. Do you think of stress as something to be rid of or to overcome?	N	S	O	F	VF
16. Do you tend to be serious, unhappy, or gloomy?	N	S	O	F	VF
17. Are you tense in the face of life's everyday vicissitudes?	N	S	O	F	VF

FIGURE 12. Rating chart for stress-prone personality characteristics.

might be identified or described. Those already mentioned should be sufficient to give an idea of how diverse the possibilities can be. By this point, you may well be asking yourself whether your style is stress-prone. To gain a better understanding of yourself and your own personality style—and whether or not you are predisposed to stress—answer the questions in the chart in Fig. 12. Circle the answer that best describes your average frequency of experiencing each feeling or attitude listed.

If you find that most of your answers are in the "Frequently" or "Very frequently" category, then you may be stress-prone. These answers imply that your attitudes, beliefs, and coping styles may actually create tension for you. Stress-proneness is not simply a matter of fixed personality types; it is a matter of *how* we think, feel, and behave. And these ways of adapting are learned, which implies that you can learn new, more functional ways of surviving. In fact, you can go beyond survival and learn to thrive. The last chapter is devoted to just that—building stress-resistant habits and attitudes. There is life beyond stress.

CHAPTER 10

BEYOND SURVIVAL

FROM COPING TO THRIVING

It appears to be a typical Monday for Chuck. Since nine o'clock he has seen one client after another, sandwiching phone calls in between, and managing two quick consultations with his partner as well. He has smoked half a pack of cigarettes before noon, not to mention his having drunk four (or was it five?) cups of strong black coffee. By lunchtime, Chuck is ravenous, but he worries about going out for lunch for fear that a hearty meal will upset his stomach and trigger the intense abdominal pain he has been experiencing intermittently over the past few months. Instead, he wolfs down milk and cottage cheese in his office and wonders whether he will be able to make it through the afternoon. His partner, Mary, tells him he has an ulcer and really ought to see someone about it. Chuck is stoic, however. He thinks it just comes with the territory.

Thus far, Chuck's story sounds like a typical stress scenario: overworked, under too much stress, coping ineffectively, and beginning to manifest the signs of stress-induced illness. But there is also something unusual taking place in Chuck's practice. What is unusual is not Chuck himself, however, nor even his incipient ulcer. What is unusual is Chuck's partner, Mary. She works a very similar schedule, seeing about the same number of clients and working about the same number of hours as Chuck does. She too returns phone calls and engages in quick consultations. She even usually eats lunch in her office. There, however, the resemblance ends. For Mary does not have an ulcer and

she seems to thrive at her job, full of energy and extremely productive. Somehow, Mary manages not only to survive, but also
to excel under the same circumstances that seem to be tearing
Chuck apart. This is what is unusual. How can two people react
to similar situations in such radically different ways?

Chuck and Mary exemplify one of the seeming paradoxes of
stress—that one person can cope, or even thrive, while another
person, subjected to similar pressures, collapses under the strain.
Part of the answer to this seeming contradiction lies in the
aspects of stress that we have previously discussed: increased
physical resistance, use of effective coping techniques, differences in cognitive style, perhaps even genetic variations! But as
significant as these factors can be, they still cannot account
entirely for the radical differences in the ways people respond to
stress. How is it possible for some people to actually confront
stress—and turn the pressures of stress to their own advantage?

This puzzling question might be answered in many ways.
One particularly forceful response comes from the European
psychiatrist Viktor Frankl. Himself a survivor of the Nazi concentration camps, Frankl examined the behavior of his fellow
prisoners in an effort to discover why some were able to survive
the horrors of the camps while millions of others perished.
Clearly, the survivors were able to maintain the will to live in
spite of unbelievable conditions. Inmates of the camps were
starved, beaten, tortured both physically and psychologically—
driven far beyond the limits of what the human body and spirit
could be thought to endure. Yet those who managed to survive
were able to leave the camps and return to at least a semblance
of normal life. What did these people know? What enabled them
to overcome the indescribable horror of the Nazi holocaust?

The answer was not what one might have expected. Physical
strength, for example, was not decisive. In fact, many of those
who survived were far from robust specimens. Nor was education a significant factor, or wealth, or devout religiosity. Frankl
finally discovered what it was that set the survivors apart, the
single, mutually shared characteristic that enabled these extraordinary people to triumph over the terror of Auschwitz or Buch-
enwald. Frankl summed up his finding in a quote taken from the

German philosopher Nietzsche: "He who has a 'why' can endure any 'how.'" Human beings, Frankl found, need a reason for being, a "why" that makes their lives meaningful and gives dimension and purpose to their actions. Those who had managed to survive the camps shared a common purpose: They had something to live for. They had a purpose for their lives.

Frankl found this insight so powerful that he created a new school of psychotherapy, logotherapy, based upon it. We too can profit from his observation, for it is precisely that sense of meaning, that perception that something makes life worth living, that lies at the heart of any effort to overcome stress and turn it to our own ends. This view has been confirmed in recent research, most particularly in the work of Suzanne Kobasa and Salvatore Maddi of the University of Chicago. These researchers have described some of the characteristics of "stress-resistant" people who manage to remain happy and healthy in the face of many demanding life changes. Their research suggests that psychological resiliency or hardiness is based on three attitudes toward life: (1) an openness to change, (2) a feeling of involvement in whatever one is doing, and (3) a sense of control over the events in one's life.

Dr. Kobasa's doctoral dissertation, for example, used a sample of 670 middle- and upper-level managers at an Illinois public utility. She found that those who experienced low levels of illness in spite of many life changes and a correspondingly high level of stress were distinctly different from other managers who encountered similar levels of stress but became more seriously ill. Interestingly enough, those who became ill in response to the stress were less committed and less emotionally engaged in their work and social lives than those who encountered the same kind of stress but remained well. For example, rather than confronting and trying to solve an emotional conflict with a spouse, the manager who would subsequently fall victim to disease would avoid dealing with the conflict at all. Those managers who remained healthy in spite of similar levels of stress would, on the other hand, seek to work out the conflict. Not surprisingly, those who dealt poorly with stress and later fell ill with greater frequency also felt that they had less control of external events.

They tended to regard themselves more from the perspective of a victim, rather than from the point of view of someone who was ready and willing to solve a problem. Furthermore, those managers who were found to be more susceptible to illness also tended to view change as threatening, while their colleagues who managed to confront similar stress without becoming sick felt that changes were challenges—opportunities for growth and achievement.

This research, together with Frankl's work, suggests that people can respond to stress in a positive and powerful way. The common ingredients in such a stress-controlling style are a strong sense of personal purpose, a feeling of control over events, and a flexible and open attitude. Taken together, these characteristics indicate the kind of person who can confront stress—and turn it to his or her own purposes.

The only problem with this insight is that it does not apply to most of us. Some people, like Chuck's partner Mary, may very well be able to meet stress on its own terms and conquer it. The rest of us, however, are left marveling. Stress still afflicts us in ways we would rather forget. And this happens in spite of our efforts to bolster our resistance and to increase our coping skills. Even given a variety of stress-fighting skills, most of us still feel at a disadvantage. Stress still seems to hold the upper hand. How can we ever overcome this apparent disadvantage?

The answer to this question is twofold. First, there is nothing easy about changing. Making a significant change in your behavior takes time, energy, and, most of all, commitment. Deciding to confront the forces of stress in your life is not something that anyone would choose lightly. If you have read this far, however, you may well be ready to act on your own behalf. This is the first step, and the most essential one. Without the desire to change, the wanting to control stress instead of the other way around, little more can be accomplished.

The second aspect to becoming able to control stress and turn it to our own advantage is learning the specific behaviors that such stress-thriving attitudes require. By examining these stress-controlling behaviors, each of us can learn important skills that will augment our personal abilities and make us better able to confront and triumph over stress. The most important stress-controlling behaviors can be summarized under ten headings.

THE TEN COMMANDMENTS OF STRESS RESILIENCY

What are the key features of the stress-resistant person? My own clinical observations suggest the following matrix of characteristics:

1. The resilient person has *decided to live.* This person is not ambivalent about living or dying. He embraces life—at home, at work, or at play.

2. Out of this decision emerges a *will to live* and specific *reasons for being.* These people not only have goals toward which they strive, but also continuously update old goals and create new ones. The nonresilient person flounders when a goal is achieved. He may become stuck in a depression rather than create a new challenge.

3. Once the person decides to live and determines why he will live, he then formulates *how* he will live. Does he want to simply get by and survive, or go beyond—to thrive? Resilient types want to live well and to thrive.

4. The resilient type has an *optimistic attitude* about life and self. This person expects life events to turn out well and in his favor. Even in the face of adversity, he expects success because he is confident in his own abilities.

5. The resilient type views himself as *master of his fate.* He is in control, and his power lies in his ability to handle whatever vicissitudes of life come along. Those who fall prey to illness typically view themselves as helpless victims. Out of that perceived helplessness, they experience anxiety and depression. Depression can be lethal.

6. The resilient type operates in an *open learning mode.* The person engages in divergent thinking, the basis for creativity. Divergent thinking occurs when a person considers many different alternatives in the appraisal of a situation. Convergent thinking, on the other hand, means that the person sees few

alternatives and options. Dr. Aaron Beck, a cognitively oriented psychiatrist, notes that convergent thinking and helplessness are core characteristics of depressed people.

7. The open learning attitude leads to the resilient person's viewing stressful situations and changes—the good and the bad—as *opportunities* and *challenges*. The resilient person views a situation as an opportunity to learn, to grow, and to enrich life.

8. The resilient person handles these challenges by engaging in a *problem-solving* (or solution-finding) *dialogue*. The stress- and illness-prone person tends to engage in series of negative thoughts that focus on failure, loss, and the expectation of a negative outcome—a runaway negative train of thought as described in the preceding chapter, on cognitive styles. The resilient person steps back, gains an overall perspective, defines the problems and task at hand, and then finds solutions.

9. The dialogue process of resiliency makes the resilient person an *active participant* in his fate. The unhealthy tend to be passive in their attitudes and behaviors. Resiliency involves accepting your feelings and thoughts, whatever they are, and then actively changing what you don't want to experience. When a resilient person doesn't like a feeling state, he will actively do something to generate a different feeling. (This process of controlling your feelings can be learned and will be discussed later.) As an active participant, the resilient type embraces life. The person is emotionally engaged in what he is doing at the time. Even when relaxing, the resilient type focuses on that; there is no point in having your mind somewhere else at the time you might be fully focused on what you are doing.

An active participant will use change to his advantage. The resilient type accepts change as inevitable and uses each situation as a unique opportunity to have some experience that enriches him. The unhealthy person tends to avoid or fear change, which is seen as a burden and a liability. His or her mind is often elsewhere dreaming about how "if only it weren't this way, then all would be well."

10. The stress-resistant type, then, is characterized by a matrix of attitudes and action styles that emphasize *responsibility*. Resilient people realize that they are responsible for their fate as

well as their health, thinking, feeling, and behavior. They carry out this responsibility through a realistic acceptance of the consequences of their actions. True responsibility entails accepting feedback, both positive and negative. A responsible person can accept success or failure without a loss of self-esteem. The responsible person uses feedback as an opportunity to learn and to improve. Responsible people *like themselves*, have *high self-esteem*, and *strive to improve*. Nonresponsible people fear feedback and alter it in such a way as to preclude learning.

Where are you on this profile?

1. Have you decided to live?
2. Do you have positive reasons for living?
3. Are you living well, or poorly?
4. Are you truly optimistic?
5. Do you see yourself in control of your life, thoughts, feelings, and actions?
6. Are you truly open to learning, to your feelings, and to divergent ways of viewing an event?
7. Are you challenged by change?
8. Do you engage in problem-solving dialogues during stressful times? Or do you spin your wheels helplessly in negative thoughts?
9. Are you an active participant who is emotionally committed to each sphere of your life?
10. Do you take responsibility for your thoughts, feelings, actions, and life?

Resiliency breeds resistance to disease and to stress. The matrix of resiliency leads to a greater likelihood of physical and mental well-being. It allows you to strive without being driven, and to go beyond mere survival to live an active and productive life.

HOW TO LEARN RESILIENCY AND RESISTANCE TO STRESS

Some of the earlier chapters may have actually elicited some apprehension. What if you had a very high score on the Holmes and Rahe Life Events Survey, so that your chances of illness or injury are high? What does it mean if you are tense, or depressed, or even already showing symptoms of disease? These questions must be raised when reading about risk of illness. If you have recognized yourself as a stress-prone person, you might be wondering, "Is it possible for me to learn to resist the impact of stressful events?" The answer is "Yes!" Attitudes, habits, and behaviors are learned. Although modern scientific methods cannot yet alter our genetic structures in a predictable way, we *can* learn new life-styles. We *can* learn and practice viable health habits. And we *can* relearn what most children know instinctively—how to relax!

You have a challenge—to learn to be resilient and strong in the face of stress, to go beyond stress and use it for your own growth. Your challenge, then, is: "How can I change into a stress-resistant person?" The following section is devoted to just that, a step-by-step procedure to develop, learn, and practice stress-resistant behaviors and attitudes.

Step 1. Decide to Live

Although to some people Step 1 may seem a given, many people are actually ambivalent about living or dying. Physicians see this all the time. For example, the research evidence is clear that cigarette smoking is hazardous to your health. When a physician tells a smoker to stop because it is affecting his or her health and the smoker refuses, that person is either ambivalent about living or wishes to die.

Sigmund Freud, in his book *Civilization and Its Discontents*, explains that the death wish *(thanatos)* has permeated civilizations, creating cycles of growth, expansion, and decline. Throughout history, man has abused himself and others through war, slavery, alcohol abuse, tobacco abuse, and abuse of food. At least one out of four Americans has, has had, or will have a smoking, drinking, or eating problem within his or her lifetime. Excessive use of cigarettes, alcohol, or food is known to be contributory to disease. If people know this, why then do they persist? Is it merely a matter of an inherent uncontrollable death wish as Freud postulated? Or is it that people don't take the time to decide? People can be rational in deciding to live, but there needs to be some reward to compete against the rewards inherent in self-destructive habits such as alcohol use.

The decision to live is not all that easy for many people. When a close relative dies, it is common to hear such statements as "Why, God? Why not me?" At times of intense loss, people seem prone to think irrationally. They may even make a private, self-fulfilling pact to die. Such thoughts as "I'm the one who deserves to die" can be debilitating. It may also be a promise. In the face of death, however, some make the other commitment— to live.

A couple I know illustrate this phenomenon. Sam and Fran were a rather conventional couple. They both worked, bought a house, and raised two children. The children grew up and even went away to college. The oldest son had some difficulties that the parents never recognized, nor dealt with. While away at college, the son became depressed. He came home one weekend and hanged himself in his parents' house. The grief and distress shook the family system to its core. Eventually, Fran and Sam separated. Each blamed the other. The father became abject and overate until he weighed over 300 pounds. He died at the early age of 46 of a coronary. His excessive eating was a form of self-abuse and punishment. He decided to die, and eventually fulfilled his wish. His wife, on the other hand, grieved openly for many years. She isolated herself, but kept on working. With the devoted support of friends, she finally came to reaffirm life. She decided to live and to embrace life once again, and she is alive and well today at the ripe old age of 75.

The decision to live or to die is the foundation for resiliency and resistance. It will influence all the subsequent steps in the process of creating your resiliency.

Ask yourself: "DO I want to live?"

If you didn't hesitate to say "Yes," then continue on to Step 2.

If you answered "I think so," then you are unsure and need to sit down with yourself and think about your indecision. The word "think" reveals ambivalence or uncertainty. Keep asking yourself the question each day until you make an affirmative decision. When the answer is clearly "Yes," then move on to Step 3, unless you wish to reinforce your reasons by reviewing Step 2.

If you answered "No," then you obviously want to die. You have two choices: You can simply die in whatever manner or at whatever pace you have chosen and forget the next nine steps, or you can explore the roots of that "No." In that case, I would recommend professional help to unravel the beliefs and attitudes that underlie that decision to die. It is seldom a rational one. Unless you make the decision affirmatively, you will certainly sabotage the next nine steps.

Let's assume that you have made the decision—that is to say, you can easily and clearly say "I want to live"; then you have created the foundation for resiliency and resistance. You can then commit yourself to yourself, to your work, to your play, and to life! As noted earlier, the stress-resistant person engages emotionally in whatever tasks he or she faces.

Step 2. Develop Positive Reasons for Living

We elaborate our decision to live through our reasons for being, our raison d'être. As noted earlier, Dr. Frankl's observations are logical as well as meaningful. Our reasons for living become goals toward which to strive, and thus provide the motivation for striving. And the goals serve as guideposts around which we can focus our time, energy, and strivings. If you have a why, you can endure any how.

It is important psychologically that a person develop positive reasons for living that promote his own life and welfare as well as the lives and welfare of those around him. Negative reasons are destructive and detract from self-respect and well-being.

Let's review the steps to formulating *your* reasons for living.

Ask yourself, "What are my reasons for living?"

Then make a list and write them down.

Review this list once a day until they are clear in your mind and you can recite them readily.

Then, when the vicissitudes of life create pressures, pull out the list and remind yourself of your "why's." Remember, they form the basis for your continuing to want to live in the face of all odds.

For clarity, consider some of the following reasons that people give themselves for living:

"I want to enjoy myself as fully as I can imagine."

"I want to raise a family and enjoy their development."

"I want to write that book. I have so much to share with people."

"I want to succeed at my work and be rich."

"I want to be the best stockbroker that I can be."

Get started and complete your written list before you continue to Step 3. Notice how the reasons listed above are framed in terms of "I want"—they place all the power, control, and responsibility in your hands. Enjoy that power. As you think about your reasons, you may notice a surge of energy. Your reasons for being create a reservoir of energy and motivation to tap when under duress.

Step 3. Decide How to Live

All of us have sets of standards by which we govern our behavior: codes of morality, or ethics, as well as rules that govern our lifestyles. Some people want to live simply and conventionally. There is an expression in German that describes this lifestyle: "Kinder, Küche, und Kirche"—children, kitchen, and church. In contrast, others may strive for a jet-set style of high fashion, fast cars, and a fast-moving and glamorous social life. One path is not better than the other. Each has its own rewards.

Decide how to live by first asking yourself: "Do I want to live well or poorly?"

Let's assume that you choose "well." The next step is to define it.

Write down how you want to live well in each of the following spheres of life. We live well in many different dimensions, and it is vital to create goals in each of the major spheres. Vague goals are seldom accomplished, but specific goals can be attained. Consider these spheres of influence:

A. The Body

1. Eating: Set specific and positive goals for what and how you will eat. The chapter on nutrition (Chapter 5) will give you some guidelines to help you develop a strong body, which is a must for resistance to disease.

2. Sleep: Select the optimal number of hours you need. Then practice the relaxation exercises to get the deepest sleep possible. Restful sleep is healing and regenerating.

3. Exercise: Set specific goals for conditioning your body. A strong body bounces back after a stressful experience. A weak body becomes weaker.

4. Sex: Set goals for frequency, styles, and partners. Many people set financial goals, but how many people develop goals for their sex lives? Be creative. A viable sex life, one in which you enjoy yourself, relax, and release tension fully, is part of the process of maintaining the psychological and biochemical balances in the body.

5. Weight: Choose your ideal weight and achieve it. Your weight is an index of how well you like yourself as well as an important factor in remaining healthy. Overweight people live shorter lives and are at higher risk for diseases such as heart disease.

6. Pleasure: Set a goal of learning to enjoy your body. Practice relaxing. Enjoy yourself in a mirror. Enjoy all your senses.

B. Work

1. Financial: Be specific and set an exact dollar-figure goal for your income—this year, next year, and so on for the next 5 years. Then list the steps to attain those goals.

2. Skills: Select some skills that you want to learn, refine, or update. Then do what you have to do to achieve them—read, practice, take courses, observe. As you attain these skills, you develop viable beliefs that you are competent.

3. Occupational or career course: Set some goals for your career or occupational path. Do you want a change? If so, when

and of what type? Write down the steps in pursuing this path. Keep your direction clear in your mind.

4. Retirement: Decide the form and set a date. Each person defines retirement differently. Some people "retire" at age 50 by working only three days per week. You may even decide not to retire until physical or mental limitations force you to stop or slow down.

C. Family

1. Intimacy: Set some specific guidelines concerning with whom and how much closeness you want. Decide what form intimacy will take. Think about how much you want to touch, hug, tickle, and play with your family. There are an infinite number of ways to get close.

2. Independence: Set goals for the degree to which you will rely on other family members to initiate and select activities. There needs to be a balance between being independent and dependent. To be too independent and sulf-sufficient is to be an island unto yourself. You can create your loneliness. To be too dependent, where you determine your actions only after your partner (or friend, or other person) decides his or her course of action, is to render yourself vulnerable to feeling abandoned or rejected.

3. Emotions: Set goals for openly expressing your feelings. Let yourself experience and express your anger, sadness, fear, disappointment, and joy directly. Suppression of feelings leads to tension in the body that can be crippling. Migraine sufferers tend to hold in their anger and are perfectionistic. People who develop colitis are excellent at worrying and holding in their fears.

4. Form: Set goals for the size and form of your family. We can create a "family" in many ways. A viable and supportive social network is vital to survival. Recent research at the University of Washington School of Medicine has revealed some fascinating phenomena. Patients on dialysis were studied in terms of risk for death and family network. High-risk patients with large and viable family networks survived longer than low-risk patients with no families. At a lecture at the Humanistic Society in San Francisco in 1976, a psychologist reviewed that study and

told an interesting anecdote. A middle-aged man was rated a high risk and expected to die, but he continued to live on. The psychologist talked to him and asked him to account for his determined survival. He simply said, "I must get home to take care of my fish!" His "family" was a single goldfish, but it gave him a reason to live.

Remember, your family can be your friends, your marriage partner, your lover, your child, or your parents. For some people, pets are their "family." Choose the form that fulfills your needs.

D. Play: This is an area often forgotten by adults. When you forget to play, you tend to become serious about life. This can lead to a loss of perspective so that stresses appear to be worse than they are when your life has a balance between work and play.

1. Types: Select activities that are fun. Write them down. Set goals for how often you will let your hair down and be frivolous and silly. If you are not smiling or laughing while playing, then you are not really playing. Tickle someone. Tell a joke. Do something outrageous once in a while.

2. Schedule: Actively determine a schedule. Ask yourself, what was one funny thing that happened to me last week? What fun thing will I do this week?

E. Relaxation

1. Type: Set goals for the type of quieting activity that you will practice. Practice until you are skilled.

2. Schedule: Set up a regular pattern for practice. Research suggests that daily relaxation leads to fewer sick days missed at work, fewer hospitalizations, and less illness.

F. Creativity–Spirituality

1. Type: Set goals in these areas. You can spiritually nourish yourself through prayer as well as painting. Do what nourishes you.

2. Schedule: Once you choose the forms of expression, decide how often you will participate. You can go to church once a month, or you can meditate in your home each day.

Remember, how you live makes a statement about who you are. It is important that you be emotionally engaged in all the spheres of your life. It is not relaxing to be working but to be thinking about how you want to play, and there can be only conflict and tension when you think about work when you are playing. The Type A personality has difficulty just relaxing without feeling guilty. This is an example of not emotionally engaging in the process of relaxing. Calling in to the office while on vacation detracts from the vacation. Commit yourself to participating fully in each of the spheres listed above. Review the list of goals and objectives once a week. When you write them down and strive to fulfill them, then you begin your commitment to engage emotionally in these areas of your life. Through this process, you realistically realize your control.

When you review your goals each week, keep your perspective. The realities of time and demands of work and family will necessitate that you vary your commitments. One week you may have to work a few more hours, which means less time for family or play; another week, your family might require more time. Don't pressure yourself by saying "I should be able to do everything." This creates self-induced conflict that will not let you engage in either sphere. When you review your lists each week, you can then examine which areas have been overemphasized for how long and which have been neglected. Then simply shift your priorities. You will be controlling the ebb and flow of your commitment.

Step 4. Think Positive and Develop an Optimistic Attitude

Earlier, we noted that a stress-resistant person is able to view obstacles and tasks in general as challenges. To view life's vicissitudes as challenges, you need an optimistic attitude. This attitude has certain core beliefs that people review mentally to maintain a positive attitude. Examples of these beliefs are:

"Life works out for the best."
"I usually end up getting what I want."
"Things work out well for me."

"I can make things turn out well."

"The world is a good place in which to live, and thus there are endless opportunities out there for me."

These beliefs, which focus on self, life, and the world, create an expectation. The optimist expects a positive outcome. In contrast, the pessimist expects a negative outcome. Whichever orientation you take toward life guides your perception and appraisal of an event, and later governs your behaviors. The optimist perceives the glass as half full, the pessimist sees it as half empty.

The following joke was told to me the other day. It captures the heart of how optimistic and pessimistic attitudes govern behavior, even when the attitudes are challenged by dissonant circumstances:

> A social psychologist decided to evaluate the degree to which attitudes are consistent and malleable.
>
> He found a true pessimist and a true optimist and was going to observe their behaviors in an experimental setting. Two observation rooms were used, each having a one-way mirror and microphones and speakers so that the researcher could hear and see what was happening.
>
> In the first room, he placed a table laden with ice cream, cakes, pies, and a box of toys, then escorted the pessimist into the room.
>
> In the second room, he placed a huge pile of horse manure, and then had the optimist enter that room.
>
> The psychologist first observed the pessimist and found him talking aloud: "That ice cream is melting. It's probably too soft. Who likes soft ice cream anyway!" While looking at the cakes and pies, he said: "They seem to be burned around the edges and were probably baked yesterday. Who needs it!" He finally turned to the toys and depressingly concluded: "Oh, why bother to play with them? I'll probably break them anyway."

Thus, the pessimist was true to form. He could find fault with even the most pleasant possibilities. On the other hand, when the psychologist then turned to observe the optimist, he saw something intriguing:

The optimist was throwing the horse manure hither and yon as though looking for something. The psychologist became worried at this wild throwing and decided to interrupt the experiment. He opened the door and asked the optimist: "What in the world is going on here? Why are you throwing the horse manure all over the place?"

The optimist turned and said smiling: "There must be a horse here somewhere!"

This is a joke, but it is not a joke. In the face of adversity, the optimist views the noxious condition as a challenge and searches for some positive resolution.

On the whole, the area of salesmanship is noted for positive thinking. Dale Carnegie and Clement Stone formulated approaches to sales that are based on an optimistic attitude about people and life. Stone, for example, talks about having a "PMA"—a "Positive Mental Attitude." In his multimillion-dollar corporations, you will hear salespeople asking one another "How is your PMA today?" Mr. Stone teaches people to develop a PMA by practicing an internal dialogue with themselves. He has people ask themselves at least several times a day, "How is your PMA today?" Thus, you train yourself to observe your attitude, or conduct an attitude check, at least several times per day.

Recently, behavioral psychologists have studied methods for developing effective cognitive coping strategies. Dr. Aaron T. Beck, a psychiatrist, has specifically researched the hypothesis that depression is the result of convergent thinking, in which people's thinking backs them into a corner, and they do not see that they have alternatives. The depressed person perceives himself as helpless and holds the view that the future is hopeless. He essentially says to himself, "Why go on if there are no rewards or reasons for living?" Severely depressed people have a very high suicide rate and have a fourfold increase in mortality during major surgical procedures. Dr. Beck's treatment then focuses on altering faulty beliefs that are negative and teaches patients new ways to view themselves, the world, and life.

Another cognitive behavioral psychologist, Dr. Donald Meichenbaum, has recently experimented with the idea of teaching people cognitive coping strategies that can help them cope with stressful life experiences. He observed that we all carry on an internal dialogue. People who experience profound negative feelings from even simple everyday life events (the person, for example, who worries about the bills, the family, and the weather, not to mention worrying about worrying) are people who carry out a negative internal dialogue. Dr. Meichenbaum has been conducting a series of treatment programs by which people are taught how to think positively. He thinks that to practice a positive affirmation such as "Every day in every way I grow stronger and healthier" is too nonspecific. There is more impact when we make statements that are specific to some feelings, action, situation, or anticipated event. For example, you are more likely to experience success in feeling more calm by practicing "As I breathe deeply and easily, I am calm and in control." Or "I enjoy giving speeches; tonight I will enjoy my talk" can be effective in reducing anxiety about giving a speech. While practicing such thoughts, you are also precluding negative thoughts.

It is clear that an optimistic attitude and a daily positive mental attitude set up a self-fulfilling prophecy—you expect some good experience and it happens. You are then rewarded and encouraged, so you continue to repeat acting and thinking positively. If you are not optimistic, how do you develop such an attitude? The following is a format that has been effective with over 100 patients of mine in the past 2 years.

If not already optimistic, then ACT as though you are. What does someone with a positive mental attitude do? Just what the pessimist does—he practices thoughts consistent with his attitude. Thus, you act as though you are optimistic by *practicing* optimistic thinking.

First, ask yourself: "Do I really want to enjoy life?"

Assuming the answer is "Yes," continue as follows:

Begin your day with a dialogue. After awakening, ask: "What is your mental attitude this morning? Are you feeling hopeful and expecting to have a good day, or are you negative?"

Whatever the answer, then ask: "How would you like to feel today?"

Assuming you want to feel good, ask yourself: "How do you want to feel? Happy? Content? Relaxed? Or exactly how?"

Select a feeling state, and then, drawing upon your knowledge of yourself, ask: "What will I need to do today to create that feeling?"

Then go ahead and enjoy your day; you have just set an emotional goal to be optimistic. *Do it* and *observe* yourself.

At lunchtime, take an ATTITUDE CHECK. Ask yourself: "How is your positive mental attitude now?" If it is negative, go through the dialogue outlined above. Write the dialogue on an index card and carry it with you. Place one by your bed within easy reach in the morning.

If you have difficulties and feel stuck, pull out your list of goals and your list of reasons for being.

It is very common for people who are pessimistic to be ruminative and obsessional—that is to say, they repeat over and over a series of negative thoughts. They practice and reinforce their own sense of gloom and doom. If you have that difficulty, then you may first have to practice a behavioral technique called THOUGHT-STOPPING. The process involves practicing turning off negative thoughts just as you would turn off a television. Thought-stopping involves three steps:

1. First, observe your own pattern of obsessional and negative thinking. Take a pad and for 1 week write down *what* the negative thoughts are and what is happening at the time you have them. Look for patterns. For example, do you detach yourself with a series of negative thoughts when you become intimate with a person? Or do you get angry, thereby distracting yourself? Negative thinking is a defense pattern that has some payoff and reward. First *observe* and then *change.*

2. Once you are skilled at knowing that you are in a negative thinking cycle, IMAGINE a big bright red stop sign and do just what it says—STOP! It often helps to make cue cards by drawing stop signs on index cards and putting them in obvious places to remind you to stop thinking negatively. Fill in the colors, too.

3. Upon stopping a negative thought sequence, replace it with POSITIVE THOUGHTS. These can be elicited by a question. Consider the following examples:

"In what ways can I enjoy the remainder of this work day?"
"How shall I stop worrying about finishing this report?"

Focus on some pleasant event in your surroundings or outside, or anticipate some positive event later: "Gosh I'm looking forward to this evening. I get to see that movie I missed." "It sure is a lovely time of year."

One of the most potent strategies for developing a positive mental attitude is to give yourself COMPLIMENTS. As I noted in Chapter 7, one great advantage of creating a positive feedback to others is that it will be returned. Think positive praises of your work, ideas, strengths, and resources. And even praise yourself for having been positive. Then notice how warm and good you feel. Remember that feeling when you think of praising others.

Finally, be sure to end your day with positive statements. For example: "You sure did a great job at work today." "You really had a pleasant time at the movie." "My life is going well."

Just before falling asleep, think about some positive experiences that you want to happen the next day. Anticipate pleasant events and end your day with positive affirmations:

"Every day in every way I grow stronger and healthier."

"Tomorrow holds some exciting possibilities for me."

"I'm going to catch up at work in the area of _____ tomorrow." "When I wake up in the morning, I will feel fresh, relaxed, calm, and alert." Then drift to sleep smiling.

Finally, if you get stuck, reread this entire chapter. Then simply remember the optimist in the room full of manure. It's all a matter of attitude.

Step 5. Take Contol of Your Life

When people feel overwhelmed by stress, they frequently carry on internal dialogues that emphasize their feelings of powerlessness and loss of control. By saying such things to themselves as "I just can't take any more of this pressure!" or "I'm at the end of my rope," such people reveal that they feel overcome by pressure and stress. These phrases also indicate that these people are using a stress-increasing cognitive style. They are interpreting the situation as one in which they have lost control.

Stress-resistant people, on the other hand, hold a different view of themselves. When they encounter events that are diffi-cult or emotionally demanding (e.g., the death of a loved one, being fired, the birth of a child), stress-resilient people accept the reality of the situation and remind themselves that they are in control. Their internal dialogue, in turn, is characterized by a recognition of this internal strength. They might say to them-selves such things as "This is rough, but I can overcome it," "The grief will pass and I'll be fine," or "I know I can do this—I just have to think it through first." Such statements show a recogni-tion of the stressful situation, but they also demonstrate an opti-mistic attitude about being able to meet the challenge of those demanding events.

Feeling in control, then, is a powerful weapon against stress. Furthermore, such an attitude can be learned. To see whether you need to develop this attitude of being in control over stress, ask yourself to what degree you see yourself as being in control of your life. If you find that you are frequently, or even very frequently, in control, then you will probably only need some fine-tuning of your ability to control stress. On the other hand, if you feel in control of your life only occasionally, or seldom, or even never, then you have plenty of work to do. Such work will pay off, though. You will learn how to control stress better in your life.

In Chapter 3, you learned how to use language association as a technique for discovering the meanings locked within stressful patterns of behavior. Now you will have an opportunity to use language as a tool once again.

How people talk reveals how they feel about controlling their lives. Take the following statements as an example:

"If she had only done what I had asked, we wouldn't be in trouble now."

"He was lucky to get that promotion."

"It's just coincidence, that's all."

"When I saw all that ice cream, I just couldn't help myself. I had to eat it."

In each of these statements, the speaker regards control as external, outside himself and acting upon him. The person actually perceives himself as powerless—and subject to fate or the whims of others. Instead of feeling in control, people who speak like this feel like victims. They fail to take responsibility for their lives and instead blame others. Do you use the language of powerlessness and blame?

For the next week, observe yourself: Notice when you blame others for what went wrong. Notice when you attribute your success or failure to some power other than you. Remember, when you blame others, you are not open to learning.

Next, observe whether or not you talk to yourself in the *language* of *helplessness*. The following statements will tell you that you believe you are helpless:

Do you say, "I *can't*. . . ."? This is equivalent to saying, "I am helpless and have no control."

Do you say, "I'll *try* to. . . ."? This is equivalent to saying, "I will put out some effort, but don't blame me when I fail." To "try" is a socially acceptable excuse for failure, and in fact a self-fulfilling promise to fail.

Do you say, "I *need*. . . ."? This is equivalent to saying, "I am helpless unless something happens."

Do you say, "I *should*. . . ."? This is equivalent to saying, "I do things because there is some externally determined set of rules or expectations that will govern my behavior."

Do you say, "I *have to*. . . ."? This is equivalent to saying, "I have no choice but to do it."

Dr. Albert Ellis's clinical approach to behavior change, called Rational Emotive Therapy, has contributed to our understanding of the language of helplessness. Each of the exemplified verbs above implies loss of control because the power is external to the speaker. Each of these phrases is based on false assumptions. Dr. Ellis's approach to behavior change is to have a person become aware of the false assumptions that underlie the language and to change these assumptions. A more effective way is to first observe the language of helplessness and then learn a new language. How do you make the focus of your power and control internal? Once you are aware that you are using the language of helplessness, stop yourself and replace it with the language of power and control. That is to say, talk to yourself affirmatively.

When faced with decisions to be made or tasks to be accomplished, say "I CAN. . . ." This statement implies that you will do it until you succeed. Even if you make a mistake, you will benefit. The mistake is an opportunity to learn. You simply learn and keep doing the task until you are successful, thereby proving that you can do what you set out to do. You reward yourself through your success.

Say "I WILL do it. . . ." In doing so, you make a commitment to carry out the task. "Trying" becomes trying to others and yourself because it is an excuse and a promise to fail!

Say "I WANT. . . ." Focus on your desires, not the expectations of others. Very young children learn very quickly to say "I want" this or that. They are then taught not to be "selfish," and usually learn by age seven that saying "I want" may not be effective in attaining their goals. They learn that when they say "I need," others feel important and are more likely to give them what they want. The child is rewarded for talking in the language of helplessness (how can someone be so terrible as to say "no" to the "needy"?), and thus, by the time he reaches adulthood, speaks it fluently.

Listen for these words: can't, try, need, should, have to. Then change to the language of power: can, will, want. Decide what is good for you and what you are willing to do—for yourself, not for the expectations of others. Use the language of power and take responsibility for your control.

Next, take control of your feelings. Did you ever say "You make me mad" or "You are driving me crazy"? These statements imply that the other person has control of your feelings. No one "makes us" feel any one way. We feel mad, sad, glad, fear, disappointment, shame, guilt, and other emotional states only when we think certain thoughts. It is true that when some loved person dies, we may feel grief and cry. But we don't have to. If you miss the person, it is probably a good idea to let yourself cry so that you don't hold in the tension that results from unexpressed grief. You can control where and when you decide to express the feelings. Whereas one person lets himself cry openly at a funeral, another person will cry later at home when alone.

You have a great deal of control over what you feel, how

intensely you feel, and how you will express the feeling. First, realize that you feel mad when you think angry thoughts. You feel fear when you think of scary images. You feel glad when you imagine happy or pleasant scenes. Did you ever wonder how actors and actresses cry or laugh on cue? They simply become skilled at imagining some event that would typically evoke such a feeling.

Your control over your feelings lies in the realm of controlling how you think and imagine events. Practice controlling your feelings.

First: Keep a diary. List a feeling you had, the thoughts that preceded it, and the context of the event. Have three columns like this:

Feelings   Thoughts   Context

Example: "I'm mad." "I think he used me." "Short-term romance when we had sex."

Second: After you have some picture of the types of situations wherein you are likely to feel a particular way, *practice a self-control dialogue.* Ask yourself: "How am I feeling?" Sample answer: "Mad." "Do I want to continue feeling this way?" Sample answer: "No." "How would I like to feel?" Sample answer: "Content." (This is your goal.) "What will I have to do to feel this way?" Sample answer: "I can go do some oil painting." (Task that achieves the goal.) When you practice this self-control dialogue, you are taking charge of your feelings.

How to Change Fear Responses. Another important aspect of gaining control of feelings is to realize that we may associate a particular feeling with a specific situation. Whenever that situation occurs, we suddenly experience the feeling we have learned to associate with it. A person who has been in a traumatizing car wreck, for example, may become fearful of driving on freeways and may develop a phobia about freeways and avoid driving on them. Or a painful love affair can elicit anxiety about becoming intimate. A person who is fired or laid off unexpectedly may become fearful about going on job interviews. These situations are similar to the experience of the famous Russian psychologist Ivan Pavlov. He was able to condition the salivary reflex of a dog to the ringing of a bell. By paired association, he rang a bell just as he presented a dog with food. The natural physiological reaction to seeing and smelling food is to salivate. After a number of pairings of the ringing of the bell with the presentation of food, the dog simply salivated when the bell rang. This process is called classical conditioning.

Later, an American psychologist demonstrated a similar type of conditioning. Dr. John Watson, in what is now considered a controversial experiment, demonstrated that a child's fear of a white rat could be generalized to a white furry object. The white furry object could bring on the child's fear response without the presence of a rat.

This is similar to what might happen in an office. Imagine that a newly hired secretary is afraid of angry men. Her first job is to work for a boss who is portly and balding. He is rough on her during her first weeks at work. He is very critical and demanding. Each time he criticizes her, she begins to sweat, tremble, and feel nauseated. She is having an anxiety reaction. After a few weeks, she finds that as soon as he enters the room, she begins to show the same signs of anxiety, even though he is being pleasant.

Let's assume that you have some specific fears that interfere with your being able to tell yourself that you are in control of your feelings. Imagine for a moment that you have a fear of going out to restaurants. On your last time out to a restaurant, you became so ill that you ran to the bathroom to vomit. Since that experience, you feel sensations of fear even when you think of going to a restaurant. You begin to avoid restaurants more and more. You find yourself looking for all kinds of excuses when friends ask you to join them for an evening out. You are afraid that you might end up going to a restaurant, and you don't want to be embarrassed by your fears. Also imagine that you are a salesperson and must take customers out to lunch. Now you find it difficult to go to work and are tense each morning. What if you have to take a customer out to lunch?

There is a solution. For one, you could decondition your fear response, or desensitize yourself to going out to restaurants. Dr. Joseph Wolpe, a South African psychiatrist, has shown that anxiety responses can be counterconditioned. That is to say, we can desensitize ourselves to the feared situation.

The methodology for desensitization is quite simple. First you learn how to relax, then you associate the relaxation with images of the feared situation. Relaxation is a response that is incompatible with fear. Dr. Wolpe found that associating the image of a feared situation with relaxation breaks the link between the fear and the situation. A great deal of research has been done with desensitization, and it works to overcome a phobia.

The first task in desensitizing yourself to some feared situation is to make a list of situations in which the fear response occurs, and rank them according to the amount of anxiety elicited. You can do this simply. First draw up a list of ten situations that elicit the fear, then assign to each a number from 1 to 100 to describe the intensity of the fear: 0 is no anxiety and 100 is total panic. Then simply rank them in order from that which creates the most anxiety to that which evokes the least. The following is an example:

1. 100 Taking an unknown prospect to a restaurant I don't know.

2. 95   Taking a known customer to a new restaurant.

3. 85   Taking a known customer to a familiar restaurant.

4. 75   Going to a new restaurant with a blind date.

5. 65   Going to a familiar restaurant with a blind date.

6. 50   Going to a new restaurant with a colleague at work.

7. 40   Going to a new restaurant with a friend.

8. 30   Going to a familiar restaurant with a friend.

9.   20   Going to a restaurant alone.

10.   10   Eating at home with friends.

Desensitization begins by practicing a relaxation response. Let's assume that you have perfected one of the responses in Chapter 4. Once relaxed, you begin with item No. 10 on this list, the scene that elicits the least amount of anxiety. After becoming completely relaxed, you imagine the scene. If you feel any tension in your body, you turn off the scene, let your mind go blank, and return to relaxing your body. After about 30 seconds of relaxation, you imagine the scene again. The goal is to be able to imagine the anxiety-provoking scene for up to 30 seconds. Once you accomplish this, you move up the list to item No. 9, and so on. The criterion for progressing to the next scene is to be able to hold the image for 30 seconds on two repeated occasions.

The desensitization process can be facilitated by taking each scene and practicing it until you feel comfortable. Thus, for example, you might learn some relaxation response in Chapter 4. Once you have succeeded, you set up an evening at home to have friends over for dinner. Just before they come, you spend time relaxing. You do that as many times as it takes for you to experience a sense of calm while eating with friends at home. You then do the same with item No. 9. You go out to restaurants alone until you are comfortable. Each time, you practice a relaxation response prior to the event.

Another alternative to desensitization is to rehearse thoughts that evoke feelings incompatible with anxiety. Dr. Donald Meichenbaum, a cognitive behaviorial psychologist, has developed programs of this type. He has observed that when a person experiences anxiety, that person is practicing thoughts that elicit sensations of fear. He observed that the phobic person practices the runaway negative dialogue. For example, a salesperson who is afraid to go to lunch goes through a series of negative dialogues that bring on the anxiety. She may have a luncheon set up one noon and begin her day with the following negative thoughts: "Oh, I have to take Mr. President out to lunch. What if I get sick in the office this morning and vomit? I'll be so nauseous at lunch that I'll blow the deal. He certainly will notice I'm upset. What will I do?" It is obvious that this type of dialogue will elicit and maintain the fear response.

An alternative to the dialogue is to practice a positive one that will elicit confidence and relaxation. Our salesperson would better begin the day by practicing a relaxation response. When she plans her day and thinks about the luncheon, she may begin to feel a bit queasy. The queasy sensations can then be used as a signal to commence a calming dialogue. Imagine her name is Joan. Joan begins to talk to herself:

How are you feeling this morning?	A bit queasy.
Do you want to feel that way?	No.
So how do you want to feel?	Calm and secure.
What will bring on those feelings?	Practicing a relaxation response and rehearsing my presentation.
So what are you going to do?	Relax and practice.

The *self-control dialogue* is a tool. It can stop the negative thinking and the anxiety. It also points to solutions and alternative thoughts. Joan might rehearse affirmations that elicit calm. During the morning, before lunch, she might repeat such meditations as:

"I am calm and in control."
"I know how to sell."
"I can just sit back and listen to the customer."
"I can end the lunch early should the need arise."
"I'm selecting the restaurant, so I'm on familiar turf."

Joan has another alternative. She can first reinterpret or reframe her experience of anxiety. This is commonly done in hypnosis. The late Dr. Milton Erickson, a premier hypnotherapist, was a master at reframing a person's experience from a negative to a positive one. First, Joan might realize that the sensations for fear and joy are the same—the body is mobilized. Then she might realize that being anxious has two meanings—fear and eagerness! When she thinks of the impending luncheon and feels her heart rate increasing, she might just simply say: "I'm really excited about this meeting. I get to meet the president of X Corporation. What an opportunity." Thus, she reframes her body's sensations in a positive frame of reference and then views the experience as an opportunity. She might also remember that a little anxiety is useful in that it mobilizes us to action. Too much anxiety immobilizes us, and too little may lead to inactivity. She might say to herself: "A little anxiety is good. I'll be on my toes and give a super presentation."

After that luncheon, which is now more likely to be successful, it is important to have Joan reward herself with praise. The reduction of the anxiety may itself be a reward, but it is useful to consciously reward ourselves as well. She might say to herself: "Joan, you were clear and articulate. You closed that deal quickly and efficiently. Great job!"

Most people will find that once they can control their anxiety, they perceive themselves as being in control.

Step 6. Be Open to Learning

The resilient person is open to difference. Varying points of view, different emotional reactions, and discrepant information are viewed as acceptable. The resilient person is not rigid about how life "should" be and doesn't try to fit his experiences into preconceived pigeonholes. Each experience is weighed and reviewed on its own merits. The resilient person accepts reality from a position of self-confidence. He knows he is okay, so there is nothing to prove.

As an example of the opposite attitude, consider the Type A personality discussed earlier. Type A's have a number of characteristics that indicate psychological rigidity and being closed to learning. The Type A person is very competitive, for instance. He strives to do things "right" and, since he believes he can do the best job, hesitates to delegate responsibility. He may even act arrogantly in his efforts to prove he is right. The Type A person is engaged in a life-and-death struggle—within himself—to prove something. This is similar to a phenomenon that is often observed with alcoholics. The male alcoholic typically uses alcohol to become more assertive and "macho," and to act with fewer inhibitions. He behaves as though his drinking were a rite of passage. This is a dynamic similar to that of the Type A personality. The Type A is out to prove something—either through monetary accomplishment or through excellence. He has a compulsion to be "right." How tense!

Remember, if you discover that you are the type of person who tries to prove you are "right" when you engage in dialogue with others, then you are in a NONLEARNING mode. That's right. If you are busy proving that you are "right," that means that the other person is "wrong." This type of belief is faulty. It also alienates people. You cannot be listening if you are busy proving a point.

Thus, the first rule in developing an open learning viewpoint is to STOP PROVING THAT YOU ARE RIGHT. Right and wrong are issues of morality, not reality.

The second step is to VIEW ERRORS AS OPPORTUNITIES. Mistakes are not "being human" (which is an excuse to not learn), they are inevitable.

The person who criticizes himself for making mistakes is busy abusing himself. That is a nonlearning mode of behavior.

The third step is to practice the LEARNING DIALOGUE. The vicissitudes of life present us with roadblocks, crises, and events that are emotionally tumultuous. In these situations, we are likely to feel uncomfortable. Use that discomfort as a signal to begin the learning dialogue. Specifically, ask yourself:

"What can I learn from this experience?"

"In what ways can I benefit from it?"

"This situation is an opportunity. For what?"

This dialogue creates what Dr. Erickson calls the learning set.

The techniques discussed above are just that—methods by which you can train yourself to be open to new learning. You can roll with the punches that way and benefit from stressful situations. But why is it easier for one person to be open and another to be defensive in times of stress? Is it a question of learning or genetics?

My own clinical observations point to the issue of self-esteem. To be closed to change is to be closed to new learning and to challenges. To be closed to change means that the person is viewing the change as a danger. Something is perceived as a threat. Even a rat of a genetically docile strain will fight when cornered by a threatening stimulus.

The person who is open to change and open to learning has positive self-esteem. Such people like themselves. They know that they are okay. There is no pressure internally to feel threatened when you know you are a good, solid person. The Type A person is driven to strive from an internal sense of insecurity. Even when the Type A arrives at the top of the corporate or economic ladder, he does not stop his relentless pursuit. He sets higher goals and standards and begins his strivings anew. There is no inner peace or contentment. Type A's have low self-esteem, but try to counter that internal insecurity by achieving higher and higher accomplishments. That is why they tend to strive for the approval of their superiors, not that of their peers.

When you hold yourself in high regard, you can strive for some goal, but you need not be driven. You will not be threatened by differences in opinion or by dissonant experiences.

Although it is not within the scope of this book to teach you how to build a high level of positive self-esteem, there are several ways to do so.

First, fill a mental library about yourself with positive volumes. Think of your assets and liabilities. Make a list of each and see which is longer. A long list of assets and a short list of liabilities suggests high self-esteem. Appreciate your assets in terms of your body, your mind, your abilities, and your sensibilities.

Note what you do well. Accept your limitations, physical and mental. Then decide which areas might benefit from updating, polishing, and new learning. Most important, praise yourself whenever you succeed. A quitter does not respect himself unless all options have been tried.

At the end of each day, review mentally, or better yet, write down, just what you did well. Set goals and achieve them. Then praise yourself for your accomplishments. Be your own best friend. Over time, you will grow to like yourself. Be flexible and open to new learning and to change. That is the essence of eustress (a term that Dr. Hans Selye coined, by analogy with such words as "euphony," to denote the good side of stress). Strive without being driven. Strive to grow and to learn.

Step 7. View Change as a Challenge

Earlier in the book, we looked at some research results that indicate that the more life changes we experience within a 2-year period, the more likely we are to become ill or injured. Other more recent research suggests that it is not simply the experience of change that generates illness, but rather how one appraises those changes. Those who remain healthy in the face of change view it as an opportunity and a challenge. Thrivers appear to hold the belief (or assumption) that they will overcome an obstacle and will benefit in the process of tackling the challenge.

Taxes, like death, are an irrevocable event. Tax time happens every April 15, whether we like it or not. It is the time when there is an increase in the frequency of coronaries, even for accountants. The stress-prone person is someone who will take an inevitable event and think negatively about it. For example, a computer executive friend of mine became depressed on April 15. In a phone conversation, he said: "Martin, I don't know why I work so hard. Is it really worth it all? I have to dole out twenty thousand dollars in taxes. This year my business is finally under way and I'm stuck; I can't seem to get ahead of these taxes!"

It is not surprising that he felt depressed or that he couldn't sleep well at night. His internal dialogue is negative. He thought of himself as helpless and expected this to continue on into the future. He also could not see any rewards for future hard work. The change he experienced, the recent success of his business, was experienced as a defeat.

In my conversation, I suggested that he view this moment as being actually an opportunity and a challenge. It was an opportunity to learn about tax sheltering and tax manipulation. He faced a challenge, not a defeat. The tone of his voice lightened as he opened his thinking: "Martin, please tell me, what can I do?" After only a couple of explanations about tax strategies such as incorporation and tax sheltering, he quickly and excitedly said, "I understand and I know whom to call!" By leading him to view his "predicament" as a challenge, I enabled him to free himself enough to see that he actually needed to learn something new. His solution was simple: Call an expert and get more information.

So how can you shift from distress to control over your feelings and actions?

The first step is awareness. Observe your thinking when you react to some change or stressful event. Is your thinking negative? If so, you are viewing the situation as an obstacle, not as an opportunity.

Use your feelings also to signal your reaction. Anxiety, fear, and depression indicate distress. You are not feeling challenged, but rather immediately or potentially defeated.

The second step is to ask yourself some questions: "How can I benefit from this situation? What can I learn here? What are my options? How can I use this to my advantage so I can enrich myself?" With these questions, you formulate a challenge for yourself. Practice these questions daily. Use them any time you feel anxious, depressed, or tense in the face of change or pressing situations.

Have these questions typed out on index cards. Keep one in your workplace and one at home. Carry one in your wallet. Practice until these questions are second nature to you.

Your success in turning around stressful events in your favor will be highly rewarding and will release new energies.

Step 8. Learn and Practice Problem-Solving Dialogues

If you are to control stress, it is essential to recognize the difference between a runaway negative dialogue and a problem-solving dialogue. Both are forms of talking to yourself, but they vary drastically in their effects. Negative dialogues fuel the stress reaction; they keep stress alive and well. Problem-solving dialogues, on the other hand, lead to solutions by replacing negative dialogues with positive ones aimed at solving your problems.

Unfortunately, many people have not yet learned about problem-solving dialogues and their usefulness in the fight against stress. Many people persist in worrisome, negative thinking, and over a period of time the body's continued mobilization in the stress reaction begins to take its toll. Patients who have angina pectoris (chest pain) are typically very anxious people. People who develop ulcers are chronic worriers. One might say that the ulcer patient "can't stomach" some stressful events, whereas the angina patient "eats his heart out" over events. Worriers are prone to many symptom complexes including migraines, chest pain, eczema, dermatitis, and ulcers. The process of worrying is a psychological defense, but it usually does not work and in fact creates more tension.

There is another way out of negative thinking cycles. When faced with a situation he doesn't like, the resilient type will accept the challenge of the situation and engage in a positive dialogue geared to discovering solutions.

For example, the computer executive discussed in Step 7 could have approached his dilemma more constructively. He could have said: "I'm really mad about my tax situation. I don't like feeling this way, nor do I want a repeat next year. What can I do differently?" This type of questioning leads to a challenge.

He continues his dialogue: "What are my possibilities? This is a specialized area in which I have little information. Who can I approach who is an expert or might lead me to one? A tax consultant—that's who I need, of course!" His mood changes to joy as he creates a solution that in turn evokes a different and positive feeling. The solution-finding dialogue leads to perceiving oneself as being in control.

The problem-solving dialogue follows several stages:

First, step back, gain a perspective, and look at your predicament. Ask yourself questions such as: "What is the roadblock or dilemma here?" Define the problem(s). Example: "I'm paying too much tax."

Second, create some objective. Ask yourself: "What do I want to accomplish?" Example: "I want to pay less tax and keep more of my income."

Third, ask yourself for some solutions: "How can I achieve that objective?" Example: "Investigate some tax shelters."

Then, if you do not find any immediate solutions, ask yourself whom you can turn to for more information or advice: "Who might have some solutions to my difficulty?" Example: "A tax consultant," Or: "My friend Martin might know someone. I trust his judgment."

Most important, though, is the fact that you practice this self-questioning daily. It needs to be automatic in order to close down a stress reaction immediately.

Step 9. Become an Active Participant

As noted earlier, the stress-resistant person is emotionally engaged in his work, family, or play. To make such a *commitment*, you must know yourself. You need to accept your feelings and thoughts and you must *clarify your values.* If you are to embrace your work and relationships, these must be of intrinsic value to you. If you are in conflict about work, then it will be difficult to focus on your work tasks, and it will be difficult to keep your mind on what you experience. If you are at work, but spend your time dreaming about being at home with your family, then you are in conflict and must be tense.

In 1979, Kobasa, Hilder, and Maddi published an article in the *Journal of Occupational Medicine* on this topic. They found that psychological "hardiness" can protect people from the destructive impact of stressful life events. A 2-year longitudinal study of 259 executives showed clearly that people with positive attitudes toward life remained healthier. One significant characteristic was that resistant types rated high on commitment. They embraced their work and their relationships. Type A personalities, on the other hand, are likely to be in conflict and will over-commit themselves to their work to the exclusion of relationships. The resilient are balanced.

To develop a stance of being an active participant in your life, it is important to clarify your values and create your commitment to each valued experience.

Ask yourself: "What is most important to me at this time in my life? Relationships? Work? Play?"

These may all be important to you. Then review the past week. How many hours did you engage in each area? If you didn't engage in it, then you were not very committed. Compare the number of hours for relationships, work, and play. Which is most, and which is least? Is your life balanced?

You will know immediately how balanced your life is at this time. If you keep telling yourself "In five years I will have more time to play with the children," then you are probably deceiving yourself. In five years, you are likely to be saying the same thing, or by then your relationships will be so distant that the children may not want to play with you! Eastern philosophies state it clearly—there is only now.

Make a specific commitment to each area. Set goals in each area so that there is time for the others. Set specific time frames to demonstrate that commitment. For example, you might decide to complete your work within a maximum of 50 hours per week. You commit yourself to spending two evenings per week with an important person (e.g., two evenings devoted to your spouse and three to the children). On Sunday night, create a schedule for the week: your work week, your relationships week, and your play week. Then simply follow your outline.

Step 10. Become Responsible

Responsibility is difficult to achieve. It means that you accept yourself, your feelings, thoughts, and actions. It means that whether you succeed or fail, the consequences are attributable to your participation. You do not blame others, and you accept feedback and mistakes as opportunities to learn and to improve yourself. You make a commitment to growth. The responsible person evaluates feedback and grows personally. The roots of responsibility lie in a core of positive self-esteem— you like yourself. Therefore, there is no threat when feedback is negative. You also welcome feedback with the attitude that feedback is useful for learning.

Imagine for a moment that you have given a speech to a professional audience. Afterward, several people pointed out to you that halfway through the speech, you lost the audience. If you act responsibly, you might engage in the following dialogue: "Okay, that speech didn't really go over that well. I noticed some people left early and others were yawning. How did I lose the audience? What can I do differently next time?" The resilient and responsible person actively searches the environment for more feedback to improve.

On the other hand, the nonresponsible type is quick to blame others, to deny, and to distort or dismiss feedback. This precludes learning. A nonresponsible reaction to the ineffective speech might be as follows: "Oh, the damn P.A. system, it was weak. Besides, what does that jerk know anyway about giving a speech!" This person is threatened and closed to learning.

CONCLUSION

You can learn to develop all the stress-resistant characteristics discussed above. The attitudes and cognitive coping patterns you have been reading about need to be practiced until they become habits. These new, habitual patterns can inoculate you against stressors and transform distress into a positive, self-enhancing force in your life.

Remember:

1. *Decide to live.*
2. Create your *reasons for being,* and develop a will to live.
3. Formulate *how* to live.
4. Develop and practice an *optimistic attitude.*

5. View yourself as the *master of your fate.* You control your own destiny.
6. Practice an *open learning mode.* Think divergently and creatively.
7. View stress and change as *challenges* and *opportunities* to learn and to grow.
8. Practice the *solution-finding dialogue* daily.
9. Become an *active participant* in your destiny. Make a balanced commitment to family, work, and play.
10. *Live responsibly.* Accept and seek all types of feedback. Strive to improve yourself. Appreciate your strengths and thrive.

By developing these new patterns for shaping stress to your own ends, you will learn as well to like, accept, and respect yourself. You will learn to perceive yourself as being in control of your life, and you will become more balanced in your commitment to relationships, work, and play. You will go beyond stress survival, and even beyond coping and stress management. You will become a master of stress. You will learn to thrive. There is life after stress—one filled with growth and joy!

BIBLIOGRAPHY

CHAPTER 1. ON THE NATURE OF STRESS

Brod, J. Circulatory changes underlying blood pressure elevation during acute emotional stress in normotensive and hypertensive subjects. *Clinical Science,* 1959, *18,* 269–270.

Cannon, W. B. *Bodily changes in pain, hunger, fear and rage.* Boston: C. T. Branford, 1953.

Cannon, W. B., & Paz, D. Emotional stimulation of adrenal secretion. *American Journal of Physiology,* 1911, *28,* 64–70.

Gray, J. A. *The psychology of fear and stress.* New York: McGraw-Hill, 1971.

Grenell, R., & Galay, S. (Eds.). *Biological foundations of psychiatry.* New York: Raven Press, 1976.

Johnson, R., & Spalding, J. *Disorders of the autonomic nervous system.* Philadelphia: F. A. Davis, 1974.

Lang, P., Rice, D., & Sternbach, R. The psychophysiology of emotion. In N. Greenfield & R. Sternbach (Eds.), *The handbook of psychophysiology.* New York: Holt, Rinehart & Winston, 1972.

Mason, J. W. A historical view of the stress field, Part I. *Journal of Human Stress,* 1975, *1* (1), 6–12.

Mason, J. W. A re-evaluation of the concept of non-specificity in stress theory. *Psychiatric Research,* 1971, *8,* 323–333.

Mason, J. W. A review of psychoendocrine research on the pituitary–adrenal cortical system. *Psychosomatic Medicine,* 1968, *30,* 576–607.

McGuigan, F. J., Sime, W. E., & Wallace, J. M. (Eds.). *Stress and tension control.* New York: Plenum, 1980.

Pelletier, K. R. *Mind as healer, mind as slayer.* New York: Delacorte Press, 1977.

Selye, H. The general adaptation syndrome and disease of adaptation. *Journal of Clinical Endocrinology,* 1946, *6,* 117–230.

Selye, H. The general adaptation syndrome and the gastrointestinal diseases of adaptation. *American Journal of Proctology,* 1951, *2,* 167–184.

Selye, H. *The stress of life.* New York: McGraw-Hill, 1956.

Selye, H. *Stress without distress.* Philadelphia: Lippincott, 1974.

Selye, H. *The stress of life* (rev. ed.) New York: McGraw-Hill, 1976.

Serbin, G. (Ed.). *Psychopathology of human adaptation.* New York: Plenum Press, 1976.

Solomon, G. F. Emotions, stress, and the central nervous system. *Annals of the New York Academy of Sciences,* 1969, *164,* 335–343.

Stokols, D. A typology of crowding experiences. In A. Baum and Y. Epstein (Eds.), *Human response to crowding.* Hillsdale, New Jersey: Lawrence Erlbaum Associates, 1976.

Weiner, H., Thaler, M., Reiser, M., & Mirsky, I. Etiology of duodenal ulcer. *Psychosomatic Medicine,* 1957, *19,* 1–10.

CHAPTER 2: THE SIGNS OF STRESS

Almy, T. P., Kern, F., & Tulin, M. Alterations in colonic function in man under stress. *Gastroenterology,* 1949, *12,* 425–436.

AMA Drug (latest ed.). Acton, Massachusetts: Publishing Services Group, Inc.

Amkraut, A., & Solomon, G. From symbolic stimulus to the pathophysiologic response: Immune mechanisms. *International Journal of Psychiatry in Medicine,* 1974, *5,* 541–563.

Berkun, M. Experimental studies of psychological stress in man. *Psychological Monographs,* 1962, *76* (Entire No. 534).

Brown, G. W. Life events and psychiatric illness. *Journal of Psychosomatic Research,* 1972, *16,* 311–320.

Dunbar, H. F. *Emotions and bodily changes.* New York: Columbia University Press, 1935.

Engle, G. Sudden and rapid death during psychological stress. *Annals of Internal Medicine,* 1971, *74,* 771–782.

Heisel, J. S. Life changes as etiologic factors in juvenile rheumatoid arthritis. *Journal of Psychosomatic Research,* 1972, *17,* 411–420.

Holmes, T. H., Trenting, T., & Wolff, H. Life situations, emotions, and nasal disease. *Psychosomatic Medicine,* 1951, *13,* 71–82.

Holmes, T. H., & Wolff, H. G. Life situations, emotions and backache. *Psychosomatic Medicine,* 1952, *14,* 18–33.

Mahl, G. F., & Brody, E. Chronic anxiety symptomatology, experimental stress and HCl secretion. *Archives of Neurological Psychiatry,* 1954, *71,* 314–325.

Mittelman, B., & Wolff, H. Emotions and gastroduodenal function. *Psychosomatic Medicine,* 1942, *4,* 5–61.

Murphy, L. B., & Moriarty, A. E. *Vulnerability, coping, and growth.* New Haven: Yale University Press, 1976.

Paykel, E., Myers, J., Dieneit, M., Klerman, G., Lindenthal, J., & Pepper, J. Life events and depression: A controlled study. *Archives of General Psychiatry,* 1969, *21,* 753–760.

Rahe, R. H. The pathway between subjects' recent life changes and their near-future illness reports: Representative results and methodological issues. In B. S. Dohrenwend and B. P. Dohrenwend (Eds.), *Stressful life events: Their nature and effects.* New York: Wiley, 1974, pp. 73–86.

Roessler, R., & Greenfield, M. (Eds.). *Physiological correlates of psychological disorders.* Madison: University of Wisconsin Press, 1962.

Shontz, F. *The psychological aspects of physical illness and disability.* New York: Macmillan, 1975.

CHAPTER 3. YOUR STRESS SELF-ANALYSIS

Altman, I. *Environment and social behavior: Privacy, personal space, territory and crowding.* Monterey, California: Brooks Cole, 1975.

Altman, I. Environmental psychology and social psychology. *Personality and Social Psychology Bulletin,* 1976, 2, 96–113.

Altman, I., & Wohlwill, J. F. (Eds.). *Human behavior and the environment: Current theory and research.* New York: Plenum, 1978.

Appley, M. H., & Trumbull, R. (Eds.). *Psychological stress: Issues and research.* New York: Appleton-Century-Crofts, 1967.

Baum, A., & Epstein, Y. (Eds.). *Human response to crowding.* Hillsdale, New Jersey: Lawrence Erlbaum Associates, 1976.

Berman, D. M. *Death on the job: Occupational health and safety struggles in the United States.* New York: Monthly Review Press, 1978.

Cobb, S., & Rose, R. Hypertension, peptic ulcer and diabetes in air traffic controllers. *Journal of the American Medical Association,* 224:4 [(23) April, 1973], 489.

Coehlo, G. V., Hamburg, D. A., & Adams, J. E. (Eds.). *Coping and adaptation.* New York: Basic Books, 1974.

Environmental and Health Monitoring in Occupational Health: Report. Geneva: WHO, 1973.

Glass, D. C., & Singer, J. E. *Urban stress.* New York: Academic Press, 1972.

Goldstein, M. J. Individual differences in response to stress. *American Journal of Community Psychology,* 1973, 1, 113–137.

Haan, N. *Coping and defending: Processes of self-environment organization.* New York: Academic Press, 1977.

Janis, I. L. *Decision making: A psychological analysis of conflict, choice, and commitment.* New York: Free Press, 1977.

Kahn, R. L., *et al. Organizational stress: Studies in role conflict and ambiguity.* New York: Wiley, 1964.

Lazarus, R. S., & Cohen, J. B. The study of stress and coping in aging. Paper given at the 5th WHO Conference on Society, Stress and Disease: Aging and Old Age. Stockholm, Sweden, June 14–19, 1976, L. Levi, Chairman.

L. Levi (Ed.). *Society, stress and disease.* Vol. 1. London: Oxford University Press, 1971.

Lowen, A. *The language of the body.* New York: Grune and Stratton, 1958.

Monat, A. Temporal uncertainty, anticipation time, and cognitive coping under threat. *Journal of Human Stress,* 1976, *2,* 32–43.

Moos, R. H. Conceptualizations of human environments. *American Psychologist,* 1973, *28,* 652–665.

Moos, R. H. Psychological techniques in the assessment of adaptive behavior. In G. V. Coelho, D. A. Hamburg, & J. E. Adams (Eds.), *Coping and adaptation.* New York: Basic Books, 1974, pp. 334–399.

Toffler, A. *Future shock.* New York: Random House, 1970.

White, R. W. Motivation reconsidered: The concept of competence. *Psychological Review,* 1959, *66,* 297–333.

CHAPTER 4. RELAXATION: YOUR FIRST LINE OF DEFENSE

Arnarson, E., & Sheffield, B. The generalization of the effects of EMG and temperature biofeedback. Paper presented at the Annual Meeting of the Biofeedback Society of America, Colorado Springs, March 1980.

Basmajian, J. (Ed.). *Biofeedback: Principles and practices for clinicians.* Baltimore: Williams & Wilkins, 1979.

Basmajian, J., & Hatch, J. Biofeedback and the modification of skeletal muscular dysfunctions. In R. Gathel & K. Price (Eds.), *Clinical applications of biofeedback.* Oxford: Pergamon, 1979.

Benson, H. Decreased blood pressure in borderline hypertensive subjects who practice meditation. *Journal of Chronic Diseases,* 1974, *17,* 163–169.

Benson, H. *The relaxation response.* New York: Morrow, 1975.

Berstein, D., & Borkovec, T. *Progressive relaxation training.* Champaign, Illinois: Research Press, 1973.

Borkovec, T., Grayson, J., & Cooper, K. Treatment of general tension: Subjective and physiological effects of progressive relaxation. *Journal of Consulting and Clinical Psychology,* 1978, *46,* 518–528.

Boudreau, L. TM and yoga as reciprocal inhibitors. *Journal of Behavior Therapy and Experimental Psychiatry,* 1972, *3,* 97–98.

Brown, B. *Stress and the art of biofeedback.* New York: Harper & Row, 1977.

Cox, D., Freundlick, A., & Meyer, R. Differential effectiveness of EMG feedback, verbal relaxation instructions, and medication placebo with tension headaches. *Journal of Consulting and Clinical Psychology,* 1975, *43,* 892–898.

Daebler, H. The use of relaxation and hypnosis in lowering high blood pressure. *American Journal of Clinical Hypnosis,* 1973, *16,* 75–83.

Green, E. E., Green, A. M., & Walters, E. D. Self regulation of internal states. London: Procedings of the International Congress of Cybernetics, 1969.

Harvey, J. Diaphragmatic breathing: A practical technique for breath control. *The Behavior Therapist,* 1978, *1,* 13–14.

Jacobson, E. *Progressive relaxation.* Chicago: University of Chicago Press, 1938.

Jacobson, E. *Modern treatment of tense patients.* Springfield, Illinois: Charles C Thomas, 1970.

Jacobson, E. *You must relax.* New York: McGraw-Hill, 1978.

Kendall, B. Clinical relaxation for neuroses and psychoneuroses. In E. Jacobson (Ed.), *Tension in medicine.* Springfield, Illinois: Charles C Thomas, 1967.

Luthe, W., & Schultz, J. H. (Ed.). *Autogenic therapy* (Vols. 1–6). New York: Grune & Stratton, 1969.

Nicassio, P., & Bootzin, R. A comparison of progressive relaxation and autogenic training as a treatment for insomnia. *Journal of Abnormal Psychology,* 1974, *83,* 253–260.

Paul, G. Physiological effects of relaxation training and hypnotic suggestion. *Journal of Abnormal Psychology,* 1969, 74, 425–437.

Paul, G. Inhibition of physiological response to stressful imagery by relaxation training and hypnotically suggested relaxation. *Behavior Research and Therapy,* 1969, *7,* 249–256.

Shoemaker, J., & Tasto, D. Effects of muscle relaxation on blood pressure of essential hypertensives. *Behavior Research and Therapy.* 1975, *13,* 29–43.

Stoyva, J. Self-regulation and stress-related disorders: A perspective on biofeedback. In D. I. Mostofsky (Ed.), *Behavior control and modifications of physiological activity.* Englewood Cliffs, New Jersey: Prentice-Hall, 1976.

Stoyva, J. Guidelines in the training of general relaxation. In J. Basmajian (Ed.), *Biofeedback: Principles and practices for clinicians.* Baltimore: Williams & Wilkins, 1979.

CHAPTER 5. RESISTING STRESS: SLEEP, EXERCISE, AND NUTRITION

Ardell, D. *High level wellness.* Emmaus, Pennsylvania: Rodale, 1977.

Balog, L. F. The effects of exercise on muscle ,ension and subsequent muscle relaxation. Unpublished doctoral dissertation, University of Maryland, 1978.

Bar-Or, O., & Buskirk, E. The cardiovascular system and exercise. In W. Johnson & E. Buskirk (Eds.), *Science and medicine of exercise and sport.* New York: Harper & Row, 1974.

Bray, G. Lipogenesis in human adipose tissue: Some effects of nibbling and gorging. *Journal of Clinical Investigation,* 1972, *51,* 537–546.

Cooper, K. H. *Aerobics.* New York: Bantam Books, 1968.

DeVries, H. The effects of exercise upon residual neuromuscular tension. Paper presented to the American Association of Health, Physical Education and Recreation National Convention, Minneapolis, May 1963.

DeVries, H. *Physiology of exercise.* Dubuque, Iowa: Wm. C. Brown, 1966.

DeVries, H. Physiological effects of exercise training regimen upon men aged 52 to 88. *Journal of Gerontology,* 1970, *25,* 325–336.

DeVries, H., & Adams, G. Electromyographic comparison of single doses of exercise and meprobamate as to effects on muscular relaxation. *American Journal of Physical Medicine,* 1972, *52,* 130–141.

Dodson, L., & Mullens, W. Some effects of jogging on psychiatric hospital patients. *American Corrective Therapy Journal,* 1969, Sept.–Oct., 130–134.

Girdano, D., & Everly, G. *Controlling stress and tension: A holistic approach.* Englewood Cliffs, New Jersey: Prentice-Hall, 1979.

Graham, D. T. Caffeine: Its identity, dietary sources, intake and biological effects. *Nutrition Reviews,* 1978, *36,* 97–102.

Greden, J. F. Anxiety or caffeinism: A diagnostic dilemma. *American Journal of Psychiatry,* 1974, *131,* 1089–1092.

Haskell, W., & Fox, S. Physical activity in the prevention and therapy of cardiovascular disease. In W. Johnson & E. Burkirk (Eds.), *Science and medicine of exercise and sport.* New York: Harper & Row, 1974.

Hodges, R. E. The effects of stress on ascorbic acid metabolism in man. *Nutrition Today,* 1970, *5,* 11–12.

Katch, F. I., & McArdle, W. D. *Nutrition, weight control and exercise.* Boston: Houghton Mifflin, 1977.

Kissen, D. M. Relationship between lung cancer, cigarette smoking, inhalation and personality and psychological factors in lung cancers. *British Journal of Medical Psychology,* 1964, *37,* 203–216.

Lappe, F. M. *Diet for a small planet.* New York: Ballantine Books, 1974.

Lazar, A. The effects of the TM program on anxiety, drug abuse, cigarette smoking and alcohol consumption. In D. Orme-Johnson, L. Domash, & J. Farrow (Eds.), *Scientific research on the TM program.* Geneva: Maharishi International University Press, 1975.

Mattlin, E. *Sleep less, live more.* New York: Ballantine Books, 1979.

Moorehouse, L., & Grass, L. *Total fitness.* New York: Simon and Schuster, 1975.

Pollock, M. L. The quantification of endurance training programs. *Exercise and sport science reviews* (Vol. 1). New York: Academic, 1973.

Pritikin, N. *The Pritikin permanent weight-loss manual.* New York: Grosset and Dunlap, 1981.

Robinson, C. H. *Normal and therapeutic nutrition.* New York: Macmillan, 1972.

Select Committee on Nutrition and Human Needs: U.S. Senate Dietary Goals for the United States (2nd ed.). Washington, D.C.: U.S. Government Printing Office, 1977.

Stephenson, P. Physiologic and psychotropic effects of caffeine on man. *Journal of the American Dietetic Association,* 1977, *71,* 240–247.

CHAPTER 6. STRESS REDUCTION AT WORK: PACING YOURSELF

Cooper, C. L., & Marshall, J. *Understanding executive stress.* New York: P.B.I., 1977.

Lakein, A. *How to get control of your time and your life.* New York: P.H. Wyden, 1973.

Le Boeuf, M. *Working smart.* New York: Warner Books, 1979.

Stein, M. L. *The T. factor: How to make time work for you.* New York: Playboy Paperbacks, 1976.

CHAPTER 7. STRESS PREVENTION AT WORK: CREATING A POSITIVE ATMOSPHERE

Assagioli, R. *Psychosynthesis.* New York: Viking Press, 1965.

Environment: The human impact. National Science Teachers Association, 1973.

Folinsbee, J., *et al.* (Eds.). *Environmental stress: Individual human adaptations.* New York: Academic Press, 1978.

Harris, T. *I'm O.K., you're O.K.* New York: Harper & Row, 1967.

Holahan, L. C. *Environment and behavior: A dynamic perspective.* New York: Plenum Press, 1977.

Klein, S. M. *Workers under stress.* Lexington: University Press of Kentucky, 1971.

Krasner, L. (Ed.). *Environmental design and human behavior: A psychology of the individual in society.* New York: Pergamon, 1980.

Trieff, N. (Ed.). *Environment and health.* Ann Arbor, Michigan: Ann Arbor Science, 1980.

Williams, J. S., Jr., *et al. Environmental pollution and mental health.* Information Resources, 1973.

CHAPTER 8. STRESS REDUCTION IN THE FAMILY: IMPROVING COMMUNICATION

Ackerman, N. W. Behavior trends and disturbances of the contemporary family. In I. Galdston (Ed.), *The family in contemporary society.* New York: International Universities Press, 1958.

Ackerman, N. W. *The psychodynamics of family life.* New York: Basic Books, 1958.

Backus, F., & Dudley, D. Observations of psychosocial factors and their relationship to organic disease. In Z. J. Kipowski, D. Lipsitt, and P. Whybrow (Eds.). *Psychosomatic medicine.* New York: Oxford, 1977.

Bateson, G., and Reusch, J. *Communication: The social matrix of psychiatry.* New York: Norton, 1951.

Berne, E. *Transactional analysis.* New York: Grove Press, 1961.

Corson, S., & Corson, E. Psychosocial influences on renal function: Implications for human pathophysiology. In L. Levi (Ed.), *Society, stress and disease* (Vol. 1). New York: Oxford University Press, 1971.

Froberg, J., Karlsson, C., Levi, L., & Lidberg, L. Physiological and biochemical stress reactions induced by psychosocial stimuli. In L. Levi (Ed.), *Society, stress and disease* (Vol. 1). New York: Oxford University Press, 1971.

Fromm, E. *The art of loving.* New York: Harper & Row, 1956.

Hall, E. T. *The silent language.* New York: Doubleday, 1959.

Henry, J. P., & Stephens, P. *Stress, health and the social environment.* New York: Springer, 1977.

Jackson, D., & Lederer, W. J. *The mirages of marriage.* New York: Norton, 1968.

Lecker, S. *The natural way to stress control.* New York: Grosset and Dunlap, 1978.

Pinneau, S. R., Jr. Effects of social support on occupational stresses and strains. Paper delivered at American Psychological Association Convention, Washington, D.C., September 1976.

Sarbin, T., & Coe, W. *Hypnosis: A social psychological analysis of influence communication.* New York: Holt, Rinehart & Winston, 1972.

Satir, V. *Conjoint family therapy.* Palo Alto, California: Science and Behavior Books, 1967.

Spiegel, J. P. Homeostatic mechanisms within the family. In I. Galdston (Ed.), *The family in contemporary society.* New York: International Universities Press, 1958.

Thomas, C. B., & Duszynski, K. R. Closeness to parents and the family constellation in a prospective study of five disease states: Suicide, mental illness, malignant tumors, hypertension and coronary heart disease. *Johns Hopkins Medical Journal,* 1974, *134,* 251–269.

Watzlawick, P., Beavin, J., & Jackson, D. *Pragmatics of human communication.* New York: W. W. Norton, 1967.

Zuk, G., and Boszormenyi-Nagy, I. *Family therapy and disturbed families.* Palo Alto, California: Science and Behavior Books, 1967.

CHAPTER 9. COGNITIVE STYLES AND STRESS-PRONENESS

Chavat, J., Dell, P., & Folkow, B. Mental factors and cardiovascular disorders. *Cardiologia,* 1964, 44, 124–141.

Eliot, R. *Stress and the major cardiovascular disorders.* Mount Kisco, New York: Futura, 1979.

Engel, G. L. Studies of ulcerative colitis. III. Nature of the psychologic process. *American Journal of Medicine,* 1955, *19,* 231–256.

Friedman, M., & Rosenman, R. H. *Type A behavior and your heart.* New York: Knopf, 1974.

Grace, W., Wolf, S., & Wolff, H. Life situations, emotions and chronic ulcerative colitis. *Journal of the American Medical Association,* 1950, *142,* 1044–1048.

Glass, D. C. *Behavior patterns, stress and coronary disease.* Hillsdale, New Jersey: Lawrence Erlbaum Associates, 1977.

Jenkins, C. D., Rosenman, R. H., & Zyzanski, S. J. Prediction of coronary heart disease by a test for the coronary-prone behavior pattern. *New England Journal of Medicine,* 1974, *23,* 1271–1275.

Lazarus, R. S., & Launier, R. Stress-related transactions between person and environment. In L. Pervin & M. Lewis (Eds.), *Perspectives in interactional psychology.* New York: Plenum Press, 1978.

LeShan, L. L., & Worthington, R. E. Personality as a factor in pathogenesis of cancer: Review of literature. *British Journal of Medical Psychology*, 1956, *29*, 49.

Lipowski, Z. J. Psychophysiological cardiovascular disorders. In A. Freedman, H. Kaplan, & B. Sadock (Eds.), *Comprehensive textbook of psychiatry*. Baltimore: Williams & Wilkins, 1974.

Machlowitz, M. M. *Workaholics: Living with them, working with them*. Reading, Massachusetts: Addison-Wesley, 1980.

Moos, R. H. MMPI inventory response patterns in patients with rheumatoid arthritis. *Journal of Psychosomatic Research*, 1964, *8*, 17.

Neufeld, R. W. J. The effect of experimentally altered cognitive appraisal on pain tolerance. *Psychonomic Science*, 1970, *20*, 106–107.

Neufeld, R. W. J. Evidence of stress as a function of experimentally altered appraisal of stimulus aversiveness and coping adequacy. *Journal of Personality and Social Psychology*, 1976, *33*, 632–646.

Pervin, L. A., & Lewis, M. (Eds.). *Perspectives in interactional psychology*. New York: Plenum Press, 1978.

Rosenman, R. H., & Friedman, M. Coronary heart disease in the Western Collaborative group study: A follow-up experience of 4½ years. *Journal of Chronic Disease*, 1970, *231*, 173–190.

Schwartz, E., & Shapiro, D. *Consciousness and self regulation. Advances in research* (Vol. 1). New York: Plenum Press, 1976.

Speisman, J. C., Lazarus, R. S., Mordkoff, A. M., & Davison, L.A. The experimental reduction of stress based on ego-defense theory. *Journal of Abnormal and Social Psychology*, 1964, *68*, 367–380.

Wolf, S., & Glass, G. B. Correlation of conscious and unconscious conflicts with changes in gastric function and structure. In H. G. Wolff, S. Wolf, *et al.* (Eds.), *Life stress and bodily disease*. Baltimore: Williams & Wilkins, 1950.

CHAPTER 10. BEYOND SURVIVAL: FROM COPING TO THRIVING

Assagnioli, R. *The art of will*. New York: Viking Press, 1973.

Beck, A. T. *Depression*. New York: Harper & Row, 1967.

Beck, A. T. *Cognitive therapy and the emotional disorders*. New York: International Universities Press, 1976.

Coopersmith, S. *The antecedents of self-esteem*. San Francisco: W. H. Freeman, 1967.

Ellis, A. *Humanistic psychology: The rational-emotive approach*. New York: Julian, 1973.

Erickson, M., Rossi, E., & Rossi, S., *Hypnotic realities*. New York: Irving, 1976.

Everly, G. S. The development of less stressful personality traits in adults through educational intervention. *Maryland Adult Education*, 1980, *2*, 63–66.

Festinger, L. *A theory of cognitive dissonance*. Evanston, Illinois: Row, Peterson, 1957.

Freud, S. *Civilization and its discontents.* New York: W. W. Norton, 1961.

Frankl, V. E. *Man's search for meaning.* New York: Washington Square Press, 1963.

Kobasa, S. C., Hilder, R. R., & Maddi, S. R. *Journal of Occupational Medicine,* 1979, *21,* 595–598.

Lazarus, R. S. *Psychological stress and the coping process.* New York: McGraw-Hill, 1966.

Lazarus, R. S. *Patterns for adjustment.* New York: McGraw-Hill, 1976.

Lefcourt, H. M. *Locus of control: Current trends in theory and research.* New York: Halstead Press, 1976.

Maltz, M. *Psychocybernetics.* New York: Pocket Books, 1966.

Meichenbaum, D., & Novaco, R. Stress inoculation: A preventive approach. In D. Spielberger & I. Sarason (Eds.), *Stress anxiety* (Vol. 5). New York: Wiley, 1978.

Moos, R., & Engel, B. T. Psychophysiological reactions in hypertensive and arthritic patients. *Journal of Psychosomatic Research,* 1962, *6,* 227–241.

Peale, N. V. *The power of positive thinking.* New York: Prentice Hall, 1952.

Seligman, M. E. P. *Helplessness: On depression, development and death.* San Francisco: W. H. Freeman, 1975.

Selye, H. *Stress without distress.* Philadelphia: Lippincott, 1974.

Selye, H. *Stress in health and disease.* Reading, Massachusetts: Butterworths, 1976.

Shapiro, J., & Shapiro, D. The psychology of responsibility: Some second thoughts on holistic medicine. *New England Journal of Medicine,* 1979, *301,* 211–212.

Vaillant, G. *Adaptation to life.* New York: Little, Brown.

Wolpe, J. *Psychotherapy by reciprocal inhibition.* Stanford: Stanford University Press, 1958.

INDEX